Multistate Corporate Tax Course

2011 EDITION

JOHN C. HEALY, MST, CPA
MICHAEL S. SCHADEWALD, PhD, CPA

.CCH

a Wolters Kluwer business

Contributors

Authors .... John C. Healy, MST, CPA
Michael S. Schadewald, PhD, CPA
Technical Review .... Sharon Brooks, CPA
Production Coordinator .... Hilary Rawk
Production .... Lynn J. Brown
Layout & Design .... Laila Gaidulis

This publication is designed to provide accurate and authoritative information in regard to the subject matter covered. It is sold with the understanding that the publisher is not engaged in rendering legal, accounting, or other professional service. If legal advice or other expert assistance is required, the services of a competent professional person should be sought.

ISBN: 978-0-8080-2456-9

No claim is made to original government works; however, within this Product or Publication, the following are subject to CCH's copyright: (1) the gathering, compilation, and arrangement of such government materials; (2) the magnetic translation and digital conversion of data, if applicable; (3) the historical, statutory and other notes and references; and (4) the commentary and other materials.

Printed in the United States of America

MULTISTATE CORPORATE TAX COURSE (2011 EDITION)

Introduction

The state tax laws are always changing. The complex interrelationship of phased-in and delayed new law effective dates, changing state revenue department rules, and an ever-changing mix of taxpayer wins and losses in the courts creates the need for the tax practitioner to constantly stay on top of the new rules and reassess tax strategies at the start of every year. The rules this year are significantly different from the rules last year, and the rules next year promise to be different from those governing this year. This is a fact of life for the modern-day state tax practitioner.

CCH's *Multistate Corporate Tax Course (2011 Edition)* is a helpful resource that provides explanations of significant laws, regulations, decisions and issues that affect multistate tax practitioners. Readers get guidance, insights and analysis on important provisions and their impact on multistate tax compliance and tax planning. This Course is the top quality tax review and analysis that every state tax practitioner needs to keep a step ahead.

Among the topics covered in the Course are:

- Principles of Multistate Corporate Income Taxation
- Apportionment Formulas
- State Tax Implications of Federal Section 338 Elections
- Treatment of Nonbusiness Income
- Post-Audit Strategies
- Nexus Issues
- Constitutional Issues

Throughout the Course you will find comments that are vital to understanding a particular strategy or idea, Examples to illustrate the topics covered, and Study Questions to help you test your knowledge. Answers to the Study Questions, with feedback on both correct and incorrect responses are provided in a special section beginning on page 203.

To assist you in your later reference and research, a detailed topical index has been included for this Course beginning on page 225.

This Course is divided into two Modules. Take your time and review each Course Module. When you feel confident that you thoroughly understand the material, turn to the CPE Quizzer. Complete one or both Module Quizzers for Continuing Professional Education credit. You can complete and return the Quizzers to CCH for grading at an additional charge. If you receive a grade of 70 percent or higher on the Quizzers, you will receive CPE credit for the Modules graded. Further information is provided in the CPE Quizzer instructions on page 233.

September 2010

COURSE OBJECTIVES

This Course was prepared to provide the participant with an overview of multistate tax issues. Upon Course completion, you will be able to:

- Identify which activities of a multistate corporation can create nexus
- Explain how state taxable income is generally calculated
- Describe the equitable relief provisions of UDITPA §18
- Differentiate between the federal Section 338(g) and Section 338(h)(10) elections
- Demonstrate how nonbusiness income is allocated
- Describe the current trends in sales and use tax audits
- Identify how physical presence affects nexus for sales and use tax purposes
- State the prohibitions covered under the Commerce Clause and the Equal Protection Clause
- List and state the origin of the four essential elements necessary for a tax to be considered unconstitutional under the Commerce Clause

CCH'S PLEDGE TO QUALITY

Thank you for choosing this CCH Continuing Education product. We will continue to produce high quality products that challenge your intellect and give you the best option for your Continuing Education requirements. Should you have a concern about this or any other CCH CPE product, please call our Customer Service Department at 1-800-248-3248.

NEW ONLINE GRADING gives you immediate 24/7 grading with instant results and no Express Grading Fee.

The **CCH Testing Center** website gives you and others in your firm easy, free access to CCH print Courses and allows you to complete your CPE Quizzers online for immediate results. Plus, the **My Courses** feature provides convenient storage for your CPE Course Certificates and completed Quizzers.

Go to **www.cchtestingcenter.com** to complete your Quizzer online.

One complimentary copy of this book is provided with certain CCH publications. Additional copies may be ordered for $37.00 each by calling 1-800-248-3248 (ask for product 0-0968-200). Grading fees are additional.

MULTISTATE CORPORATE TAX COURSE (2011 EDITION)

Contents

Principles of Multistate Corporate Income Taxation

This chapter discusses the basic principles and some advanced concepts of multistate corporate income taxation, including:

- Nexus
- Apportionment
- Combined unitary reporting
- Tax-planning strategies

LEARNING OBJECTIVES

Upon completing this chapter, the student will be able to:

- Identify which activities of a multistate corporation can create nexus
- Explain how state taxable income is generally calculated
- Describe the different types of apportionment formulas
- Explain the difference between consolidated statements and unitary reporting, and describe how states stand on this issue
- Describe several basic multistate tax-planning strategies
- Explain the cost-of-performance rule and market-based approach for sourcing sales
- Describe the different ways in which nexus can be created
- Identify which states currently impose non-income taxes

INTRODUCTION

Forty-five states and the District of Columbia impose some type of income-based tax on corporations.

Nevada, Ohio, South Dakota, Washington, and Wyoming do *not* levy a corporate income tax. However, Ohio does impose a gross receipts tax called the *commercial activity tax*, and Washington imposes a gross receipts tax called the *business and occupation tax*. Texas imposes a tax on gross margin, called the *margin tax*, and Michigan imposes both a modified gross receipts tax and a business income tax.

The corporate income taxes of California, Florida, New York, and a number of other states are formally franchise taxes imposed on, for example, the privilege of doing business in the state. Nevertheless, because the value of the franchise is measured by the income derived from that privilege, the tax is computed in essentially the same manner as a direct income tax.

This course on multistate corporate income taxation is organized into two sections, as follows:

1. Basic Principles
   - Nexus
   - Computation of State Taxable Income
   - Distinction Between Business and Nonbusiness Income
   - Apportionment Formulas
   - Sales Factor
   - Property Factor
   - Payroll Factor
   - Consolidated Returns and Combined Unitary Reporting
   - Concept of a Unitary Business Group
   - Basic Multistate Tax Planning Strategies

2. Advanced Concepts
   - Nexus
   - Specialized Industry Apportionment Formulas
   - Sourcing Sales of Services
   - Non-Income Taxes–Michigan, Ohio, Texas and Washington
   - Mechanisms Used by States to Limit Income Shifting
   - Pass-Through Entities

BASIC PRINCIPLES

Nexus

Constitutional Nexus. A threshold issue for any corporation operating in more than one state is determining the states in which it must file returns and pay income tax. A state has jurisdiction to tax a corporation organized in another state only if the out-of-state corporation's contacts with the state are sufficient to create nexus.

Historically, states have asserted that virtually any type of in-state business activity creates nexus for an out-of-state corporation. This approach reflects the reality that it is politically more appealing to collect taxes from out-of-state corporations than to raise taxes on in-state business interests. The desire of state lawmakers and tax officials to, in effect, export the local tax burden is counterbalanced by the Due Process Clause and Commerce Clause of the U.S. Constitution, both of which limit a state's ability to impose a tax obligation on an out-of-state corporation.

The landmark case on constitutional nexus is *Quill Corp. v. North Dakota* [504 US 298 (1992)]. Quill was a mail-order vendor of office supplies that solicited sales through catalogs mailed to potential customers in North Dakota and made deliveries through common carriers. Quill was incorporated in Delaware and had facilities in California, Georgia, and Illinois.

Quill had no office, warehouse, retail outlet, or other facility in North Dakota, nor were any Quill employees or representatives physically present in North Dakota. During the years in question, Quill made sales to roughly 3,000 North Dakota customers and was the sixth largest office supply vendor in the state.

Under North Dakota law, Quill was required to collect North Dakota use tax on its mail-order sales to North Dakota residents. Quill challenged the constitutionality of this tax obligation. The Supreme Court held that Quill's economic presence in North Dakota was sufficient to satisfy the Due Process Clause's *minimal connection* requirement.

On the other hand, the Court ruled that an economic presence was not, by itself, sufficient to satisfy the Commerce Clause's *substantial nexus* requirement. Consistent with its ruling 25 years earlier in ***National Bellas Hess, Inc. v. Department of Revenue***, the Court ruled that a substantial nexus exists only if a corporation has a *nontrivial* physical presence in a state [386 US 753 (1967)]. In other words, the Court ruled that a physical presence is an essential prerequisite to establishing constitutional nexus—at least for sales and use tax purposes.

The Court did not address the issue of whether the physical presence test also applied for income tax purposes, which has resulted in a significant amount of controversy and litigation (see discussion below under the heading of Economic Nexus).

Public Law 86-272. Congress enacted Public Law 86-272 in 1959 to provide multistate corporations with a limited safe harbor from the imposition of state income taxes. Specifically, Public Law 86-272 prohibits a state from imposing a *net income tax* on a corporation organized in another state if the corporation's only in-state activity is:

1. Solicitation of orders by company representatives
2. For sales of tangible personal property
3. Orders that are sent outside the state for approval or rejection
4. Orders that, if approved, are filled by shipment or delivery from a point outside the state

Although Public Law 86-272 can provide significant protections for a multistate business, it has several important limitations:

1. It applies *only* to taxes imposed on net income and provides no protection against the imposition of a sales and use tax collection obligation, property taxes, gross receipts taxes (e.g., Ohio commercial activity tax, or Washington business and occupation tax), or corporate franchise taxes on net worth or capital.

2. It protects only sales of tangible personal property. It does not protect activities such as leasing tangible personal property, selling services, selling or leasing real estate, or selling or licensing intangibles.

3. For businesses that send employees into other states to sell tangible personal property, it applies only if those employees limit their in-state activities to the solicitation of orders that are sent outside the state for approval and, if approved, are filled by a shipment or delivery from a point outside the state.

> **EXAMPLE**
>
> If a salesperson exercises an authority to approve orders within a state, the company does *not* qualify for protection under Public Law 86-272.
>
> Likewise, Public Law 86-272 does not protect the presence of a salesperson who performs non-solicitation activities within a state (eg. repairs, customer training, or technical assistance).

Although Public Law 86-272 does not define the phrase solicitation of orders, the meaning of the phrase was addressed by the U.S. Supreme Court in *Wisconsin Department of Revenue v. William Wrigley, Jr., Co.* [505 US 214 (1992)].

In this case, the Court defined *solicitation of orders* as encompassing "requests for purchases" as well as "those activities that are entirely ancillary to requests for purchases—those that serve no independent business function apart from their connection to the soliciting of orders."

Examples of activities that might serve an independent business function, apart from the solicitation of orders, include:

- Installation and start-up
- Customer training
- Engineering and design assistance
- Technical assistance
- Maintenance and repair
- Credit and collection

QUESTIONS

> **1.** Which of the following states does *not* impose a corporate income tax?
>   **a.** Alabama
>   **b.** California
>   **c.** Florida
>   **d.** South Dakota

> **2.** Which of the following is *not* true of P.L. 86-272?
>   **a.** It applies *only* to a net income tax.
>   **b.** It protects *only* sales of intangible personal property.
>   **c.** For businesses that send employees into other states to sell tangible personal property, it applies *only* if those employees limit their in-state activities to the solicitation of orders that are approved out-of-state and are filled by shipment or delivery from a point outside the state.

Computation of State Taxable Income

Most states that impose a corporate income tax use either the corporation's federal taxable income before the net operating loss and special deductions (federal Form 1120, Line 28) or the corporation's net federal taxable income (federal Form 1120, Line 30) as the starting place for computing state taxable income.

The states that do not tie the computation of state taxable income directly to a corporation's federal tax return typically adopt the majority of the federal provisions governing items of gross income and deduction in defining the state tax base.

A corporation's state income tax liability generally is computed using the following steps:

1. **State Tax Base:** Begin with the amount of federal taxable income (Line 28 or Line 30 of the federal corporate income tax return, Form 1120). Add or subtract the state addition and subtraction modifications. The resulting amount is the *state tax base*.
2. **Apportionable Business Income:** If applicable, add to (or subtract from) the state tax base the total net allocable nonbusiness income (loss). The resulting amount is the total *apportionable business income* (loss).
3. **Business Income/Loss:** Multiply the total apportionable business income (loss) by the state's apportionment percentage. The resulting amount is the *business income* (loss) apportioned to the state.
4. **State Taxable Income/Loss:** Add to (or subtract from) the business income apportioned to the state the total net allocable nonbusiness income (loss), if applicable, that is allocated to the state. The resulting amount is the *state taxable income* (loss).
5. **State Tax Liability:** Multiply the state taxable income by the state tax rate to determine the *state tax liability* before credits.
6. **Net Income Tax Liability:** Subtract the state's tax credits from the state tax liability to arrive at the *net income tax liability* for the state.

Using the federal tax base as the starting point for computing state taxable income is referred to as piggybacking.

Conformity with federal provisions simplifies tax compliance for multistate corporations, but complete conformity with the federal tax laws would effectively cede control over state tax policy to the federal government.

States also must be wary of the effects of federal tax law changes on state tax revenues. Although federal taxable income generally is used as the starting point in computing state taxable income, numerous state modifications are required both to reflect differences in federal and state policy objectives and to eliminate income that a state is constitutionally prohibited from taxing.

The modifications to federal taxable income vary significantly among the states. Common *addition* modifications include the following:

- Interest income received on state and municipal debt obligations
- State income taxes
- Federal net operating loss carryover deductions
- Federal dividends-received deductions
- Royalties and interest expense paid to related parties
- Expenses related to state tax credits
- Federal domestic production activities deduction under Section 199
- Expenses related to income that is exempt for state tax purposes
- Federal bonus depreciation under Section 168(k)
- Federal Section 179 asset expensing

Common subtraction modifications include the following:

- Interest income received on federal debt obligations
- State net operating loss carryover deductions
- State dividends-received deductions
- Expenses related to federal tax credits
- Federal Subpart F income with respect to foreign subsidiaries
- Federal Section 78 gross-up income

Distinction Between Business and Nonbusiness Income

In 1957, a group of state tax officials promulgated the Uniform Division of Income for Tax Purposes Act (UDITPA) to provide uniformity among the states with respect to the taxation of multistate corporations. UDITPA has been adopted, at least in part, by many states.

In an attempt to distinguish income derived from a corporation's regular trade or business from income derived from any activities that are unrelated to that trade or business, UDITPA makes a distinction between *business income* and *nonbusiness income.*

Under the UDITPA approach, a taxpayer apportions a percentage of its business income to each state in which it has nexus, but specifically allocates the *entire* amount of any nonbusiness income to a single state (UDITPA Secs. 4 and 9). Therefore, the principal consequence of classifying an item as nonbusiness income is that the income is excluded from the tax base of every nexus state, except the state in which the nonbusiness income is taxable in full (e.g., the state of commercial domicile).

Because the classification of an item as nonbusiness income can effectively remove the income from the tax base of one or more nexus states, the business versus nonbusiness income distinction has historically been an area of significant controversy between taxpayers and state tax authorities.

The distinction between business and nonbusiness income is related to the constitutional restrictions on the ability of a state to tax an out-of-state corporation. Based on these constitutional protections, taxpayers have challenged the ability of nexus states to tax an item of income that the taxpayer believes has no relationship to the business activity conducted in the state.

As the Supreme Court stated in *Allied-Signal, Inc. v. Division of Taxation* [504 US 768 (1992)], "the principle that a State may not tax value earned outside its borders rests on the fundamental requirement of both the Due Process and Commerce Clauses that there be 'some definite link, some minimum connection, between a state and the person, property or transaction it seeks to tax'" [*Miller Bros. Co. v. Maryland,* 347 US 340, 344-345 (1954)].

EXAMPLE

The taxpayer in *Mobil Oil Corp. v. Commissioner of Taxes* was an integrated petroleum company that was incorporated and commercially domiciled in New York [445 US 425 (1980)]. Mobil challenged Vermont's ability to tax the dividends that it received from its foreign subsidiaries.

The essence of Mobil's argument that Vermont could *not* constitutionally tax the foreign dividends was that the activities of the foreign subsidiaries were unrelated to Mobil's business activities in Vermont, which were limited to distributing petroleum products. Stating that "the linchpin of apportionability in the field of state income taxation is the unitary business principle," the Supreme Court ruled that Vermont *could* tax an apportioned percentage of the dividends Mobil received from its foreign subsidiaries, because those subsidiaries were part of the same integrated petroleum enterprise as its distribution activities in Vermont.

In other words, because they were received from unitary subsidiaries, the dividends were includible in Mobil's apportionable business income. The Court also indicated that if the business activities of the foreign subsidiaries had "nothing to do with the activities of the recipient in the taxing state, due process considerations might well preclude apportionability, because there would be no underlying unitary business."

Each state is free to adopt its own definitions of business and nonbusiness income, subject to the constitutional constraints discussed above.

Most states have adopted a definition of *nonbusiness income* that more or less conforms to the UDITPA definition of nonbusiness income, which is "all income other than business income" [UDITPA §1(e)]. Thus, the key is the definition of business income.

According to UDITPA §1(a), *business income* is:

> ... income arising from transactions and activity in the regular course of the taxpayer's trade or business and includes income from tangible and intangible property if the acquisition, management, and disposition of the property constitute integral parts of the taxpayer's regular trade or business operations.

Therefore, under UDITPA, an item of income is classified as business income if it either arises from a transaction in the regular course of the taxpayer's business (transactional test), or from property that is an integral part of the taxpayer's business (functional test) [MTC Reg. IV.1.(a)].

The *transactional test* looks at the frequency and regularity of the income-producing transaction in relation to the taxpayer's regular trade or business. The critical issue is whether the transaction is frequent in nature, as opposed to a rare or extraordinary event.

In contrast, the *functional test* looks at the relationship between the underlying income-producing asset and the taxpayer's regular trade or business. The critical issue is whether the asset is integral, as opposed to incidental, to the taxpayer's business operations.

When an item of income is determined to be nonbusiness income, most states allocate the income to a specific state under guidelines similar to Sections 4 through 8 of UDITPA and the related Multistate Tax Commission (MTC) regulations. The basic thrust of these rules is that nonbusiness income derived from real and tangible personal property is allocable to the state in which the property is physically located, whereas nonbusiness income derived from intangible property is allocable to the state of commercial domicile (except for royalties, which are allocable to the state where the intangible asset is used). The MTC is an agency of state governments that was established in 1967 to promote fairness and uniformity in state tax laws.

STUDY QUESTIONS

---

3. Which of the following is an *advantage* of state conformity to federal tax provisions?

   a. It simplifies tax compliance for multistate corporations.
   b. Federal tax law changes affect state tax revenues.
   c. Complete conformity with federal tax laws would effectively cede control over state tax policy to the federal government.

4. Which of the following is *not* a true statement regarding UDITPA?

   a. UDITPA was promulgated to provide uniformity among the states with respect to the taxation of multistate corporations.
   b. Under the UDITPA approach, a taxpayer apportions a percentage of its business income to each state in which it has nexus.
   c. UDITPA makes no distinction between business and nonbusiness income.

Apportionment Formulas

A taxpayer's right to apportion its income is not automatic or elective; rather, it is a privilege that must be warranted by the corporation's activities.

The requirements for establishing the right to apportion income vary from state to state, but generally include:

- Carrying on business in another state
- Maintaining a regular place of business in another state
- Being taxable in another state

Some states take the restrictive position that permits apportionment only if the corporation is actually filing returns and paying tax in another state.

Once a corporation has established its right to apportion income, the next step is to compute the applicable state apportionment percentages using the formulas provided by each taxing state. These formulas are usually based on the relative amounts of property, payroll, and/or sales that the corporation has in each taxing state.

These formulas reflect the notion that a corporation's business activity in a state is properly measured by the amount of property, payroll, and sales in the state. These three components of an apportionment formula are referred to as *factors*. For any given state, each factor equals the ratio of the corporation's property, payroll or sales in the state to its property, payroll or sales everywhere.

Factor weights vary from state to state. At present, about 10 states use a three-factor apportionment formula that equally weights sales, property, and payroll. Most states use a modified three-factor formula, under which the sales factor is assigned more weight than the property or payroll factors.

About 15 states double weight the sales factor (i.e., 50 percent sales, 25 percent property, and 25 percent payroll). Roughly a dozen states use a single-factor sales-only formula, including:

- Colorado
- Georgia
- Illinois
- Iowa
- Maine
- Michigan
- Nebraska
- New York
- Oregon
- Texas
- Wisconsin

Several other states have enacted legislation to adopt a sales-only formula. Effective in 2011, California will permit taxpayers to elect to use a sales-only formula. Likewise, Indiana, Minnesota and South Carolina are adopting sales-only formulas, effective in 2014, 2011, and 2011, respectively.

Effective in 2010, Pennsylvania weights the sales factor 90 percent, and property and payroll factors five percent each.

Assigning more weight to the sales factor than to the property or payroll factor tends to increase the percentage of an out-of-state corporation's income that is subject to tax, because the out-of-state corporation's principal activity in the state—sales of its product—is weighted more heavily than its payroll and property activities. At the same time, assigning more weight to the sales factor tends to reduce the tax on in-state corporations that have nationwide sales, as well as significant amounts of property and payroll in the state (factors that are given relatively less weight in the apportionment formula).

The standard three-factor formula was designed to apportion the income of multistate manufacturing and mercantile businesses and may not fairly apportion the income of businesses in other industries. To address this issue, many states provide special rules for computing apportionment percentages for businesses in certain industries. Typically, these special rules involve the modification or exclusion of the conventional factors or the use of unique, industry-specific factors.

Examples of industries for which states provide *special apportionment factor rules* include:

- Airlines
- Railroads
- Trucking companies
- Financial institutions
- Television and radio broadcasters
- Publishers
- Telecommunication services companies
- Mutual funds
- Pipelines
- Ship transportation companies
- Professional sports franchises

In theory, apportionment prevents double taxation of a corporation's income. However, because each state is free to choose its own apportionment formula and make its own rules for computing the factors, apportionment does not provide a uniform division of a taxpayer's income among the taxing states.

There are significant differences among the states in terms of factor weights, as well as variations in the computation of the factors themselves. This diversity can result in more than 100 percent of a corporation's income being subject to state taxation.

Another potentially adverse consequence of apportionment occurs when a taxpayer's operations in one state result in a loss, but the corporation's overall operations are profitable. In such cases, the apportionment process will assign a percentage of the corporation's overall profit to the state in which the loss was incurred, even though no profit was generated by the taxpayer's operations in that state.

To address these issues, UDITPA §18 and the tax laws of most states allow a corporate taxpayer to petition for relief when the application of the state's apportionment formula does not fairly represent the taxpayer's business activity in the state. In such situations, UDITPA §18 lists several possible alternatives to the standard formula, including the use of separate accounting, the exclusion of one or more factors, the inclusion of one or more additional factors, or some other method that provides a more equitable apportionment of the taxpayer's income.

Case law indicates, however, that there is a presumption that a state's apportionment method is equitable. In other words, to receive relief from distortions caused by the state's standard formula, a corporation must prove by clear and convincing evidence that the apportionment method in question grossly distorts the amount of income actually earned in the state. For the most part, corporations have been unsuccessful in proving that a state's apportionment provisions are inequitable.

Sales Factor

Under UDITPA §15, the sales factor is a fraction whose numerator is the total sales of the taxpayer in the state during the tax period and whose denominator is the total sales of the taxpayer everywhere during the tax period.

$$\text{Sales Factor} = \frac{\text{Total Sales of the Taxpayer in the State During the Tax Period}}{\text{Total Sales of the Taxpayer Everywhere During the Tax Period}}$$

Because the sales factor is used to apportion a corporation's business income, only sales that generate apportionable business income are includible in the fraction.

Nonbusiness sales are excluded from the sales factor. Under UDITPA §1(g), the term *sales* means all gross receipts of the taxpayer other than receipts related to nonbusiness income. Consistent with this expansive view of the sales factor, MTC Regulation IV.15(b) provides that the sales factor generally includes all gross receipts derived by the taxpayer from transactions and activities in the regular course of its trade or business. Examples include:

- Gross receipts from sales of inventory
- Gross receipts from sales of services
- Interest
- Dividends
- Rentals
- Royalties
- Other gains derived from other business assets and activities

Also, receipts from transactions with a related corporation generally are included in the sales factor—unless a consolidated or combined return is filed with the related corporation, in which case intercompany receipts generally are excluded from the sales factor.

Under UDITPA §16(a), sales of tangible personal property are assigned to the sales factor numerator of the state into which the goods are delivered or shipped. This so-called *destination test* reflects the original purpose of including a sales factor in the apportionment formula, which was to provide tax revenue to the states in which customers are located.

UDITPA §16(b) contains two *exceptions* to the destination test:

1. Sales to the U.S. government are assigned to the state from which the goods are shipped, rather than to the state in which the purchaser is located.
2. If the seller is not taxable in the destination state (in which case there is no sales factor numerator to which to assign the sale under the destination test), the sale is thrown back into the sales factor numerator of the state from which the goods are shipped—commonly referred to as throwback.

The rationale for throwback is to make sure that all of a company's sales are assigned to the numerator of some state's sales factor. Despite the logical basis for adopting a throwback rule, many states do not require throwback—primarily because that makes the state a more desirable place to locate a manufacturing or distribution facility from which to ship goods.

The lack of a throwback rule results in *nowhere sales*, which are sales that are included in the denominator but not in the numerator of the sales factor.

Under UDITPA §17, any sales other than sales of tangible personal property are considered in-state sales if the income-producing activity is performed in the state. This *income-producing activity rule* applies to:
- Fees for services
- Rental income
- Income from intangibles (interest, dividends, royalties, and capital gains)

Under MTC Reg. IV.17(2), the term income-producing activity applies to each separate item of income and means the transactions and activity engaged in by the taxpayer in the regular course of its trade or business. Examples include the:
- Rendering of personal services by employees or the use of tangible or intangible property by the taxpayer in performing a service
- Sale, rental, leasing, licensing or other use of real property
- Rental, leasing, licensing or other use of tangible personal property
- Sale, licensing or other use of intangible personal property

If the income-producing activity is performed in two or more states, the sale is assigned to the state in which the greater proportion of the income-producing activity is performed, based on cost of performance (UDITPA §17). Under MTC Reg. IV.17(3), the term *costs of performance* means direct costs determined in a manner consistent with generally accepted accounting principles and in accordance with accepted conditions or practices in the trade or business of the taxpayer.

Direct costs include material and labor costs that have a causal relationship with the sale in question. *Indirect costs*, which include general and administrative expenses that are not associated with any specific sale, are *not* taken in account in determining the costs of performance.

Property Factor

Under UDITPA §10, the property factor is a fraction whose numerator is the average value of the taxpayer's real and tangible personal property owned or rented and used in the state during the tax year and whose denominator is the average value of all the taxpayer's real and tangible personal property owned or rented and used everywhere during the tax year.

$$\text{Property Factor} = \frac{\text{Average Value of the Taxpayer's Real and Tangible Personal Property Owned or Rented and Used in the State During the Tax Year}}{\text{Average Value of the Taxpayer's Real and Tangible Personal Property Owned or Rented and Used Everywhere During the Tax Year}}$$

Under MTC Reg. IV.10(a), the definition of *real and tangible personal property* includes:

- Land
- Buildings
- Machinery
- Stocks of goods
- Equipment
- Other real and tangible personal property

Intangible property, such as accounts receivable and marketable securities, generally is excluded from the property factor.

Property owned by the corporation is typically valued at its average original cost plus the cost of additions and improvements, but without any adjustments for depreciation. A few states require property to be included at its net book value or federal adjusted tax basis. Rented property is included in the property factor at a value equal to eight times the annual rental.

Only property that is used in producing *apportionable business income* is included in the property factor. Therefore, *excluded* property includes:

- Construction-in-progress
- Property that has been permanently withdrawn from service
- Property that is used for producing nonbusiness income generally

Property that is temporarily idled, however, generally remains in the property factor.

Although the average value of the property is usually determined by averaging the beginning and ending property values, many states allow the average value to be calculated on a monthly or quarterly basis if the use of the annual computations substantially distorts the actual value of the property. This may occur if a significant amount of property is acquired or disposed of near the beginning or the end of the year.

Payroll Factor

Under UDITPA §13, the payroll factor is a fraction whose numerator is the total amount paid in the state during the tax year by the taxpayer for compensation and whose denominator is the total compensation paid everywhere during the tax year. For this purpose, compensation generally includes:

- Wages
- Salaries
- Commissions
- Any other form of remuneration paid or accrued to an employee that is taxable to the employee for federal income tax purposes

Payments made to an independent contractor or to any other person who is not properly classifiable as an employee generally are excluded from the payroll factor. Compensation related to the production of nonbusiness income is also excluded from the payroll factor. In addition, a few states exclude executive compensation from the payroll factor in an attempt to make the state a more desirable place to locate a headquarters office.

The rules for computing an employee's compensation and for assigning that compensation to a particular state parallel those used to compute the employer's federal and state unemployment taxes. Federal Form 940, *Employer's Annual Federal Unemployment Tax Return,* summarizes taxable compensation amounts on a state-by-state basis and is often used to compute state payroll factors.

When computing the numerator of the payroll factor for a particular state, note that an employee's compensation is included in the numerator for that state if they perform services exclusively within that state. If an employee performs services both within and without a state, the *entire* amount of the employee's compensation is still generally assigned to a single state, based on a hierarchy of factors, including (in the order in which they are applied) the employee's base of operations, where the employee is directed from, and the employee's state of residence (UDITPA §14).

STUDY QUESTIONS

5. Assigning more weight to the sales factor than to the property or payroll factor tends to *decrease* the percentage of an out-of-state corporation's income that is subject to tax. *True or False?*
   a. True
   b. False

6. Under UDITPA, sales of tangible personal property are generally assigned to the sales factor numerator of the state:
   a. From which the goods are shipped
   b. In which the goods are delivered or shipped
   c. Where the company is commercially domiciled

Consolidated Returns and Combined Unitary Reporting

For financial reporting purposes, a parent corporation must issue consolidated financial statements that include all of its majority-owned subsidiaries.

For federal income tax purposes, an affiliated group of corporations may elect to file a federal consolidated income tax return (Code Sec. 1501). Thus, a federal consolidated return is not mandatory, and the members of an affiliated group have the option of filing federal returns on a separate-company basis. Filing a federal consolidated return is a popular election, primarily because it allows the group to offset the losses of one affiliate against the profits of other affiliates.

An *affiliated group* is defined as one or more chains of includible corporations connected through stock ownership with a common parent that is an includible corporation, provided that the common parent directly owns 80 percent or more of at least one of the other includible corporations, and stock meeting the 80 percent test in each includible corporation other than the common parent must be owned directly by one or more of the other includible corporations [Code Sec. 1504(a)].

An *includable corporation* is any corporation other than an exempt corporation, life insurance company, foreign corporation, Section 936 corporation, RIC, REIT, DISC or S corporation [Code Sec. 1504(b)].

The states that impose corporate income taxes employ a wide variety of filing options for groups of commonly controlled corporations. This makes it difficult to generalize about state filing options.

Roughly speaking, the different state filing options fall into one of the following categories:
- Mandatory separate-company returns
- Elective consolidated returns
- Mandatory combined unitary reporting
- Discretionary combined unitary reporting
- A hybrid system, which includes both elective consolidated returns and discretionary combined unitary reporting

The lack of uniformity in state filing options means that tax practitioners must carefully analyze the filing options available in any given nexus state.

Mandatory Separate-company Returns. Three states—Delaware, Maryland, and Pennsylvania—require each member of a commonly controlled group of corporations to compute its income and file a return as if it were a *separate* economic entity. Under this mandatory separate-company return approach, consolidated returns and combined unitary reporting are *not* permitted or required under any circumstances.

The filing of separate-company returns provides taxpayers with the opportunity to create legal structures and intercompany transactions that shift income from affiliates based in high-tax states to affiliates based in low-tax states.

> **EXAMPLE**
>
> If a multistate corporation's only activities in a high-tax state are sales and distribution, which are often relatively low-margin activities, and if the high-tax state allows separate-company returns, the corporation may be able to insulate its higher-margin assets and activities from taxation in the high-tax state by forming a sales subsidiary that is responsible for marketing products in that state.

Disadvantages of the separate-company return approach include the:

- Inability to offset the losses of one affiliate against the profits of other affiliates
- Need to develop defensible arm's-length transfer prices for intercompany transactions

Elective Consolidated Returns. Roughly 20 states (including Alabama, Florida, Georgia, Iowa, and South Carolina) generally allow affiliated corporations to file separate-company returns but also permit such corporations to elect to file a state consolidated return if certain conditions are met. The qualification requirements for including an affiliated corporation in a state consolidated return vary from state to state.

In terms of stock ownership requirements, most states piggyback on the federal rule requiring 80 percent or more ownership. A number of states also require that an affiliated group file a federal consolidated return as a prerequisite to filing a state consolidated return.

Examples of additional *restrictions* that a state may impose for including a specific affiliate in a state consolidated return include:

- Having nexus in the state
- Deriving income from sources in the state
- Not being subject to a special apportionment formula

The *advantages* of filing a consolidated return include:

- The ability to offset the losses of one affiliate against the profits of other affiliates
- Elimination of intercorporate dividends
- Deferral of gains on intercompany transactions
- The use of credits that would otherwise be denied because of a lack of income

A major disadvantage of filing a consolidated return is that it can prevent a taxpayer from creating legal structures and intercompany transactions to shift income from affiliates based in high-tax states to affiliates based in low-tax states.

Combined Unitary Reporting. Twenty-three states require members of a unitary business group to compute their taxable income on a combined basis. These states include Alaska, Arizona, California, Colorado, Hawaii, Idaho, Illinois, Kansas, Maine, Massachusetts, Michigan, Minnesota, Montana, Nebraska, New Hampshire, New York (for related corporations that have substantial intercorporate transactions), North Dakota, Oregon, Texas, Utah, Vermont, West Virginia, and Wisconsin. The District of Columbia will require combined reporting starting in 2011.

Combined reporting is a methodology for apportioning the business income of a taxpayer corporation that is a member of a commonly controlled group of corporations engaged in a unitary business. Generally speaking, the taxpayer member's apportioned business income is determined by multiplying the aggregate business income of all the members of the unitary business group by an apportionment percentage that is based on factors—the denominators of which include the factors everywhere of all group members, and the numerators of which include the in-state factors of only the taxpayer member.

Despite its surface-level resemblance to a consolidated return, combined unitary reporting *differs* from a federal consolidated return in a number of important respects:

1. *Apportionment methodology versus type of return.* A federal consolidated return involves the filing of a single return for a group of affiliated corporations, and the computation of the group's federal income tax as if the group were a single economic entity. In contrast, combined unitary reporting is not so much a type of return as the name given to the calculations (akin to a spreadsheet) by which a unitary business group apportions its income.

2. *Common ownership requirements.* Inclusion in a state consolidated return generally requires 80 percent or more ownership (which piggybacks on the ownership threshold for inclusion in a federal consolidated return), whereas membership in a combined unitary report generally requires more than 50 percent ownership.

3. *Unitary business requirement.* To be included in a combined report, an affiliate must be engaged in the same trade or business as the other group members, as exhibited by such factors as centralized management, functional integration, and economies of scale. This unitary business test is not a requirement for inclusion in an elective consolidated return.

4. *Worldwide combination.* Consistent with the federal approach to consolidation, affiliates organized in a foreign country generally are not included in a state consolidated return. On the other hand, states have the ability to require the inclusion of foreign country affiliates in a combined unitary report.

Despite these differences, the advantages and disadvantages of consolidated returns and combined reporting are similar.

A primary *disadvantage* of both filing options is that they can limit a taxpayer's ability to use intercompany transactions to shift income from affiliates based in high-tax states to affiliates based in low-tax states.

A major *advantage* of both filing options is that losses of one affiliate can be offset against the profits of other affiliates. In addition, the effect of apportioning income on a combined basis may be to shift income from a high-tax state to a low-tax state.

Numerous states, including New Jersey, North Carolina, and Virginia, generally allow commonly controlled corporations to file separate-company returns but also require or permit a combined unitary report if certain conditions are satisfied. A common reason for requiring a combined report is the state tax authority's determination that a combined report is necessary to clearly reflect the group's income earned in the state or to prevent the evasion of taxes.

> **EXAMPLE**
>
> New Jersey does not permit an affiliated group to elect to file a consolidated return, nor does it require a unitary group to compute its income on a combined basis. Thus, every corporation with nexus in New Jersey is generally considered a separate entity and must file its own return.
>
> The Director of the Division of Taxation may, however, require members of an affiliated group or a controlled group to file a consolidated return "if the taxpayer cannot demonstrate by clear and convincing evidence that a report by a taxpayer discloses the true earnings of the taxpayer on its business carried on in this State" (N.J. Rev. Stat. 54:10A-10.c.).

Concept of a Unitary Business

Combined unitary reporting requires a determination of whether two or more corporations are engaged in a unitary business.

Unfortunately, there is no simple, objective definition of what constitutes a *unitary business*. In fact, over the years the courts have developed a number of different tests for determining the existence of a unitary business.

As one Supreme Court Justice observed, "the unitary business concept ... is not, so to speak, unitary." Because of the many judicial interpretations of a unitary business, it is not always clear which of the available tests should be applied. In addition, even if a taxpayer knows which test will be used, the subjective nature of the tests makes them difficult to apply with any certainty.

Generally, a vertically integrated business, in which each separate affiliate or division performs an interdependent step that leads to a finished product only when the steps are combined, will be treated as unitary.

A horizontally integrated business, in which there are parallel operations in different geographic locations (e.g., a chain of retail stores), will generally be considered unitary if there is centralized management.

A conglomerate may or may not be considered unitary, depending on whether there is strong centralized management, as exhibited by a centralized executive force and shared staff functions, as well as economies of scale in the form of common employee pension and benefit plans, common insurance policies, and so on.

As mentioned above, the courts have developed a number of different tests for determining the existence of a unitary business, including the:

- Three-unities test
- Contribution or dependency test
- Flow-of-value test
- Factors-of-profitability test

Three-unities test. The three-unities test requires the presence of [*Butler Bros. v. McColgan,* 315 US 501 (1942)]:

1. Unity of ownership
2. Unity of operation
3. Unity of use

Unity of ownership generally is satisfied when 50 percent or more of the corporation's stock is owned directly or indirectly by another corporation in the group.

Unity of operation is evidenced by the performance of certain staff functions by one of the corporations on behalf of the entire group, such as centralized purchasing, advertising, accounting and legal services, and human resource functions.

Unity of use is associated with common executive forces and general systems of operations and is evidenced by major policy decisions that are made by centralized management, intercompany product flow, and services that are provided by one affiliate to other group members.

Contribution or dependency test. The contribution or dependency test focuses on whether the enterprise's in-state business operations depend on, or contribute to, the enterprise's out-of-state business operations [*Edison Cal. Stores, Inc. v. McColgan,* 176 P.2d 697 (Cal. 1947)]. Examples of business activities that may be considered contributing factors are:

- Substantial borrowing from out-of-state operations to finance in-state operations
- Transfers of top-level executives, manufacturing equipment, or materials from out-of-state operations to in-state operations

Flow-of-value test. Under the flow-of-value test, "some sharing or exchange of value … beyond the mere flow of funds arising out of a passive investment" is needed to establish the existence of a unitary business [*Container Corp. of Am. v. Franchise Tax Bd.,* 463 US 159 (1983)].

Factors-of-profitability test. The factors-of-profitability test looks to functional integration, centralization of management, and economies of scale to determine the existence of a unitary business [*Allied-Signal, Inc. v. Division of Taxation,* 504 US 768 (1992)].

In addition to judicial interpretations, state-specific statutes and regulations are important sources of authority regarding what constitutes a unitary business group. Like their judicial counterparts, however, they generally leave much to be desired in terms of providing detailed and objective guidance.

The MTC regulations portray the concept of a unitary business as follows:

> A unitary business is a single economic enterprise that is made up either of separate parts of a single business entity or of a commonly controlled group of business entities that are sufficiently interdependent, integrated and interrelated through their activities so as to provide a synergy and mutual benefit that produces a sharing or exchange of value among them and a significant flow of value to the separate parts [MTC Reg. IV.1.(b)].

More specifically, a unitary business is characterized by significant flows of value evidenced by the following factors:

1. **Functional integration**—This includes product flow among affiliates and centralized functions such as advertising, accounting, purchasing, manufacturing, and financing. Examples include common marketing programs, transfers or pooling of technical information or intellectual property, common distribution systems, common purchasing, and common or intercompany financing.
2. **Centralization of management**—Joint participation of corporate directors and officers in the management decisions that affect the different business units. Indicators of centralized management include interlocking boards of directors, interchange of personnel at upper management levels, and required parent company approval on major policy decisions.
3. **Economies of scale**—Centralized purchasing, centralized administrative functions, etc.

The MTC regulation also identifies same type of business, steps in a vertical process, and strong centralized management as indicators of a unitary business.

STUDY QUESTIONS

---

7. Which of the following states does not require each member of a commonly controlled group of corporations to file separate-company returns?

   a. Arizona
   b. Delaware
   c. Maryland

8. Inclusion in a state elective consolidated return generally requires 50 percent or more common ownership. ***True or False?***

   a. True
   b. False

Basic Multistate Tax Planning Strategies

The objectives of multistate income tax planning are to:
- Structure an organization's business activities
- Create the optimal mix of legal entities in order to minimize state income tax costs

Planning techniques generally involve an attempt either to reduce the total amount of the organization's taxable income subject to apportionment or to minimize the apportionment percentage in a given state.

In determining which activities or entities to alter, the tax planner must carefully analyze the effects that each change has on the corporation's total state tax liability to ensure that the taxes saved in one state are not offset by tax increases in other states. Therefore, effective state tax planning requires a review of a corporation's activities in *all* states and an understanding of the apportionment formulas and other tax laws of the states in which the corporation does business.

Moreover, any tax planning strategy must be reviewed in light of practical business considerations and the additional administrative or operational costs that might be incurred in implementing the strategy.

The remainder of this section briefly discusses the following selected planning opportunities:
- Selecting the states in which to be taxed
- Establishing the right to apportion income
- Engaging structure planning techniques
- Using the most beneficial group filing method

Selecting the States in Which to Be Taxed. When a corporation has only a limited connection with a state, it may be possible to discontinue that activity by using an alternative means of accomplishing the same result.

EXAMPLE

If maintaining a corporate office in a state creates an undesired nexus, the corporation might avoid nexus by providing the sales representatives with an office allowance rather than a formal company office.

When nexus is created by sales representatives performing repair and maintenance services in the state, one strategy would be to separately incorporate the sales division that operates in the state.

Assuming the state does not require combined reporting, this would prevent the state from taxing the profits attributable to the parent corporation's out-of-state assets and activities. Such a technique will be successful *only* if the incorporated division is a bona fide business operation and the state does not successfully assert that the corporation continues to have nexus under the concepts of affiliate or agency nexus (discussed below). In addition, the pricing of any sales or services between the new subsidiary and the parent corporation must be at arm's length.

Although most planning techniques are designed to avoid nexus, there are situations in which a corporation can benefit from establishing nexus in a state.

Creating nexus in a particular state can be *beneficial* if the corporation:
- Currently does not have the right to apportion its income
- Wants to avoid the application of a sales throwback rule by creating nexus in a destination state
- Wants to have a loss affiliate create nexus in a state that allows only nexus affiliates to join in filing a state consolidated return.

Establishing nexus may be simple to accomplish because of the relatively low threshold for creating constitutional nexus and the limited nature of the protection afforded by Public Law 86-272.

Establishing the Right to Apportion Income. A corporation that has nexus in only one state may *not* apportion its income and therefore is subject to tax on 100 percent of its income in that state.

By establishing the right to apportion its income, the taxpayer may be able to reduce its state income tax costs substantially, particularly if the corporation is domiciled in a high-tax state. The income that is removed from the tax base of the state of domicile may escape state taxation altogether if the state in which the corporation establishes nexus does not impose a corporate income tax or imposes a corporate income tax but has more liberal nexus rules than the state of domicile.

Another major factor in determining the tax benefit of apportioning income is whether the state from which the taxpayer is shipping goods has a sales throwback rule. Many states do not require throwback, in which case sales in states where the taxpayer does not have nexus are not assigned to the numerator of any state's sales factor (called *nowhere sales*).

To acquire the right to apportion its income, the corporation generally must have nexus in at least one state other than its state of domicile. Whether a corporation's activities or contacts in another state are considered adequate to justify apportionment is generally determined by reference to the tax laws of the domicile state.

To apportion its income, a corporation must typically:

- Carry on business in another state
- Maintain an office or other regular place of business in another state, OR
- Be taxable in another state

Some states take the restrictive position that apportionment is permitted *only* if the corporation is actually filing returns and paying tax in another state. A corporation should analyze its current activities in and contacts with other states to determine which activities or contacts, if any, could be redirected so that the corporation will be granted the right to apportion its income.

Structure Planning Techniques. Numerous states allow a group of commonly controlled corporations to file returns on a separate-company basis. This can provide a taxpayer with the opportunity to create legal structures and intercompany transactions that shift income from affiliates based in certain high-tax states to affiliates based in low-or no-tax states.

For example, if a high-tax state allows separate-company reporting, and a multistate corporation's only activity in that state is sales and distribution (which are often relatively low-margin activities), the corporation may be able to insulate its out-of-state assets and activities from taxation in the high-tax state by forming a sales subsidiary that is responsible for marketing its products in the state.

Another example of structure planning is a financial institution that holds a significant portfolio of marketable securities. The taxpayer may be able to realize significant tax savings by transferring the securities to an intangible property holding company domiciled in Delaware (which does not tax the income of a corporation whose only activities in the state are the maintenance and management of intangible property or the collection and distribution of income from such property).

Historically, large corporations (in particular, retailers) used Delaware trademark holding companies to avoid state income taxes. By transferring valuable trademarks and trade names to an intangible property holding company domiciled in Delaware, and then licensing the use of the intangibles back to the operating companies, a corporation could potentially avoid state taxation of the income attributable to the intangible assets. States have significantly curtailed the use of trademark holding companies by enacting combined reporting requirements, related-party expense add-back provisions, and economic nexus statutes.

Structure planning can also be used to take advantage of net operating losses in states that do not allow any form of consolidated or combined reporting. One way to use such losses is to merge an unprofitable affiliate into a profitable affiliate. Another potential strategy for better utilizing an affiliate's net operating losses is to convert the unprofitable affiliate into a single member limited liability company (LLC). A single-member LLC is generally treated as a *disregarded entity* for both federal and state income tax purposes and, therefore, the use of a single-member LLC effectively produces the same result as a consolidated return.

> **NOTE**
>
> Care must be taken when dealing with single-member LLCs because some states impose entity-level taxes on such entities.

Using the Most Beneficial Group Filing Method. In states that permit an affiliated group to elect to file a consolidated return, such an election can be beneficial when one affiliate has losses that can be offset against the income generated by other affiliates.

Other potential *benefits* of filing a consolidated return include:
- The elimination of intercorporate dividends
- Deferral of gains on intercompany transactions
- The use of credits that would otherwise be limited by the lack of income

In choosing whether to file a consolidated return, the corporation should determine whether the advantages of a consolidated return can be realized without adverse consequences.

For example, a corporation that is eligible to file a consolidated return in a given state may choose not to do so if it has significant losses on intercompany transactions and would lose the deduction as a result of the election. On the other hand, another member of the same affiliated group may elect to file a consolidated state return in another state to defer recognition of intercompany gains.

A major *disadvantage* of filing a consolidated return is that it can limit a taxpayer's ability to use intercompany transactions that shift income from affiliates based in high-tax states to affiliates based in low-tax states.

Most states that permit affiliated corporations to file a consolidated return have adopted a reporting-consistency requirement similar to that imposed for federal consolidated return purposes. Thus, once an election to file a consolidated return is made, the affiliated group generally must continue to file on a consolidated basis—unless the group receives permission from state tax authorities to file separate-company returns.

STUDY QUESTIONS

> **9.** Assume a manufacturer wants to establish nexus in a state to avoid throwback of its sales into that state. Which of the following activities would most likely create income tax nexus in that state?
>
> **a.** A sales representative engaging in non-solicitation activity
> **b.** A sales representative soliciting orders for tangible personal property
> **c.** Providing a sales representative with a company car that is used only in solicitation activities
>
> **10.** It is *always* beneficial to file a consolidated return in states that permit that election. ***True or False?***

ADVANCED CONCEPTS

Nexus

Economic Nexus. In *Quill,* the U.S. Supreme Court ruled that a corporation satisfies the Commerce Clause's *substantial nexus* requirement only if the taxpayer has a physical presence in the state.

Yet, in *Geoffrey, Inc. v. South Carolina Tax Commission*, the South Carolina Supreme Court held that a trademark holding company that licensed its intangibles for use in South Carolina had nexus for income tax purposes despite the lack of any tangible property or employees in South Carolina [437 S.E.2d 13 (S.C. 1993), *cert. denied* 510 US 992, 1993].

Geoffrey was the trademark holding company of the toy retailer, Toys "R" Us. Geoffrey was incorporated and domiciled in Delaware and had a license agreement with South Carolina retailers allowing them to use its trademarks and trade names, including the Toys "R" Us trademark. The court held that licensing intangibles for use in the state was sufficient to satisfy the minimum connection and substantial nexus requirements of the Due Process Clause and the Commerce Clause. The *Geoffrey* court did *not* follow the precedent established by *Quill,* because it believed that ruling applied only to the issue of nexus for sales and use tax purposes.

Since 1993, there has been a significant amount of litigation related to the *Geoffrey* court's interpretation of the Commerce Clause's substantial nexus requirement. In addition, many states have enacted "economic nexus" standards that are based on the amount of sales or income derived from sources within a state. In addition, the highest courts in several other states have ruled that a physical presence is not an absolute prerequisite to income tax nexus.

In *Lanco, Inc. v. Division of Taxation*, the New Jersey Supreme Court ruled that the Delaware trademark holding company of the clothing retailer Lane Bryant had income tax nexus in New Jersey, even though it had no physical presence in the state [908 A.2d 176 (N.J. 2006); *cert. denied*, U.S. Sup. Ct., 06-1236, June 18, 2007]. The court concluded that "the better interpretation of *Quill* is the one adopted by those states that limit the Supreme Court's holding to sales and use taxes." The court also stated that "we do not believe that the Supreme Court intended to create a universal physical-presence requirement for state taxation under the Commerce Clause."

In *Tax Commissioner v. MBNA America Bank, N.A.*, the taxpayer was a Delaware bank that issued credit cards, extended unsecured credit, and serviced the credit card accounts of customers nationwide [640 S.E.2d 226 (W. Va. 2006); *cert. denied*, U.S. Sup. Ct., 06-1228, June 18, 2007]. Although MBNA did not have a physical presence in West Virginia, during one of the tax years in question, it derived over $10 million of gross receipts from West Virginia customers. The West Virginia Supreme Court of Appeals ruled that the physical presence test "applies only to state sales and use taxes and not to state business franchise and corporation net income taxes," and that MBNA had "a significant economic presence sufficient to meet the substantial nexus" test under the Commerce Clause.

In *Capital One Bank and Capital One F.S.B. v. Commissioner of Revenue*, the Massachusetts Supreme Judicial Court ruled that, despite the lack of any physical presence in the state, the two out-of-state credit card banks had substantial nexus in Massachusetts, because of the "purposeful, targeted marketing of their credit card business to Massachusetts customers ... and their receipt of hundreds of millions of dollars in income from millions of transactions involving Massachusetts residents and merchants" [No. SJC-10105 (Mass. Sup. Jud. Ct., Jan. 8, 2009); *cert. denied*, U.S. Sup. Ct., No. 08-1169, June 22, 2009].

Likewise, in *Geoffrey, Inc. v. Commissioner of Revenue*, the Massachusetts Supreme Judicial Court ruled that, despite the lack of a physical presence in the state, a Delaware trademark holding company that received royalty income from licensing trademarks to affiliated entities which used the trademarks for retail business activities in Massachusetts had income tax nexus in Massachusetts [No. SJC-10106, Mass. Sup. Jud. Ct., Jan. 8, 2009; *cert. denied*, U.S. Sup. Ct., No. 08-1207, June 22, 2009)].

Agency Nexus. Under the *Quill* decision, a corporation generally has constitutional nexus in any state in which it has property or employees located on a regular basis. What if, rather than conducting business in a state through employees (dependent agents), a corporation conducts business through independent contractors (independent agents)? Do the in-state activities of independent agents, acting on an out-of-state corporation's behalf, create constitutional nexus?

In *Scripto, Inc. v. Carson*, the U.S. Supreme Court addressed the issue of whether the Florida marketing activities of 10 independent sales representatives created Florida sales tax nexus for Scripto, a Georgia corporation that manufactured writing instruments [362 US 207 (1960)]. The Court held that for nexus purposes, the distinction between employees and independent contractors was "without constitutional significance," and that "to permit such formal 'contractual shifts' to make a constitutional difference would open the gates to a stampede of tax avoidance." In the Court's opinion, the critical fact was that the activities of the independent agents in Florida helped to create and maintain a commercial market for Scripto's goods. Thus, the presence of independent agents engaged in continuous local solicitation created Florida sales and use tax nexus for Scripto.

The Supreme Court reaffirmed these principles 25 years later in *Tyler Pipe Industries, Inc. v. Department of Revenue*, holding that the activities of an independent contractor residing in Washington were sufficient to create constitutional nexus for the out-of-state principal for purposes of the Washington business and occupation tax (a type of gross receipts tax) [483 US 232 (1987)]. As in *Scripto,* the Court held that the critical test was "whether the activities performed in this state on behalf of the taxpayer are significantly associated with the taxpayer's ability to establish and maintain a market in this state for the sales."

In addition to protecting solicitation activities of employee-salespersons, Public Law 86-272 protects certain in-state activities conducted by independent contractors. Specifically, the law provides that independent contractors can engage in the following in-state activities on behalf of an out-of-state corporation without creating income tax nexus for the principal:

1. Soliciting sales
2. Making sales
3. Maintaining an office

Thus, unlike employees, independent agents are permitted to maintain an in-state office without creating nexus for the principal.

The Supreme Court's decisions in *Scripto* and *Tyler Pipe* establish the principle that the use of independent agents to perform continuous local solicitation creates constitutional nexus for an out-of-state principal. Relying on these decisions, in Nexus Bulletin 95-1 (1995), the MTC took the position that the mail-order computer industry's practice of providing warranty services through third-party service providers creates constitutional nexus for sales and use tax purposes.

Affiliate Nexus. A number of states have taken the position that the existence of common ownership between a corporation that has a physical presence in a state (e.g., an in-state brick-and-mortar retailer) and an out-of-state corporation that has no physical presence in the state but makes substantial sales in the state (e.g., an affiliated out-of-state mail-order vendor) is sufficient to create constitutional nexus for the out-of-state mail-order affiliate. As with agency nexus, most of the litigation concerns the issue of nexus for sales and use tax purposes.

For example, in *SFA Folio Collections, Inc. v. Tracy,* SFA Folio (Folio), a New York corporation, sold clothing and other merchandise by direct mail to customers in Ohio and delivered the merchandise using common carriers [73 Ohio St. 3d 119, 652 N.E. 2d 693 (1995)]. Folio had no property or employees in Ohio, but Folio's parent corporation, Saks & Company, owned another subsidiary, Saks Fifth Avenue of Ohio (Saks-Ohio), which operated a retail store in Ohio.

Ohio tax authorities argued that Folio had *substantial nexus* in Ohio, because it was a member of an affiliated group that included a corporation that operated a store in Ohio and therefore was required to collect Ohio sales tax on its mail-order sales to Ohio customers. The state's position was based on a nexus-by-affiliate statute that the Ohio Legislature had enacted, as well as the argument that Saks-Ohio was an *agent* of Folio.

The agency argument was based on the fact that Saks-Ohio accepted some returns of Folio sales and distributed some Folio catalogs. The Ohio Supreme Court rejected the affiliate nexus argument, reasoning that to impute nexus to Folio merely because a sister corporation had a physical presence in Ohio ran counter to federal constitutional law and Ohio corporation law. The court also rejected the agency nexus argument because Saks-Ohio accepted Folio's returns according to its own policy (not Folio's) and charged the returns to its own inventory (not Folio's).

Consistent with the Ohio Supreme Court's ruling in *SFA Folio,* other states have generally been unsuccessful in their attempts to argue that common ownership, by itself, creates nexus for an out-of-state affiliate [See, e.g., *Current, Inc. v. State Bd. of Equalization,* 24 Cal. App. 4th 382, 29 Cal. Rptr. 2d 407 (Ct. App. 1994); *SFA Folio Collections, Inc. v. Bannon,* 217 Conn. 220, 585 A.2d 666 (1991); *Bloomingdale's By Mail, Ltd. v. Commonwealth,* 130 Pa. Commw. 190, 567 A.2d 773 (Commw. Ct. 1989)]. On the other hand, if an in-state affiliate functions as an agent for the out-of-state affiliate, the Supreme Court's decisions in *Scripto* and *Tyler Pipe* provide a basis for arguing that the activities of the in-state affiliate creates nexus for an out-of-state affiliate.

In *Borders Online, Inc.*, the California Court of Appeals ruled that an out-of-state online retailer had a substantial nexus in California for sales and use tax purposes, because an affiliated corporation that sold similar products in brick-and-mortar stores in California performed return and exchange activities for the online retailer [No. A105488 (Cal. Ct. of App., May 31, 2005)]. The brick-and-mortar affiliate was considered to be an authorized *representative* of the online retailer because the online retailer posted a notice on its Web site that returns could be made to the brick-and-mortar retailer, and the brick-and-mortar retailer's acceptance of returns was an integral part of the online retailer's sales operations. Therefore, under the relevant state statute, the online retailer was considered to be engaged in business in California and subject to the obligation to collect use tax on sales to California residents.

In *Barnesandnoble.com LLC v. State Bd. of Equalization*, the California Superior Court ruled that an in-state brick-and-mortar affiliate's distribution of coupons that provided a discount on an online purchase did not create sales and use tax nexus for the related Internet retailer. The retail stores did *not* act as the Internet vendor's agent or representative [No. CGC-06-456465 (Cal. Super. Ct., Oct. 11, 2007)]. The court concluded that "[a]n essential element is that the agent (or representative) must have the authority to bind the principal." In the present case, the in-state retailer had no such authority and could do nothing but pass out the coupons created and distributed by Internet vendor.

A number of states have enacted affiliate nexus statutes for sales and use taxes. For example, in H.B. 360 (Mar. 3, 2008), Idaho amended its definition of a *retailer engaged in business in this state* for sales and use tax collection purposes to include a retailer with substantial nexus in the state. A retailer has *substantial nexus* with Idaho if *both* of the following apply:

1. The retailer and an in-state business maintaining one or more locations within Idaho are related parties.
2. The retailer and the in-state business use an identical or substantially similar name, trade name, trademark, or goodwill to develop, promote, or maintain sales, or the in-state business provides services to, or that inure to the benefit of, the out-of-state business related to developing, promoting, or maintaining the in-state market.

The above provisions do *not* apply to a retailer that had less than $100,000 in sales in Idaho in the previous year.

Deliveries in Company-Owned Trucks. A corporation generally has constitutional nexus in any state in which it has property or employees located on a regular basis. Thus, a number of state courts have held that the regular and systematic presence of company-owned delivery trucks driven by company employees is sufficient to create sales and use tax nexus [E.g., *Brown's Furniture, Inc. v. Wagner,* No. 78195 (Ill. 1996); *Town Crier, Inc. v. Zehnder,* No. 1-98-4251 (Ill. App. Ct. 2000); *John Swenson Granite Co. v. State Tax Assessor,* 685 A.2d 425 (Me. Super. Ct. 1996)].

For income tax purposes, Public Law 86-272 shields an out-of-state corporation from taxation if its only in-state activity is:

1. Solicitation of orders by company representatives
2. For sales of tangible personal property
3. The orders are sent outside the state for approval or rejection
4. If approved, orders are filled by shipment or delivery from a point outside the state

Over the years, taxpayers have taken the position that the phrase *shipment or delivery* implies that a seller is protected by Public Law 86-272, regardless of whether it ships the goods into the state using a common carrier or its own delivery trucks. Some states, however, have taken the position that the seller's use of its own trucks to make deliveries is not protected by Public Law 86-272.

State supreme courts in Massachusetts and Virginia have ruled that deliveries in company-owned trucks is a protected activity under Public Law 86-272 [*National Private Truck Council v. Virginia Department of Taxation,* 253 Va. 74, 480 S.E.2d 500 (1997); and *National Private Truck Council v. Commissioner of Revenue,* 688 N.E.2d 936 (Mass. 1997), *cert. denied*].

In 2001, the MTC revised its Statement of Information Concerning Practices of Multistate Tax Commission and Signatory States Under Public Law 86-272 by removing from the list of unprotected activities the following item: "Shipping or delivering goods into this state by means of private vehicle, rail, water, air or other carrier, irrespective of whether shipment or delivery fee or other charge is imposed, directly or indirectly, upon the purchaser." Several state revenue departments have also indicated that deliveries using company-owned trucks is protected by Public Law 86-272 [Rev. Rul. 24-01-01, Neb. Dept. of Rev. (Feb. 22, 2001); Decision No. 2005-05-10-22, Okla. Tax Comn. (May 10, 2005); and Ala. Reg. 810-27-1-4-.19 (Feb. 28, 2006)].

De Minimis Rule. The existence of a *de minimis* rule in the nexus arena is supported by numerous authorities. With respect to constitutional nexus, the Supreme Court has ruled that the Commerce Clause requires a *substantial nexus* in a state [*Complete Auto Transit, Inc. v. Brady,* 430 US 274 (1977)]. In addition, in *Quill,* the taxpayer held title to a few floppy diskettes that were located in North Dakota.

The Supreme Court indicated that, although title to a few floppy diskettes located in a state "might constitute some minimal nexus, in *National*

Geographic Society v. California Bd. of Equalization, 430 US 551, 556 (1977), we expressly rejected a 'slightest presence' standard of constitutional nexus" [*Quill Corp. v. North Dakota,* 504 US 298 n.8 (1992)]. Thus, the presence of a few floppy diskettes did *not* satisfy the substantial nexus requirement of the Commerce Clause. With respect to Public Law 86-272, in *Wrigley* the Supreme Court indicated that a *de minimis* level of in-state non-solicitation activities does not cause a company to lose the protection afforded by Public Law 86-272.

State courts in Illinois and Michigan have adopted the "more than a slightest presence" test articulated in *Orvis Co., Inc. v. Tax Appeals Tribunal* and *Vermont Information Processing Inc. v. Tax Appeals Tribunal,* in which the New York Court of Appeals concluded that, although a physical presence is required to satisfy the *Quill substantial nexus* requirement, the in-state physical presence need not be substantial; instead, it must be "demonstrably more than a slightest presence" [Nos. 138, 139 (N.Y. 1995)].

In *Brown's Furniture v. Wagner,* the Illinois Supreme Court concluded that "the Orvis court stated—correctly, we believe—the rule regarding substantial nexus" [No. 78195 (Ill. 1996)]. Likewise, in *MagneTek Controls, Inc. v. Michigan Department of Treasury,* the Michigan Court of Appeals stated that "we conclude that the court in *Orvis* correctly understood *Quill* and enunciated an appropriate test for applying *Quill*" [No. 181612 (Mich. Ct. App. 1997)].

STUDY QUESTIONS

11. In which of the following cases did the court determine that the taxpayer had *no* nexus because of a lack of physical presence?

a. *Geoffrey, Inc. v. South Carolina Tax Commission*
b. *Lanco, Inc. v. New Jersey Division of Taxation*
c. *West Virginia Tax Commissioner v. MBNA America Bank, N.A.*
d. *Quill Corp. v. North Dakota*

12. Based on the court decisions discussed previously, in which of the following situations is it most likely that the company has income tax nexus?

a. A related corporation has a physical presence in the state, but the company itself does not. The operations of the in-state affiliate have nothing to do with those of the taxpayer.
b. The company does not have any service technicians based in the state. However, the company's out-of-state technicians travel to the state to provide repair services, as needed. During the current year, these technicians spend roughly two weeks in the state.
c. The company makes deliveries into the state using company-owned trucks.

Specialized Industry Apportionment Formulas

The UDITPA equally weighted three-factor apportionment formula was designed to apportion the income of multistate manufacturing and mercantile businesses and may not fairly apportion the income of businesses in other industries.

For example, the conventional UDITPA property and payroll factors are difficult to compute for property and payroll that is regularly in motion, such as that of interstate trucking companies, airlines, and railroads. In addition, since its adoption in 1957, the UDITPA §17 income-producing activity rule for sourcing sales of services has been controversial.

Many commentators have argued that its effect is often to merely mimic the property and payroll factor, rather than measure the customer base within a state. The drafters of UDITPA foresaw the limitations of the standard UDITPA apportionment formula, and, under Section 2, specifically excluded from UDITPA certain service businesses, including *financial organizations* (bank, trust company, savings bank, private banker, savings and loan association, credit union, investment company or insurance company), and *public utilities* (defined as any business entity that owns or operates for public use any plant, equipment, property, franchise or license for the transmission of communications, transportation of goods or persons or the production, storage, transmission, sale, delivery or furnishing of electricity, water, steam, oil, oil products or gas).

To address these issues, many states provide special rules for computing apportionment percentages for businesses in certain industries. Typically, these special rules involve the modification or exclusion of the conventional factors or the use of unique, industry-specific factors. Examples of industries for which states provide special apportionment factor rules include airlines, railroads, trucking companies, financial institutions, television and radio broadcasters, publishers, telecommunication services companies, mutual funds, pipelines, ship transportation companies, and professional sports franchises.

In many cases, the equitable relief provisions of UDITPA §18, which numerous states have incorporated into their statutes, serve as the basis for state revenue departments to adopt specialized formulas. UDITPA §18 provides that if the standard apportionment formula does not fairly reflect a taxpayer's in-state business activity, tax authorities may require the exclusion of one or more of the factors or the inclusion of additional factors that will fairly represent the taxpayer's business activity in the state.

Under Section 18, the MTC has promulgated special apportionment regulations covering:

- Construction contractors [MTC Reg. IV.18(d)]
- Airlines [MTC Reg. IV.18(e)]
- Railroads [MTC Reg. IV.18(f)]
- Trucking companies [MTC Reg. IV.18(g)]
- Television and radio broadcasters [MTC Reg. IV.18(h)]
- Publishers [MTC Reg. IV.18(j)]

The MTC has also promulgated a model statute for apportioning the income of financial institutions (Nov. 17, 1994). In July 2008, the MTC approved a proposed model regulation for the apportionment of income from telecommunications services.

Sourcing Sales of Services

UDITPA §17. UDITPA provides two different rules for determining the numerator of the sales factor. UDITPA §16 applies to sales of tangible personal property, and UDITPA §17 applies to all sales other than sales of tangible personal property. UDIPTA §17 is a catch-all provision, which applies to fees from services, rental income, as well as interest, dividends, royalties, and gains derived from the sale of intangible property.

Most states employ some variation of the UDITPA §17 income-producing activity rule to source sales of services. Under UDITPA §17(a), sales of services are attributed to the state in which "the income producing activity is performed."

> **EXAMPLE**
>
> A consulting firm receives a $100,000 fee for services performed by the taxpayer's employees at its offices in State P. Regardless of where the client is located, the $100,000 sale is attributed to State P, because that is where the underlying income-producing activity (i.e., employee services) is performed.

Under UDIPTA §17(b), if the income-producing activity is performed in two or more states, the sale is attributed to the state in which a greater proportion of the income-producing activity is performed than in any other state, based on the *costs of performance*. Thus, in order to source sales of services under the UDITPA income-producing activity rule, the taxpayer must first determine what activity produced the income.

Once the taxpayer has identified the applicable income-producing activity, a cost-of-performance analysis is conducted. This involves determining the costs associated with the activity, as well as the states in which those costs were incurred.

The cost-of-performance rule is an all-or-nothing approach, whereby the *entire* sale is attributed to the single state in which the greater proportion of the costs of performance is incurred.

EXAMPLE

A consulting firm receives a $100,000 fee for services performed by its employees. Seventy percent of the costs of performance are incurred in State P, and 30 percent of the costs of performance are incurred in State Q.

Under UDIPTA §17(b), the entire $100,000 sale is attributed to State P, because that is where the greater proportion of the income-producing activity is performed (based on costs of performance), and none of the $100,000 sale is attributed to State Q—despite the significant amount of costs of performance incurred in State Q.

UDITPA does not define the terms *income-producing activity* or *costs of performance*, but additional guidance is provided by the MTC regulations. Under MTC Reg. IV.17(2), the term *income-producing activity* applies to each separate item of income and means the transactions and activity engaged in by the taxpayer in the regular course of its trade or business. Examples of *income-producing activity* include:

- The rendering of personal services by employees or the use of tangible or intangible property by the taxpayer in performing a service
- The sale, rental, leasing, licensing or other use of real property
- The rental, leasing, licensing or other use of tangible personal property
- The sale, licensing or other use of intangible personal property

The mere holding of intangible personal property is not, by itself, an income-producing activity.

Under MTC Reg. IV.17(3), the term *costs of performance* means direct costs determined in a manner consistent with generally accepted accounting principles and in accordance with accepted conditions or practices in the trade or business of the taxpayer. Direct costs include material and labor costs that have a causal relationship with the sale in question. In other words, a direct cost is a cost that was incurred for a specific purpose and is traceable to that purpose.

EXAMPLE

The direct costs associated with a service contract for maintaining business equipment would include both the cost of repair parts and the compensation costs of the service technicians.

Indirect costs, which include general and administrative expenses that are not associated with any specific sale, are not taken into account in determining the costs of performance. In 2007, the MTC approved an amendment to MTC Reg. IV.17 to include in the taxpayer's cost of performance payments to an agent or independent contractor for the performance of personal services and the utilization of tangible and intangible property that give rise to the particular item of income.

MTC Reg. IV.17(4)(B)(c) provides a special rule for applying the UDITPA income-producing activity rule to gross receipts for the performance of "personal services," under which a lump-sum payment for personal services performed in two or more states is prorated among the states in proportion to the time spent in each state, based on the premise that the services performed in each state constitute a separate income-producing activity. The regulation does not define what constitutes "personal services."

Market-Based Source Rules. The original purpose of the sales factor was to include in the apportionment formula a measure of the taxpayer's customer base within a given state. However, unlike the UDITPA §16 destination test for inventory sales, the UDITPA §17 income-producing activity rule for sales of services does not accurately measure a service company's customer base when the seller (service provider) performs services in one state and the purchaser (service recipient) is located in another state.

When UDITPA was drafted in 1957, it was rare for a service provider and service recipient to be located in different states. Today, however, it is more common for customers to do business with out-of-state service providers. In such cases, the income-producing activity rule no longer measures the customer base within a state, but instead tends to mimic the property and payroll factors.

Due in part to this weakness of the income-producing activity rule, some states have adopted a market-based approach for sales of services, whereby receipts from services are attributed to a state based on where the service recipient is located. In addition to providing a more accurate measure of the taxpayer's customer base, this approach has the political appeal of reducing the tax burden on service providers that have in-state facilities but provide services primarily to out-of-state customers.

A market-based rule for services also creates an incentive for regional and national service providers to locate their facilities within the state's borders. Because most states use the income-producing activity rule, a market-based source rule can result in nowhere income for service providers that locate their facilities within the state. Finally, the tax revenue on in-state service providers that is lost from switching from the income-producing activity rule to a market-based rule may be partially offset by increased taxes on out-of-state service providers that make sales to in-state customers.

The states that have adopted a market-based approach for sales of services include California (effective in 2011), Georgia, Illinois, Iowa, Maine, Maryland, Michigan, Minnesota, Utah, and Wisconsin.

Non-Income Taxes—Michigan, Ohio, Texas and Washington

Most states link their corporate tax structures to the federal net income tax model, primarily for ease of administration. Some states, however, base their corporate tax systems on different models, or impose specialized corporate taxes in addition to a regular corporate income tax.

Michigan Business Tax. Michigan imposes a 4.95 percent business income tax and a 0.80 percent modified gross receipts tax. Taxpayers pay the sum of the two new taxes. There is currently an annual surcharge equal to 21.99 percent of a taxpayer's Michigan business tax. The surcharge is capped at $6 million per year.

The business income tax base is a taxpayer's federal taxable income, adjusted for numerous addition and subtraction modifications. The modified gross receipts tax base is a taxpayer's gross receipts reduced by purchases from other firms, which includes acquisitions of inventory, depreciable assets, materials, and supplies. Both taxes apply to business entities generally, including C corporations, S corporations, partnerships, limited liability companies, and sole proprietorships.

A unitary business group must compute both the business income tax and the modified gross receipts tax on a combined basis. The term *unitary business group* is defined as:

1. A group of U.S. persons, other than a foreign operating entity, one of which owns or controls more than 50 percent of the ownership interests with voting rights of the other U.S. persons, and
2. That has business activities or operations which result in a flow of value between or among persons included in the unitary business group or has business activities or operations that are integrated with, are dependent upon, or contribute to each other

Ohio Commercial Activity Tax. Ohio imposes a *commercial activity tax* (CAT) on a business entity's gross receipts. The tax rate is 0.26 percent. The CAT applies to C corporations, S corporations, partnerships, and limited liability companies.

Generally, items that are treated as gross receipts for federal income tax purposes are treated as gross receipts for CAT purposes. There are important exceptions, however.

> **EXAMPLE**
>
> Interest (except on credit sales), dividend, and capital gain income is not subject to the CAT.

A taxable gross receipt is a gross receipt sitused to Ohio. Sales of inventory are attributed to Ohio if the property is received in Ohio by the purchaser, rents and royalties are attributed to Ohio if the property is located or used in Ohio, and fees for services are attributed to Ohio in the proportion that the purchaser's benefit in Ohio bears to the purchaser's benefit everywhere. Thus, examples of taxable gross receipts include sales of property delivered to locations within Ohio, rents from property used in Ohio, and fees for services where the purchaser receives the benefit in Ohio.

Two or more commonly controlled corporations may elect to compute the CAT as a *consolidated elected taxpayer*. If this election is made, receipts received between members of the group are not subject to the CAT. However, all commonly owned entities that are part of the group are included in the group, including entities that do not have nexus in Ohio on a separate-company basis. If the election is not made, any taxpayers with common ownership of more than 50 percent must file as a *combined taxpayer*. A combined taxpayer may not exclude receipts between members of the group. However, combined taxpayers only need to include in the group those members who have nexus with Ohio.

Texas Margin Tax. Texas imposes a business *margin tax*. Taxable entities include C corporations, S corporations, limited liability companies, and partnerships. Certain entities are exempt from the margin tax, including sole proprietorships, general partnerships with direct ownership entirely composed of natural persons, and certain passive entities. A taxable entity's margin is the lowest of three amounts:

1. Total revenue minus cost of goods sold
2. Total revenue minus compensation
3. 70 percent of total revenue

The tax rate is 0.5 percent for taxpayers primarily engaged in retail or wholesale trade, and 1 percent for all other businesses.

Taxable entities that are part of an affiliated group engaged in a unitary business must file a combined group report and compute their margin tax as if they were a single taxable entity. An "affiliated group" means a group of one or more taxable entities in which a controlling interest is owned by a common owner or owners, either corporate or noncorporate, or by one or more of the member entities. A controlling interest means more than 50 percent direct or indirect ownership.

A taxable entity that conducts business outside the United States is *excluded* from the combined report if 80 percent or more of its property and payroll are assigned to locations outside the United States. A unitary business means a single economic enterprise that is made up of separate parts of a single entity or of a commonly controlled group of entities that are sufficiently interdependent, integrated, and interrelated through their activities so as to provide a synergy and mutual benefit that produces a sharing or exchange of value among them and a significant flow of value to the separate parts.

Washington Business and Occupation Tax. The State of Washington imposes a gross receipts tax called the *business and occupation tax* (B&O tax). The B&O tax applies to C corporations, S corporations, partnerships, and sole proprietorships. The B&O tax rate varies with the type of business activity. The four primary business activity classifications are retailing, wholesaling, manufacturing, and service and other activities. The applicable tax rates are 0.471% for retailing, 0.484% for wholesaling, 0.484% for manufacturing, and 1.5% for service and other activities.

The B&O tax is imposed on a seller's gross receipts derived from business activities conducted within the State of Washington. Since the tax is a gross receipts tax, there are generally no deductions from the B&O tax for labor, materials, taxes, or other costs of doing business. Taxable gross receipts generally include:

- Gross proceeds from sales of goods delivered to customers located in Washington, except for sales of goods that an in-state retailer or wholesaler delivers to customers located outside of Washington
- Gross receipts from sales of services rendered in Washington
- The value of products manufactured in Washington

STUDY QUESTIONS

13. A corporation sells a service. Sixty-percent of the income-producing activity is performed in State A, 30 percent in State B, and 10 percent in State C. Under the cost-of-performance rule in UDITPA §17(b), how is the sale allocated?

a. 60 percent to State A, 30 percent to State B, and 10 percent to State C

b. 34 percent to State A, 33 percent to State B, and 33 percent to State C

c. 100 percent to State A

14. Under a market-based approach for sourcing sales of services, receipts from services are attributed to a state based on where the service recipient is located. **_True or False?_**

Mechanisms Used by States to Limit Tax Base Erosion

A principal planning objective is to create legal structures that minimize the state income taxes of the business enterprise as a whole. Through the use of separately incorporated affiliates and intercompany transactions (loans, licenses, inventory sales, etc.), income can be shifted from operations in high-tax states to operations in low-tax states. Such strategies are made possible by the large number of states that require or permit the filing of separate-company returns, whereby each member of an affiliated group that has nexus in a state computes its income and files a return as if it were a separate and distinct economic entity.

States employ a number of mechanisms to limit the ability of multistate businesses to use related party structures and transactions to shift income. As discussed below, these include the theory of economic nexus, the judicial doctrines of economic substance and business purpose, combined reporting, Code Sec. 482-type reallocation provisions, and related party expense addback provisions.

Economic Nexus. The highest courts in several states have ruled that an economic presence, such as the licensing of trademarks for use within the state by affiliated companies, is sufficient to create constitutional nexus for income tax purposes [*Geoffrey, Inc. v. South Carolina Tax Commission,* 437 S.E.2d 13 (S.C. 1993), *cert. denied* 510 US 992 (1993); *Lanco, Inc. v. Division of Taxation,* No. A-89-05 (N.J. Sup. Ct., Oct. 12, 2006); *cert. denied,* U.S. Sup. Ct., 06-1236 (2007); *Commissioner v. MBNA America Bank, N.A.,* No. 33049 (W.V. Sup. Ct. of App., Nov. 21, 2006); *cert. denied,* U.S. Sup. Ct., 06-1228 (2007); and *Capital One Bank and Capital One F.S.B. v. Commissioner of Revenue,* No. SJC-10105 (Mass. Sup. Jud. Ct., Jan. 8, 2009); *cert. denied,* U.S. Sup. Ct., No. 08-1169 (2009)].

Economic Substance and Business Purpose. In *Gregory v. Helvering,* the U.S. Supreme Court has ruled that a transaction is respected only if it has economic substance and serves a business purpose other than tax avoidance [293 US 465, 1935]. The states have invoked the judicial doctrines of economic substance and business purpose as an argument to, for example, disallow deductions for royalty payments made by an operating company to a trademark holding company.

For example, in *Syms Corp. v. Commissioner of Revenue,* the Massachusetts Supreme Judicial Court ruled that the transfer and licensing back of trademarks between a retailer and its trademark holding company was a sham transaction, and therefore no deduction was allowed for the royalty payments [No. SJC-08513 (Mass. Sup. Jud. Ct., Apr. 10, 2002)]. On the other hand, in *The Sherwin-Williams Co. v. Commissioner of Revenue,* the Massachusetts Supreme Judicial Court ruled that two trademark holding companies had economic substance and served valid business purposes [No. SJC-08516 (Mass. Sup. Jud. Ct., Oct. 31, 2002)].

Combined Reporting. Requiring an out-of-state trademark holding company or financing company to file a combined report with an in-state operating company eliminates the tax benefits of intercompany royalty and interest payments. When computing the unitary group's combined income, the in-state operating company's royalty and interest expense deductions are offset by the royalty and interest income of the out-of-state holding and financing companies.

For example, New Jersey does not permit an affiliated group to elect to file a consolidated return nor require all unitary groups to compute their tax on a combined basis. Thus, every corporation with nexus in New Jersey generally is considered a separate entity and must file its own return. The Director of the Division of Taxation may, however, require members of an affiliated group or a controlled group to file a consolidated return "if the taxpayer cannot demonstrate by clear and convincing evidence that a report by a taxpayer discloses the true earnings of the taxpayer on its business carried on in this State" [N.J. Rev. Stat. 54:10A-10.c.].

Section 482-Type Reallocation. Code Sec. 482 authorizes the IRS to reallocate income among commonly controlled corporations whenever necessary to prevent the evasion of taxes or to clearly reflect the income of the related entities. Congress enacted Section 482 to ensure that commonly controlled corporations report and pay tax on their actual share of income arising from intercompany transactions. Many states have enacted Section 482-type statutes, although the details of these statutes vary significantly from state to state.

For example, Florida tax authorities may make adjustments to clearly reflect a taxpayer's income if an arrangement exists between related entities that causes a taxpayer's income to be "reflected improperly or inaccurately" [Fla. Stat. ch. §220.44].

Related Party Expense Add Back Provisions. Another technique that many states use to limit income shifting is to require corporations to add back any royalty or interest payments made to related parties when computing state taxable income (hereinafter, referred to as "addback provisions").

Although the different state addback provisions share many common themes, there are significant differences, particularly with respect to the circumstances under which an exception applies and the related party expense need not be added back. Therefore, it is essential to thoroughly analyze each state's specific provisions to ensure compliance.

State related party expense addback provisions are generally targeted at interest expenses and intangible expense. Most states define *interest expense* by referring to Code Sec. 163. States generally define *intangible expenses* to include not only royalties, but also a broad range of other costs, expenses, and losses related to intangible property.

State addback provisions are designed to prevent taxpayers from using intercompany licensing and financing arrangements to avoid corporate income taxes. Under the general rules, however, state addback provisions apply automatically to all related party intangible and interest expenses, including those related party payments that are motivated by legitimate business purposes rather than tax avoidance.

As a consequence, each state provides some relief in the form of exceptions from the automatic addback requirement. These exceptions are complex and vary from state to state.

There are some common themes, however, including *exceptions* that apply when:

- The related payee's corresponding income is subject to tax in another U.S. state or a foreign country
- The related payee pays the amount to an unrelated person
- The addback adjustment produces an unreasonable result
- The taxpayer and the state tax authorities agree to an alternative adjustment

Pass-Through Entities

States generally conform to the federal tax treatment of S corporations and partnerships as pass-through entities, as well as the federal *check-the-box* classification of an LLC as a partnership or a disregarded entity.

Despite this broad conformity, numerous states impose entity-level taxes on S corporations, partnerships, and LLCs. Examples include California, Illinois, Massachusetts, Michigan, Ohio, Pennsylvania, Tennessee, Texas and Washington.

STUDY QUESTION

15. Which of the following is *not* a mechanism used by states to limit tax base erosion?

a. Separate-company reporting
b. Combined reporting
c. Economic nexus

Apportionment Formulas

This chapter discusses the methods by which states allocate and apportion income from multistate businesses. It also explains specialized industry formulas and reviews recent developments related to state apportionment.

LEARNING OBJECTIVES

Upon completing this chapter, the professional will be able to:

- Discuss how income is allocated among states
- Explain how income is apportioned among states
- Describe the equitable relief provisions of UDITPA §18
- Indicate some of the recent state apportionment developments
- List industries that use specialized apportionment formulas
- Indicate some of the recent state specialized apportionment formula developments

GENERAL APPORTIONMENT FORMULAS

Overview

When a corporation does business in more than one state, such that the corporation is or could be taxed by more than one state, the question arises as to how to determine the portion of the corporation's income attributable to each state.

When, as is often the case, a corporation consists of separate but interdependent departments and divisions that are integrated vertically or horizontally, it is generally not possible to assign the corporation's income precisely among the several states in which it does business.

Because the results obtained by using a separate accounting method for each business unit are often arbitrary, states use allocation and apportionment procedures to determine the portion of a corporation's income that is attributable to a particular state.

Allocation

Allocation generally refers to the assignment of nonbusiness income to a particular state.

Generally, *nonbusiness income* means all income other than business income, and *business income* means income that arises from the regular course of the taxpayer's trade or business, or is derived from property that is an integral part of the taxpayer's regular trade or business operations.

> **EXAMPLE**
>
> Rental income received by a manufacturing corporation for a piece of real property that is located outside the state in which the corporation carries on its manufacturing activities and that is not related to those manufacturing activities is *nonbusiness income.*

Nonbusiness income is usually allocated to the state in which the property generating the income is located or, in the case of income from intangible property, to the state in which the corporation has its commercial domicile.

Apportionment

A corporation that is taxable in more than one state has the constitutional right to have its income fairly apportioned among the taxing states [*Complete Auto Transit v. Brady,* 430 US 274 (1977)]. A taxpayer apportions its income by computing the percentage of its business income that is taxable in each nexus state using the formulas provided by those states.

To determine a state's apportionment percentage:

1. A ratio is established for each of the factors included in the state's formula. Each ratio is calculated by comparing the level of a specific business activity within a state to the total corporate activity of that type.
2. The ratios are then appropriately weighted and summed to determine the corporation's apportionment percentage for each state.

Apportionment does not necessarily provide a uniform division of a corporation's income among the nexus states (i.e., a corporation's apportionment percentages may not sum to 100 percent) because each state is free to choose the type and number of factors it will use as indicative of the amount of business activity conducted within its borders. Moreover, each state makes its own rules for computing the factors included in its apportionment formula. The lack of uniformity can result in either double taxation or *nowhere income.*

In 1957, state tax officials promulgated the Uniform Division of Income for Tax Purposes Act (UDITPA), which is a model law for apportioning the income of a corporation that is taxable in two or more states. UDITPA provides for the use of an equally weighted three-factor formula that includes a:

1. Sales factor
2. Property factor
3. Payroll factor

In *Moorman Manufacturing Co. v. Bair* [437 US 267 (1978)], the Supreme Court ruled that a three-factor formula is *not* constitutionally required, and that Iowa could use a sales-only apportionment formula. Consistent with its prior rulings, the Court stated that a state's choice of apportionment formulas generally will be upheld—unless a taxpayer can prove by clear and cogent evidence that the formula attributes income to the state that is out of all appropriate proportion to the business transacted by the taxpayer in that state.

At present, about 10 states use a three-factor apportionment formula that equally weights sales, property, and payroll. Most states use a *modified* three-factor formula, under which the sales factor is assigned more weight than the property or payroll factors. Many states double weight the sales factor (i.e., 50 percent sales, 25 percent property, and 25 percent payroll).

Roughly a dozen states use a single-factor sales-only formula—including Colorado, Georgia, Illinois, Iowa, Maine, Michigan, Nebraska, New York, Oregon, Texas, and Wisconsin. Minnesota is phasing in a sales-only formula from 2007 through 2014, and Indiana is phasing in a sales-only formula from 2007 through 2011. Effective in 2010, Pennsylvania weights the sales factor 90 percent, and the property and payroll factors 5 percent each.

Under current law, most California taxpayers are required to use a three-factor formula that includes a property factor, a payroll factor, and a double-weighted sales factor. Effective for tax years beginning on or after January 1, 2011, however, a taxpayer may make an annual election to use a single factor sales-only formula (S.B. 15. Feb. 20, 2009).

> **NOTE**
>
> The election is not available to a taxpayer that derives more than 50 percent of its gross business receipts from conducting an agricultural, extractive, banking or financial business activity.

The political appeal of an apportionment formula that weights the sales factor more heavily than the property and payroll factors is that it tends to reduce the tax liabilities of corporations that are based in the state, while potentially increasing the tax liabilities of out-of-state corporations. Specifically, placing more weight on the sales factor tends to pull a larger percentage of an out-of-state corporation's income within the taxing jurisdiction of the state because the corporation's major activity within the state—sales of its product—is weighted more heavily than its payroll and property activities.

For corporations that are based in the state, however, placing more weight on the sales factor provides tax relief because those corporations generally own significantly more property and incur more payroll costs (factors that are given relatively less weight in the apportionment formula) within the state than do out-of-state corporations.

If a state uses a three-factor apportionment formula and one of the factors is not present—e.g., a corporation has no payroll—generally the computation of the apportionment percentage is adjusted accordingly.

> **EXAMPLE**
>
> If a state uses an equally weighted three-factor formula and the taxpayer has no payroll, the apportionment percentage is determined by dividing the sum of the property and sales factors by two [e.g., *Rentco Trailer Corp. v. Director of Revenue*, No. 97-001373 RI (Mo. Admin. Hearing Comm., July 31, 1998)].

STUDY QUESTIONS

1. A business is taxable in States A, B, and C. It is commercially domiciled in State A. The business sells a parcel of land located in State B. The sale is *not* in the regular course of the taxpayer's trade or business, and the land is *not* an integral part of the taxpayer's regular business operations. Where should the income arising from the sale be allocated and apportioned?

  a. State A only
  b. State B only
  c. States A, B and C

2. Which of the following is *true* of apportionment?

  a. Apportionment assures a uniform division of a corporation's income among the states in which it has nexus.
  b. Apportionment refers to the specific assignment of nonbusiness income to a particular state.
  c. A taxpayer apportions its income by computing the percentage of its business income that is taxable in each state in which the taxpayer has nexus.

Right to Apportion

Not all corporations are entitled to apportion their income. The requirements for establishing the right to apportion income vary from state to state, but they generally entail:

- Carrying on business in another state
- Maintaining a regular place of business in another state or
- Being taxable in another state

Some states take the restrictive position that permits apportionment *only* if the corporation is actually filing returns and paying tax in another state.

New Jersey. In *River Systems, Inc. v. Division of Taxation*, the New Jersey Tax Court ruled that the income of a New Jersey corporation was 100 percent taxable in New Jersey [No. A-2741-01T3 (N.J. Super. Ct., Mar. 14, 2003)]. The court ruled that the taxpayer's use of telemarketers in New York did not satisfy New Jersey's statutory requirement that, in order to apportion its income, a taxpayer must "maintain a regular place of business" *outside* New Jersey (N.J.S.A. Sec. 54:10A-6).

In *New Jersey Natural Gas Co. v. Division of Taxation*, the New Jersey Tax Court ruled that the taxpayer must allocate all of its income to New Jersey, because the employee's home office in Connecticut did not constitute a *regular place of business* outside New Jersey [Nos. 000240-2005 and 007284-2005 (N.J. Tax Ct., Apr. 17, 2008)].

In order for an out-of-state location to be considered the taxpayer's *regular place of business*, the taxpayer must either own or rent the facility in its own name and must be directly responsible for the expenses incurred in maintaining the place of business. In this case, the taxpayer did not own or rent the employee's home and the employee was contractually responsible for all expenses related to the home office.

In December 2008, New Jersey enacted legislation to eliminate the requirement that a corporation have a *regular place of business* in another state in order to apportion its income, effective for tax years beginning on or after July 1, 2010 [A.B. 2722, Dec. 19, 2008].

Missouri. In *Jay Wolfe Imports Missouri, Inc. v. Director of Revenue*, the Missouri Supreme Court ruled that a Missouri car dealership located two blocks from the Missouri-Kansas state line was not entitled to apportion its income because it derived income from sources entirely in Missouri [No. SC89568 (Mo. Sup. Ct., May 5, 2009)]. The fact that some out-of-state customers purchased cars and then drove them back to their out-of-state addresses did not mean that the sales themselves were conducted partly within and partly outside the state.

Missouri law provides that sales partly within and partly without the state occur only if the seller's shipping point and the purchaser's destination point are in different states. In this case, the dealership did not *ship* cars purchased at its Missouri facility to out-of-state customers. Instead, the out-of-state customers completed their sales transactions and took possession of their purchased car in Missouri and then drove them to their out-of-state addresses.

In *Moberly Regional Center v. Director of Revenue*, the Missouri Administrative Hearing Commission ruled that a hospital located in and transacting business in Missouri that contracted with an affiliated out-of-state company to perform management functions was *not* entitled to apportion its income because it did not employ any labor or capital outside Missouri [No. 07-0283 RI (Mo. Admin. Hearing Comm., Oct. 6, 2008)]. Paying an affiliated out-of-state company to perform management services did not constitute the employment of labor outside the state of Missouri.

All of the hospital's employees and property were located in Missouri, and all of its patients were treated in Missouri. The hospital did not earn any income in any other state and thus has no income to apportion between Missouri and any other state.

In *TSI Holding Co. v. Director of Revenue*, a case dealing with the Missouri franchise tax, the Missouri Supreme Court ruled that three related Missouri investment holding companies were not entitled to apportion their income because they did business solely in Missouri [Nos. SC85179, SC85180, and SC85181 (Mo. Sup. Ct., Nov. 4, 2003)]. The corporations did not do business in any other state, did not have offices in any other state, and did not file franchise tax returns in any other state.

Massachusetts. In *Tech-Etch, Inc. v. Commissioner of Revenue*, the Massachusetts Appeals Court ruled that a Massachusetts manufacturer was not entitled to apportion its income in connection with sales of goods shipped to customers located in foreign countries, because the taxpayer failed to establish that it was taxable in another state or foreign country [No. 05-P-1012 (Mass. App. Ct., Nov. 3, 2006)].

Equitable Relief Provisions

The divergent apportionment formulas used by the states, along with different rules for computing the factors in each state's formula, can result in a corporation's being subject to tax on more than 100 percent of its income.

An equally adverse consequence of apportionment may result when the operations in a state result in a loss, as determined by a separate geographic accounting. When a corporation as a whole generates a profit, the use of an apportionment formula results in the corporation's incurring an income tax liability in the state in which the loss operation is located—even though no profit is generated in that state.

To provide relief in extreme situations, UDITPA §18 provides that if the standard allocation and apportionment provisions do not fairly represent the extent of the taxpayer's business activity in a state, the taxpayer may petition for, or the tax administrator may require, with respect to all or any part of the taxpayer's business activity, if reasonable:

- Use of separate accounting
- Exclusion of any one or more of the factors:
- Inclusion of one or more additional factors,
- Employment of any other method that will result in "an equitable allocation and apportionment of the taxpayer's income"

For example, California's equivalent of UDITPA §18, California Revenue and Taxation Code §25137 (Equitable Adjustment of Standard Allocation or Apportionment), states:

> If the allocation and apportionment provisions of this act do not fairly represent the extent of the taxpayer's business activity in this state, the taxpayer may petition for or the Franchise Tax Board may require, in respect to all or any part of the taxpayer's business activity, if reasonable:
>
> (a) Separate accounting;
> (b) The exclusion of any one or more of the factors;
> (c) The inclusion of one or more additional factors which will fairly represent the taxpayer's business activity in this state; or
> (d) The employment of any other method to effectuate an equitable allocation and apportionment of the taxpayer's income.

California Code of Regulations Title 18, §25137, states that "Section 25137 may be invoked only in specific cases where unusual fact situations (which ordinarily will be unique and nonrecurring) produce incongruous results under the apportionment and allocation provisions contained in these regulations."

There is a presumption developed by judicial precedent that a state's apportionment provisions are equitable. Thus, the taxpayer must do more than merely demonstrate that there is an inequity in its tax liability under the state's apportionment formula.

To receive relief from the state's standard formula, the corporation generally must prove by clear and convincing evidence that the apportionment formula grossly distorts the amount of income actually earned in the state. For the most part, corporations have found it difficult to prove that a state's standard apportionment provisions are inequitable [E.g., *Hans Rees' Sons, Inc. v. North Carolina*, 283 US 123 (1931); *Moorman Mfg. Co. v. Bair*, 437 US 267 (1978); *Container Corp. of Am. v. Franchise Tax Bd.*, 463 US 159 (1983); *Unisys Corp. v. Pa. Bd. of Fin. and Rev.*, 812 A2d 448 (Pa. Sup. Ct. 2002); and *Colgate-Palmolive Company, Inc. v. Bower* (No. 01 L 50195, Ill. Cir. Ct., Cook Cty., Oct. 15, 2002)].

See *Home Interiors & Gifts, Inc. v. Strayhorn* for an example of a fact pattern in which a state court ruled that a taxpayer's income was not fairly apportioned [No. 03-04-00660-CV (Tex. Ct. of App., Sept. 22, 2005)].

STUDY QUESTION

> **3.** Which of the following statements is true?
>   **a.** Apportionment can result in a corporation incurring an income tax liability in a state where there is a loss and no profit is generated.
>   **b.** All corporations are permitted to apportion their income.
>   **c.** UDITPA §18 allows the use of an alternative formula only if it is requested by the taxpayer.

Recent Developments

Arizona. Prior to 2007, Arizona used a double-weighted sales formula. In 2005, Arizona enacted legislation that gives taxpayers the option to use an alternative apportionment formula, under which the sales factor is weighted for tax years beginning:

- In 2007—60 percent
- In 2008—70 percent
- After 2008—80 percent

The alternative formulas are available, however, only if one or more corporations make more than $1 billion of new capital investments in the state (H.B. 2139, May 20, 2005).

California. Under current law, most California taxpayers are required to use a three-factor apportionment formula that includes a property factor, a payroll factor, and a double-weighted sales factor. Effective for tax years beginning on or after January 1, 2011, however, a taxpayer may make an annual election to use a single-factor sales-only formula (S.B. 15. Feb. 20, 2009).

> **NOTE**
>
> The election is not available to a taxpayer that derives more than 50 percent of its gross business receipts from conducting an agricultural, extractive, banking, or financial business activity.

Colorado. For tax years beginning on or after January 1, 2009, Colorado has adopted a single-factor sales formula (H.B. 1380, May 20, 2008). For tax years beginning before 2009, Colorado permitted corporations to choose between an equally weighted three-factor formula, and a two-factor (property and sales) formula.

Georgia. For tax years beginning before 2006, Georgia used a double-weighted sales formula. In 2005, Georgia enacted legislation to phase in a sales-only formula over a three-year period. The sales factor was weighted for tax years beginning (H.B. 191, Apr. 6, 2005):

- In 2006—80%
- In 2007—90 %
- After 2007—100%

Indiana. For tax years beginning before 2007, Indiana used a double-weighted sales formula. In 2006, Indiana enacted legislation to phase in a sales-only formula from 2007 through 2011.

The sales factor is weighted for tax years beginning (H.B. 1001, Mar. 24, 2006):

- In 2007—60 percent
- In 2008—70 percent
- In 2009—80 percent
- In 2010—90 percent
- After 2010—100 percent

Kansas. A manufacturer that built a new facility in Kansas costing at least $100 million, employed at least 100 new employees at the facility after July 1, 2007 and prior to December 31, 2009, and paid the employees higher than average wages, could use a sales-only apportionment formula (S.B. 240, Mar. 20, 2007). If certain requirements are met, the Kansas Secretary of Revenue may extend the deadline until June 30, 2010 (H.B. 2270, Mar. 27, 2009).

Louisiana. For tax years beginning before 2006, Louisiana used a double-weighted sales formula. For tax years beginning after 2005, a taxpayer whose apportionable income is derived primarily from the business of manufacturing or merchandising uses a sales-only apportionment formula (H.B. 679, July 1, 2005).

Michigan. Effective December 31, 2007, Michigan repealed its single business tax and replaced it with a 4.95 percent business income tax and a 0.80 percent modified gross receipts tax that apply to business activity occurring on or after January 1, 2008 (S.B. 94, July 12, 2007). The business income tax base and modified gross receipts tax base are both apportioned using a sales-only apportionment formula.

Minnesota. For tax years beginning before 2007, Minnesota used a 75-12.5-12.5 apportionment formula weighted in favor of sales. In 2005, Minnesota enacted legislation to phase in a sales-only formula over an eight-year period beginning in 2007. The sales-only formula will be fully phased in by 2014 (H.F. 138, July 14, 2005).

New Mexico. In 2009, New Mexico extended the time period for a manufacturer's optional use of a double-weighted sales apportionment formula from 2010 through 2019 (H.B. 75, Apr. 7, 2009).

North Carolina. Effective for tax years beginning after 2009, a *capital investment corporation* may apportion its business income using a sales-only formula, rather than North Carolina's standard double-weighted sales formula. To qualify, a corporation must invest at least $1 billion to construct a facility within a designated development area (S.B. 575, June 3, 2009). According to a press release issued by the governor, the legislation was enacted to encourage Apple Inc. to locate a new data center in North Carolina.

Oregon. For tax years beginning on or after July 1, 2005, Oregon adopted a sales-only formula (S.B. 31, Sept. 2, 2005). Oregon used a double-weighted sales formula for tax years beginning after 1990 and before May 1, 2003, and it used an 80-10-10 formula weighted in favor of sales for tax years beginning on or after May 1, 2003 and before July 1, 2005 (Ore. Dept. of Rev., Reg. §150-314.650).

Pennsylvania. Pennsylvania used a weighted apportionment formula as follows for tax years beginning:

- Before 2007—60-20-20 (60 percent weight on sales, and a 20 percent weight on property and on payroll)
- After 2006—70-15-15 [70 percent weight on sales, and a 15 percent weight on property and on payroll (H.B. 859, July 12, 2006)]
- After 2008—83-8.5-8.5 (83 percent weight on sales, and an 8.5 percent weight on property and on payroll)
- After 2009—90-5-5 [90 percent weight on sales, and a 5 percent weight on property and on payroll (H.B. 1531, Oct. 13, 2009)]

South Carolina. For tax years beginning after 2006, taxpayers whose principal business is manufacturing or any form of collecting, buying, assembling, or processing goods and materials in South Carolina, or selling, distributing, or dealing in tangible personal property in South Carolina, apportion their income using a sales-only formula. Prior to 2007, such taxpayers used a double-weighted sales formula.

However, for tax years beginning in 2007 through 2010, these taxpayers must apportion their income using both a double-weighted sales formula and a sales-only formula. If the calculation using the sales-only formula reduces the amount of income apportioned to South Carolina, 20 percent of the reduction is allowed for tax years beginning in 2007, 40 percent for tax years beginning in 2008, 60 percent for tax years beginning in 2009, and 80 percent for tax years beginning in 2010 (H.B. 4874, June 14, 2006).

Utah. For tax years beginning before 2006, Utah used an equally weighted three-factor formula. For tax years beginning after 2005, a taxpayer may elect to use a double-weighted sales formula in lieu of the equally weighted formula. A taxpayer making the election will not be allowed to revoke it for five tax years (H.B. 78, Mar. 18, 2005).

Vermont. Effective for tax years beginning on or after January 1, 2006, the sales factor will be double weighted (H.B. 784, June 7, 2004). Prior to 2006, Vermont used an equally weighted three-factor apportionment formula.

Virginia. Effective for tax years beginning on or after July 1, 2011, but before July 1, 2013, manufacturing companies may elect to use a triple-weighted sales apportionment formula. For tax years beginning on or after July 1, 2013, but before July 1, 2014, manufacturers may elect to use a quadruple-weighted sales formula.

For tax years beginning on or after July 1, 2014, manufacturers may elect to use a sales-only formula. A manufacturer that makes this election is required to maintain a base-year level of employment in Virginia, and must certify that the average weekly wages of its full-time employees are greater than the lower of the state or local average weekly wages for the taxpayer's industry (H.B. 2437, Apr. 14, 2009).

Wisconsin. For tax years beginning before 2006, Wisconsin used a double-weighted sales formula. In 2003, Wisconsin enacted legislation to phase in a sales-only formula. The sales factor was weighted for tax years (S.B. 197, July 31, 2003):

- Beginning in 2006—60 percent
- Beginning in 2007—80 percent
- After 2007—00 percent

STUDY QUESTION

> **4.** Which of the following states require most taxpayers to use a *sales-only* apportionment formula?
>
>   **a.** California and Vermont
>   **b.** Georgia and Wisconsin
>   **c.** North Carolina and Pennsylvania

SPECIALIZED INDUSTRY FORMULAS

Overview

The UDITPA equally weighted three-factor property, payroll and sales formula was designed to apportion the income of multistate manufacturing and mercantile businesses. It may not fairly apportion the income of businesses in other industries.

> **EXAMPLE**
>
> The conventional UDITPA property factor is difficult to compute for property that regularly moves back-and-forth across state lines, such as the transportation equipment used by interstate trucking companies, airlines and railroads.

Likewise, the UDITPA §17 income-producing activity rule for sourcing sales of services has been controversial since its adoption in 1957. Many commentators have argued that its effect is often merely to mimic the property and payroll factor, rather than to measure the customer base within a state.

The drafters of UDITPA foresaw the limitations of the standard UDITPA apportionment formula, and, specifically excluded from UDITPA certain service businesses under §2—including financial organizations and public utilities.

Financial organizations include banks, trust companies, savings banks, private bankers, savings and loan associations, credit unions, investment companies, and insurance companies. *Public utilities* are defined as any business entity which owns or operates for public use any plant, equipment, property, franchise, or license for the transmission of communications, transportation of goods or persons, or the production, storage, transmission, sale, delivery, or furnishing of electricity, water, steam, oil, oil products or gas.

To address these issues, many states provide special rules for computing apportionment percentages for businesses in certain industries. Typically, these special rules involve the modification or exclusion of the conventional factors, or the use of unique, industry-specific factors.

In some instances, a primary motive for adopting specialized industry apportionment rules is to provide an economic incentive for certain businesses to maintain or locate operations within the state. Some industries for which states provide special apportionment rules include the following:

- Airlines
- Railroads
- Trucking companies
- Financial institutions
- Television and radio broadcasters
- Publishers
- Telecommunication services companies
- Mutual funds
- Pipelines
- Ship transportation companies
- Professional sports franchises

Often the equitable relief provisions of UDITPA §18, which numerous states have incorporated into their statutes, serve as the basis for state revenue departments to adopt specialized formulas. UDITPA §18 provides that if the standard apportionment formula does not fairly reflect a taxpayer's in-state business activity, tax authorities may require the exclusion of one or more of the factors, or the inclusion of additional factors which will fairly represent the taxpayer's business activity in the state.

Under §18, the Multistate Tax Commission (MTC) has promulgated special apportionment regulations covering:

- Construction contractors (MTC Reg. IV.18(d))
- Airlines (MTC Reg. IV.18(e))
- Railroads (MTC Reg. IV.18(f))
- Trucking companies (MTC Reg. IV.18(g))
- Television and radio broadcasters (MTC Reg. IV.18(h))
- Publishers (MTC Reg. IV.18(j))

The MTC has also promulgated a model statute for apportioning the income of financial institutions (Nov. 17, 1994). In July 2008, the MTC approved a model regulation for the apportionment of income from telecommunications services.

As a general rule, only those taxpayers engaged in the type of business activity for which the special apportionment rules were developed are permitted to apply the special rules [e.g., *Cooper Tire & Rubber Co. v. Limbach*, 70 Ohio St. 3d 347 (1994); *TTX Co. v. Whitley*, No. 1-98-3604 (Ill. App. Ct., Mar. 31, 2000)]. In most instances, when a corporation is required to use a specialized apportionment formula, *all* of its income is apportioned using that formula.

> ### ■ EXAMPLE
>
> In *Texaco-Cities Service Pipeline Company v. McGaw*, the Illinois Supreme Court ruled that the taxpayer's gain from the sale of its 90 percent interest in a pipeline was apportionable under Illinois's sales-only apportionment formula for transportation services businesses [182 Ill. 2d 269 (1998)].
>
> However, in *Buckeye Pipeline Co. v. Commonwealth*, a one-percent general partner of four limited partnerships engaged in the interstate transportation of petroleum products through pipelines was permitted to use the single-factor revenue barrel mile apportionment formula for pipeline companies to apportion the portion of its gross receipts attributable to its distributive share of partnership receipts [689 A.2d 366 (Pa. Commw. Ct. 1997)].
>
> It was also required to use the standard three-factor formula to apportion gross receipts attributable to management fees received from the partnerships.

STUDY QUESTION

> **5.** Under UDITPA §2, financial organizations and public utilities are specifically *excluded* from having to use the standard UDITPA apportionment formula. *True or False?*

Airlines

Many states provide special apportionment formulas for airlines. MTC Reg. IV.18(e), which the MTC adopted in 1983, addresses the apportionment of a multistate airline's business income. As discussed below, this regulation modifies the standard three-factor property, payroll, and sales formula primarily by basing the computation of the factor numerators on the ratio of in-state aircraft departures—weighted by the cost and value of aircraft, to the total departures everywhere (similarly weighted). Some states have adopted the MTC approach, in whole or in part. Other states have adopted their own special formulas, such as formulas based on revenue miles.

Property Factor. In general, the property factor denominator includes the average value of all owned and rented real and tangible personal property used by the airline in its trade or business. The numerator includes all owned and rented property used in the state. MTC Reg. IV.18(e) provides a special rule for sourcing aircraft ready for flight.

Aircraft ready for flight are defined as aircraft owned or acquired through rental or lease that are in the possession of the taxpayer and are available for service on the taxpayer's routes. Such aircraft are includible in a particular state's numerator, based on the ratio of in-state departures and weighted by the cost and value of aircraft, to the total departures everywhere (similarly weighted).

Payroll Factor. The denominator of the payroll factor includes all compensation paid everywhere by the airline, and the numerator is the total compensation paid in the state. MTC Reg. IV.18(e) provides a special rule for sourcing compensation paid to flight personnel. The payroll of such employees is includible in the state's payroll factor numerator, based on the ratio of in-state departures and weighted by the cost and value of aircraft, to the total departures everywhere (similarly weighted).

Sales Factor. Under MTC Reg. IV.18(e), the sales factor denominator includes all revenues that the airline derives from transactions and activities in the regular course of its trade or business, except for passive income and net gains or losses from the sale of aircraft. The sales factor numerator is the taxpayer's total in-state revenue, which includes the sum of:
- The total transportation revenue multiplied by the ratio of in-state departures, weighted by the cost and value of aircraft, to the total departures everywhere (similarly weighted), PLUS
- Any nonflight revenues directly attributable to the state

Railroads

Many states provide special apportionment formulas for railroads. MTC Reg. IV.18(f), which the MTC adopted in 1981, addresses the apportionment of a multistate railroad's business income. The manner in which the regulation modifies the standard equally weighted three-factor formula is summarized below.

Property Factor. In general, the property factor denominator includes the average value of all owned and rented real and tangible personal property used by the railroad in its trade or business. Railroad cars owned by other railroads and temporarily used by the taxpayer for a per diem charge are *not* included in the property factor as rented property—whereas, railroad cars owned by the taxpayer and temporarily used by other railroads for a per diem charge *are* included in the property factor.

The numerator includes all owned and rented property used in the state. A special rule applies to sourcing mobile property, such as passenger cars, freight cars, locomotives and freight containers, which are located inside and outside of the state during the year. Such property is included in the property factor numerator based on the ratio of the locomotive-miles or car-miles in the state to the locomotive-miles or car-miles outside of the state.

Payroll Factor. The denominator of the payroll factor includes *all* compensation paid everywhere by the railroad, and the numerator is the total compensation paid in the state. A special rule applies to sourcing compensation paid to enginemen and trainmen performing services on interstate trains. The payroll of such employees is included in the state's payroll factor numerator based on the compensation required to be reported by such employees for purposes of determining their state personal income tax liabilities.

Sales Factor. Under MTC Reg. IV.18(f), the sales factor denominator includes all revenues derived by the railroad from transactions and activities in the regular course of its trade or business—except per diem and mileage charges.

The sales factor numerator is the railroad's total revenues in the state. The taxpayer in-state revenues from hauling freight, mail, and express, include the entire amount of the receipts from *intrastate shipments* (i.e., the shipment both originates and terminates within the state); and a pro-rata portion of the receipts from *interstate shipments* (i.e., shipments passing through, into, or out of the state)—determined by the ratio of the miles traveled by the shipment in the state, to the total miles traveled by the shipment from its point of origin to its destination.

Likewise, the taxpayer's in-state revenue from hauling passengers includes the entire amount of the receipts from the intrastate transportation of passengers. It also includes a pro-rata portion of the receipts from the interstate transportation of passengers—determined by the ratio of the revenue passenger miles in the state, to the revenue passenger miles everywhere. The in-state portion of any revenues, other than revenue from hauling freight, passengers, mail and express, is determined under the standard UDITPA rules for *sourcing sales.*

STUDY QUESTIONS

6. For purposes of apportioning the income of an airline, MTC Reg. IV.18(e) provides that:

    a. The total cost of aircraft ready for flight is includible in a particular state's property factor numerator.

    b. The payroll of flight personnel is includible in the state's payroll factor numerator based on the ratio of in-state arrivals, to the total arrivals everywhere—both weighted by the cost and value of aircraft.

    c. The sales factor numerator equals the sum of the taxpayer's in-state transportation revenues, plus any nonflight revenues directly attributable to the state.

Trucking Companies

Many states provide special apportionment formulas for trucking companies. MTC Reg. IV.18(g), which the MTC adopted in 1986 and amended in 1989, addresses the apportionment of a multistate trucking company's business income.

As discussed below, this regulation modifies the standard equally three-factor formula primarily by basing the computation of the factor numerators on the ratio of the mobile property miles in the state to the mobile property miles everywhere. Some states have adopted the MTC approach, in whole or in part. Other states have adopted their own special formulas, such as formulas based on revenue miles.

MTC Reg. IV.18(g) defines a *trucking company* as a motor common carrier, a motor contract carrier, or an express carrier which primarily transports tangible personal property of others by motor vehicle for compensation.

Property Factor. In general, the property factor denominator includes the average value of all owned and rented real and tangible personal property used by the trucking company in its trade or business.

The numerator includes all owned and rented property used in the state. A special sourcing rule applies to motor vehicles and trailers (*mobile property*), which is included in the state's numerator based on the ratio of mobile property miles in the state to total mobile property miles. A *mobile property mile* is defined as the movement of a unit of mobile property a distance of one mile, whether loaded or unloaded.

Payroll Factor. The denominator of the payroll factor includes *all* compensation paid everywhere by a trucking company, and the numerator is the total compensation paid in a particular state.

A special rule applies to *sourcing compensation* paid to employees performing services within and without the state. The payroll of such employees is includible in the state's payroll factor numerator, based on the ratio of mobile property miles in the state to total mobile property miles.

Sales Factor. Under MTC Reg. IV.18(g), the sales factor denominator includes all revenue derived from transactions and activities in the regular course of the trucking company's trade or business.

The sales factor numerator is the trucking company's total revenues in the state. The taxpayer in-state revenues from hauling freight, mail and express, include the entire amount of the receipts from *intrastate shipments* (i.e., the shipment both originates and terminates within the state). They also include a pro-rata portion of the receipts from *interstate shipments* (i.e., shipments passing through, into, or out of the state)—determined by the ratio of the mobile property miles traveled by the shipment in the state to the total mobile property miles traveled by the shipment from its point of origin to its destination.

The in-state portion of any revenues, other than revenue from hauling freight, mail and express, is determined under the standard UDITPA rules for sourcing sales.

Television and Radio Broadcasters

Some states provide special apportionment formulas for television and radio broadcasters. MTC Reg. IV.18(h), which the MTC adopted in 1990 and amended in 1996, addresses the apportionment of a multistate television or radio broadcaster's business income.

The regulation covers taxpayers engaged in broadcasting over the public airwaves, by cable, satellite transmission, or by any other means of communication. The manner in which the regulation modifies the standard equally weighted three-factor formula is summarized below.

Property Factor. In general, the property factor denominator includes the average value of all owned and rented real and tangible personal property used by the broadcaster in its trade or business. However, outer-jurisdictional, film and radio programming property are *excluded* from the property factor.

Outer-jurisdictional property includes orbiting satellites, undersea transmission cables, and like property that is owned or rented by the taxpayer and used in its broadcasting business but is not physically located in any particular state. Discs and similar medium containing film or radio programming and intended for sale or rental by the taxpayer for home viewing or listening are included in the property factor.

The numerator includes owned and rented property used in the state, as determined under the standard UDITPA rules for sourcing property.

Payroll Factor. The denominator of the payroll factor includes *all* compensation—including residual and profit participation payments paid to employees, including that paid to directors, actors, newscasters and other talent in their status as employees.

The numerator includes the total compensation paid in the state, as determined under the standard UDITPA rules for sourcing payroll.

Sales Factor. Under MTC Reg. IV.18(h), the sales factor denominator includes all gross receipts that the broadcaster derives from transactions and activities in the regular course of its trade or business.

The sales factor numerator is the broadcaster's gross receipts in the state. *Gross receipts*, including advertising revenue, from television film or radio programming in release to or by television and radio stations is pro-rated to a state based on an audience factor. The *audience factor* equals the ratio of the broadcaster's in-state viewing (listening) audience to its total viewing (listening) audience. A cable television system's audience factor is the ratio of the system's in-state subscribers to its total subscribers.

Receipts from the sale, rental, or licensing of discs and similar media intended for home viewing or listening are sourced under the standard UDITPA rules for sourcing sales of *tangible personal property*.

STUDY QUESTION

---

7. Which of the following statements is *not* true?

   a. MTC Reg. IV.18(h) provides special rules for apportioning the income of broadcasting companies, but *only* for companies that broadcast by cable.
   b. Some states have adopted their own special formulas for trucking companies, such as formulas based on revenue miles.
   c. Under MTC Reg. IV.18(g), a *trucking company* is a business that primarily transports the tangible personal property of others by motor vehicle for compensation.

Publishing

Some states provide special apportionment formulas for taxpayers engaged in the publishing, sale, licensing, or other distribution of books, newspapers, magazines, periodicals, trade journals or other printed material. MTC Reg. IV.18(j), which the MTC adopted in 1993, modifies the standard equally weighted three-factor formula as summarized below.

Property Factor. In general, the property factor denominator includes the average value of all owned and rented real and tangible personal property—including outer-jurisdictional (e.g., orbiting satellites and undersea transmission cables) used by the publisher in its trade or business.

The numerator includes owned and rented property used in the state. Outer-jurisdictional property is pro-rated to a state, based on the ratio of number of uplink and downlink transmissions in the state to the total number of uplink and downlink transmissions everywhere. If uplink and downlink information is not available, outerjurisdictional property is pro-rata to the state based on the ratio of the amount of time the property was used to make transmissions in the state to the total amount of time the property was used for transmissions everywhere.

Payroll Factor. The denominator of the payroll factor includes *all* compensation paid everywhere by the taxpayer, and the numerator is the total compensation paid in the state, as determined under the standard UDITPA rules for sourcing payroll.

Sales Factor. Under MTC Reg. IV.18(j), the sales factor denominator includes all gross receipts derived by the taxpayer from transactions and activities in the regular course of its trade or business, and the sales factor numerator is the taxpayer's gross receipts in the state.

Gross receipts derived from the sale of printed materials are sourced to the state in which the material is delivered or shipped to the purchaser or subscriber. A *throwback rule* applies if the purchaser or subscriber is the U.S. government or the taxpayer is not taxable in a state in which the printed materials are shipped or delivered.

Gross receipts derived from advertising and the sale or rental of the taxpayer's customer lists are pro-rated to the state, based on the taxpayer's circulation factor. A separate circulation factor is computed for each publication of printed material. It equals the ratio of the in-state purchasers and subscribers to the purchasers and subscribers everywhere, as determined by reference to rating statistics.

Telecommunications Services

Some states provide special apportionment formulas for telecommunications service companies. The MTC has promulgated a Proposed Model Regulation for Apportionment of Income from the Sale of Telecommunications and Ancillary Services.

For this purpose, the term *telecommunications service* means the electronic transmission of voice, data, audio, video, or any other information or signals, and it includes a transmission, conveyance, or routing in which computer processing applications are used to act on the content for purposes of transmission, conveyance, or routing—without regard to whether such service is referred to as voice over Internet protocol services (VOIP) or is classified by the Federal Communications Commission as enhanced or value-added.

The term *telecommunications service* includes, but is not limited to, the following services:
- Wireline
- Fixed wireless
- Mobile wireless
- Paging
- Prepaid calling
- Prepaid wireless calling
- Private communication
- Value-added non-voice data
- Coin-operated telephone services
- Pay telephone services

Property Factor. In general, the property factor denominator includes the average value of all owned and rented real and tangible personal property used by the telecommunications service company in its trade or business. Outer-jurisdictional property, however, is excluded from the property factor.

Outer-jurisdictional property is property that is owned or rented by the taxpayer and used in its telecommunications service business, but that is not physically located in any particular state—including things like:

- Orbiting satellites
- Undersea transmission cables

The numerator includes owned and rented property used in the state, as determined under the standard UDITPA rules for *sourcing property*.

Payroll Factor. The denominator of the payroll factor includes *all* compensation paid everywhere by the taxpayer, and the numerator is the total compensation paid in the state, as determined under the standard UDITPA rules for sourcing payroll.

Sales Factor. The sales factor denominator includes all gross receipts that the taxpayer derives from transactions and activities in the regular course of its telecommunications service business.

The sales factor numerator includes all gross receipts of the taxpayer from sources within the state. The regulation provides numerous specialized sourcing rules for sales of telecommunications services.

> **EXAMPLE**
>
> Gross receipts from the sale of mobile telecommunications services, other than air-to-ground radiotelephone service and prepaid calling service, are attributed to the state when the customer's place of primary use is in the state pursuant to the Mobile Telecommunications Sourcing Act.

Financial Institutions

Some state impose special franchise taxes on banks and other financial institutions, while other states subject financial institutions to the state's standard corporate income tax. In addition, many states provide special apportionment formulas for financial institutions.

In 1994, the MTC adopted a model statute for apportioning the income of a financial institution, which adopts the standard UDITPA equally weighted three-factor apportionment formula. The manner in which the model statute modifies the computation of the property, payroll, and sales factors is summarized below.

Property Factor. In general, the property factor denominator includes the average value of all owned and rented real and tangible personal property used by the financial institution in its trade or business. The property factor also includes two *intangible* assets, loans and credit card receivables, which are valued at their average outstanding principal balance—without regard to any reserve for bad debts, but reduced by any amount written-off for Federal income tax purposes.

The property factor numerator includes owned and rented real and tangible personal property that is physically located or used in the state. A loan is attributed to the state if it is properly assigned to a regular place of business of the taxpayer within the state.

A loan is *properly assigned* to the place of business with which it has a preponderance of substantive contacts, as determined by such activities as the solicitation, investigation, negotiation, approval and administration of the loan. The location of credit card receivables is determined in the same manner as loans.

Payroll Factor. The denominator of the payroll factor includes *all* compensation paid everywhere by the taxpayer, and the numerator is the total compensation paid in the state, as determined under the standard UDITPA rules for sourcing payroll.

Sales Factor. The sales factor denominator includes all gross receipts that the financial institution derives from transactions and activities in the regular course of its trade or business.

The sales factor numerator is the financial institution's gross receipts in the state. Interest from loans secured by real property is attributed to the state in which the real property is located; whereas, interest from loans not secured by real property is attributed to the state in which the borrower is located. Interest from credit card receivables and fees charged to card holders is attributed to the state in which the billing address of the card holder is located.

Net gains from the sale of loans and loan servicing fees are sourced in the same manner as the loan interest. Likewise, net gains from the sale of credit card receivables are sourced in the same manner as the interest on the credit card receivables.

Interest, dividends and net gains from investment and trading assets and activities are attributed to the state if such receipts are properly assigned to a regular place of business of the taxpayer within the state, based on where the day-to-day decisions regarding the assets or activities occur.

Finally, under a throwback rule, all receipts which would be assigned to a state in which the taxpayer is not taxable are attributed to the state in which the financial institution has its commercial domicile.

Insurance Companies

Many states do not subject insurance companies to the state's standard corporate income tax. Those states that do impose a corporate income tax on insurance companies generally require insurance companies to apportion their income using a single-factor premiums formula. The MTC has not promulgated a special apportionment formula for insurance companies.

STUDY QUESTIONS

---

8. Which of the following statements is **not** true under MTC Reg. IV.18(j) concerning apportionment for publishers?

   a. For purposes of the property factor, outer-jurisdictional property should *always* be pro-rated to a state based on the ratio of the amount of time the property was used to make transmissions in the state to the total time the property was used for transmissions everywhere.

   b. The payroll factor is determined based on the standard UDITPA rules for sourcing payroll.

   c. With regards to the sales factor, a throwback rule applies if the purchaser or subscriber is the U.S. government or the taxpayer is not taxable in a state in which the printed materials are shipped or delivered.

9. States usually require insurance companies to apportion their income using a *single-factor* property apportionment formula. ***True or False?***

Recent Developments

Alaska. In determining their Alaska property, payroll, and sales factors, water transport companies (i.e., companies engaged in the transportation of goods or passengers by ship or barge) must use a *days-spent-in-port* ratio that represents the number of 24-hour days spent in Alaska ports during the tax year divided by the total number of days spent in all ports during the tax year (Alaska Dept. of Rev., Reg. §15 ACC 19.1490, effective Aug. 8, 2007).

Colorado. For tax years beginning on or after January 1, 2009, a mutual fund service corporation that provides management, distribution, and administrative services for a regulated investment company must source mutual fund sales to Colorado based on the percentage of shareholders in the regulated investment company that are domiciled in the state (H.B. 1311, May 18, 2009).

Delaware. For tax years beginning on or after January 1, 2009, an asset management corporation may apportion income using a single-factor gross receipts formula. An *asset management corporation* is a corporation that derives 90 percent or more of its gross receipts from investment services (S.B. 213, June 3, 2008).

Illinois. As detailed below, Illinois made numerous changes to its apportionment rules in 2007 (S.B. 1544, Aug. 16, 2007) and 2008 (S.B. 783, Jan. 11, 2008). These changes generally are effective for tax years ending on or after December 31, 2008.

Income derived by a financial organization is apportioned to Illinois based on the ratio of the receipts from sources within Illinois or otherwise attributable to the State's marketplace, to the receipts everywhere.

Receipts from investment or trading assets and activities are attributed to Illinois if they are properly assigned, based on the preponderance of substantive contacts, to a fixed place of business of the taxpayer within Illinois. If the fixed place of business that has a preponderance of substantive contacts cannot be determined, the asset or activity is assigned to the state in which the taxpayer's commercial domicile is located [35 Ill. Comp. Stat. §5/304(c)].

Receipts from the sale of telecommunications services or mobile telecommunications service are attributed to Illinois, with certain exceptions, if the customer's service address is in the state [35 Ill. Comp. Stat. Sec, 5/304(a)(3)(B-5)].

Income from providing airline transportation services is apportioned to Illinois based on the ratio of revenue miles in the state to revenue miles everywhere. A *revenue mile* is the transportation of one passenger or one net ton of freight the distance of one mile for consideration [35 Ill. Comp. Stat. Sec, 5/304(d)].

Income from providing transportation services other than airline services is apportioned using a formula, the numerator of which includes:

- All receipts from any movement or shipment of people or goods that both originates and terminates in Illinois, PLUS
- That portion of the receipts from movements or shipments of people or goods passing through, into, or out of Illinois, that is determined by the ratio that the miles traveled in Illinois bears to total miles from point of origin to point of destination

The denominator is all receipts derived from the movement or shipment of people or goods [35 Ill. Comp. Stat. Sec, 5/304(d)].

Kansas. Effective June 20, 2008, if a unitary group includes one or more members engaged in railroad or interstate motor carrier operations and one or more members not engaged in railroad or interstate motor carrier operations, a three-factor formula is used to apportion the income of the entire unitary group to those members engaged in railroad or interstate motor carrier operations. Then, a single-factor mileage formula is used to apportion the income of each member engaged in railroad or interstate motor carrier operations to Kansas (Kan. Dept. of Rev., Regs. §92-12-114).

Kentucky. For tax years beginning on or after January 1, 2008, a passenger airline determines its property, payroll, and sales factors by multiplying the total average value of its aircraft, total flight personnel compensation, and total transportation revenues, by the ratio of Kentucky revenue passenger miles to total revenue passenger miles (H.B. 258, Apr. 9, 2008).

Massachusetts. In November 2007, the Massachusetts Department of Revenue issued new regulations for apportioning income derived from sales of electricity, unforced capacity, electricity brokerage services, ancillary services related to electricity, electricity transmission and distribution services, and from buying and selling financial instruments related to electricity (830 Mass. Code Regs. 63.38.10, effective for tax years beginning on or after Nov. 30, 2007).

Michigan. Effective in 2007, media receipts from sales by taxpayers whose business activities include television programming or live radio are attributable to Michigan if *both*:
- The commercial domicile of the customer is in Michigan, AND
- The customer has a direct connection with the taxpayer pursuant to a contract under which the media receipts are derived

Media receipts from the sale of advertising to a customer who is commercially domiciled in Michigan and who receives some of the benefit of the advertising sale in Michigan are attributable to Michigan in proportion to the extent that the customer receives benefit from the advertising in Michigan.

Media receipts from the sale of advertising to a customer who is a broadcaster and who receives some of the benefit of the advertising in Michigan are proportioned based on the ratio that the broadcaster's listening or viewing audience in Michigan bears to its total listening or viewing audience everywhere (H.B. 5460, Dec. 27, 2007).

Minnesota. For tax years beginning on or after January 1, 2010, receipts from management, distribution, or administrative services performed by a corporation or trust for a mutual fund are attributed to the state in which the shareholders of the fund reside for purposes of computing the Minnesota sales factor (H.B. 3149, May 29, 2008).

Oregon. Effective for tax years beginning after 2006, insurance companies must use a sales-only apportionment formula (S.B. 179, June 28, 2007). Under prior law, insurance companies used an equally weighted three-factor formula.

Pennsylvania. In *FedEx Ground Package System, Inc. v. Pennsylvania*, the Pennsylvania Commonwealth Court ruled that the numerator of a trucking company's revenue miles apportionment formula should be computed by multiplying the total number of miles that the company transported packages in Pennsylvania by the company's average receipts per mile for transporting packages "in Pennsylvania" (rather than the average receipts per mile "everywhere," which was the Department of Revenue's standard practice) [Nos. 302 F.R. 2003 and 303 F.R. 2003 (Penn. Commw. Ct., Apr. 27, 2007)].

For this purpose, *revenue mile* means the average receipts derived from the transportation by the taxpayer of persons or property one mile. During the tax year in question, FedEx's average receipts per mile everywhere were $3.93 per mile, and its average receipts per mile in Pennsylvania were $2.94.

The court determined that its interpretation follows the plain language of the statute and is consistent with the principle that an apportionment factor numerator should only reflect activity in Pennsylvania. The Pennsylvania Supreme Court affirmed the lower court's decision [Nos. 55-56 MAP 2007 (Pa. Sup. Ct., Dec. 27, 2007)].

Utah. For tax years beginning on or after January 1, 2008, an airline determines its property, payroll, and sales factors by multiplying the total average value of its mobile flight equipment, total flight personnel compensation, and total transportation revenues, by the ratio of Utah revenue ton miles to total revenue ton miles. Separate computations are made for each aircraft type (S.B. 237, Mar. 17, 2008).

STUDY QUESTION

> **10.** In 2007 and 2008, Illinois made numerous apportionment changes which generally apply to tax years ending on or after December 31, 2008. These included which of the following?
>
> **a.** Income from providing airline services is apportioned to Illinois based on a sales factor, the denominator of which includes all receipts derived from the movement or shipment of people or goods.
>
> **b.** Receipts from the sale of telecommunications services are attributed to Illinois if the call is completed in Illinois.
>
> **c.** Income of a financial organization is apportioned to Illinois based on the ratio of the receipts from sources within or otherwise attributable to Illinois's marketplace, to the receipts everywhere.

State Tax Implications of Federal Section 338 Elections

This chapter explains the federal tax implications of Internal Revenue Code Sec. 338 elections and how those elections are treated by the states.

LEARNING OBJECTIVES

Upon completing this chapter, the professional will be able to:

■ Explain the significance of a federal Section 338 election
■ Differentiate between the federal Section 338(g) and Section 338(h)(10) elections
■ Describe the state tax treatment of Section 338(g) and Section 338(h)(10) elections

FEDERAL TAX TREATMENT

Background

The acquisition by one corporation (*acquirer*) of the business operations of another corporation (*target*) can be accomplished through the purchase of either the target corporation's assets or the target corporation's stock.

Asset Purchase

If the acquisition is structured as an *asset purchase*, the target recognizes gain or loss on the sale of its assets, and the acquirer takes a basis in the assets equal to the purchase price (i.e., *market value*).

In other words, the basis of the acquired assets gets stepped-up or stepped-down to market value. However, the acquirer does not inherit the net operating loss (NOL) carryforwards, earnings, profits, and other tax attributes of the target corporation, these tax attributes remain with the target, which may use any of its NOL carryforwards to offset the gains from the asset sale.

Stock Purchase

If the acquisition is structured as a *stock purchase*, once the acquirer obtains a controlling interest in the stock of the target corporation, the acquirer may do one of the following:

- Continue to operate the target as a separate subsidiary
- Liquidate the target to obtain direct control of the target's assets

In a stock purchase where the acquirer continues to operate the target as a separate subsidiary, only the target *shareholders* recognize gain or loss. Neither the acquirer nor the target recognize any gain or loss on the acquisition, there is no change in the basis of the target's assets, and the target's NOL carryforwards and other tax attributes remain with the target.

If the acquirer liquidates the target, then:

- The subsidiary liquidation is generally tax-free to both the acquirer and target under Internal Revenue Code (Code) Secs. 332 and 337,
- The target's basis in its assets carries over to the acquirer (i.e., there is no step-up or step-down to market value), AND
- The target's tax attributes carry over to the acquirer.

A corporation making a qualifying stock purchase also has the option to make a Section 338 election. If the acquirer makes a Section 338 election, then the purchase of a controlling interest in the target's stock is treated as if it were an *asset purchase*. As a result, the target recognizes gain or loss on the fictional asset sale, and the acquirer takes a basis in the target's assets equal to the purchase price of the stock plus the liabilities assumed (i.e., market value).

Section 338 reflects the judicial principle that the purchase of a target corporation's stock in order to obtain the target's assets should be treated as a single transaction involving the acquirer's acquisition of the target's assets [see, e.g., ***Kimbell-Diamond Milling Co. v. Commissioner***, 187 F.2d 718 (CA-5, 1951)]. In 1954, Congress codified this principle by enacting Section 334(b)(2), which was replaced by Section 338 in 1982.

STUDY QUESTION

> **1.** If an acquisition is structured as a *stock purchase*, then:
>
>   **a.** The acquirer may either continue to operate the target as a separate subsidiary or liquidate the target.
>
>   **b.** The acquirer takes a basis in the assets equal to the purchase price of the stock plus the liabilities assumed.
>
>   **c.** The acquirer does not inherit *any* NOL carryforwards, which remain with the target.

Section 338(g) Election

Under Section 338(g), a corporation that makes a qualifying stock purchase may elect to have the target corporation treated as if *both* of the following have occurred:

- On the stock acquisition date, the target sells all of its assets at fair market value in a single transaction
- On the day after the stock acquisition date, the target is a new corporation that purchases all of the old target's assets

> **NOTE**
>
> The acquirer acts alone in making a Section 338(g) election and the election has no effect on the seller of the target corporation stock.

The acquirer is eligible to make a Section 338(g) election if, within a 12-month acquisition period, the acquirer obtains by purchase at least 80 percent of both the total voting power and total value of the stock of the target corporation.

> **NOTE**
>
> Stock acquired from a related party or stock acquired in a tax-free transaction (e.g., a Section 351 transaction) is not taken into account in applying the 80 percent ownership test.

The acquirer must make a Section 338(g) election no later than the fifteenth day of the ninth month beginning after the month in which the acquisition date occurs. The acquisition date is the first day during the 12-month acquisition period on which the 80 percent stock ownership requirement is satisfied. The election is made on federal Form 8023, *Elections Under Section 338 for Corporations Making Qualified Stock Purchases.*

In effect, a Section 338(g) election results in a hypothetical asset sale by the target corporation (old target) to a new corporation (new target). The old target must recognize gains and losses on the hypothetical asset sale, after which the old target no longer exists for federal income tax purposes and its tax attributes do not carry over to the new target but, instead, expire.

Thus, a Section 338 election triggers immediate gain recognition with respect to the target corporation's appreciated assets. The target's gains on the deemed asset sale are in addition to any gain recognized by the target's shareholders on the actual sale of the target's stock.

> **PLANNING POINTER**
>
> Because a Section 338 election triggers immediate gain recognition with respect to the target corporation's appreciated assets, it is generally not beneficial to make a Section 338(g) election unless the target corporation has NOL carryforwards that can be used to offset the gains triggered by the deemed asset sale.

Any gain or loss resulting from the deemed asset sale is included in the final tax return of the old target. That final return covers the old target's final tax year, which ends at the close of the stock acquisition date. When the old target is a member of an affiliated group filing a consolidated return, absent a Section 338(h)(10) election (which is discussed in the next section), the old target is disaffiliated from that group immediately before its deemed sale of assets under Section 338(g), and must file a final return on a separate company basis that includes *only* the gain or loss from the deemed asset sale and certain carryforward items (Treas. Reg. §1.338-10(a)(2)). The separate final return is referred to as a *one-day return.*

The new target is considered to be a newly formed corporation for federal income tax purposes, and the basis of the assets acquired from old target gets stepped-up or stepped-down to market value. The acquirer may, but is not required to, liquidate the new target corporation. If the new target is liquidated, the new target's stepped-up or stepped-down basis in its assets carries over to the acquiring corporation.

The price at which the old target is deemed to have sold all of its assets to the new target is referred to as the "aggregate deemed sales price" (Treas. Reg. §1.338-4); whereas, the price at which the new target is deemed to have paid to purchase the old target's assets is referred to as the "adjusted grossed-up basis (Treas. Reg. §1.338-5)." Both amounts are determined by reference to the acquiring corporation's basis in the target's stock and the liabilities of old target.

To compute its gains and losses, old target allocates the deemed sales price among its assets under rules substantially similar to those applicable to purchase price allocations under Section 1060, which generally requires the use of the residual method to allocate the purchase price of applicable asset acquisitions among the individual assets purchased. The new target applies the same allocation principles to allocate the deemed sales price among the assets it acquired (Treas. Reg. §1.338-6).

Under these principles, the deemed sales price is allocated among seven asset classes in priority order, starting with Class I assets (cash and cash equivalents), then Class II assets, then Class III assets, and so on, with any residual amount allocated to Class VII assets (goodwill and going concern value). The amount allocated to a specific asset, other than the Class VII assets, cannot exceed the asset's fair market value. To report the basis allocation, both old target and new target must attach to their respective federal tax returns Form 8883 (Asset Allocation Statement Under Section 338).

STUDY QUESTION

> **2.** Which of the following is required for an acquirer to make a Section 338(g) election?
>
> **a.** Within a 12-month acquisition period, the acquirer must make a qualified purchase of at least 80 percent of both the total voting power and total value of the stock of the target corporation.
>
> **b.** The acquirer must make a Section 338(g) election no later than the 15th day of the 12th month beginning after the month in which the acquisition occurs.
>
> **c.** The election must be made on Form 8883.

Section 338(h)(10) Election

Section 338(h)(10) provides a special election that is available when one corporation is purchasing the stock of another corporation that is either an S corporation or a member of an affiliated group of corporations. As with a Section 338(g) election, a Section 338(h)(10) election triggers a deemed sale of the target corporation's assets that results in both gain or loss recognition and a step-up or step-down in the basis of the target's assets.

In contrast to a Section 338(g) election, however, the gain or loss on the actual sale of the target's stock is ignored. Therefore, a Section 338(h)(10) election results in a *single* level of taxation, rather than the two levels of taxation associated with a Section 338(g) election. For this reason, Section 338(h)(10) elections are more popular than Section 338(g) elections.

A Section 338(h)(10) election may be made if the target corporation is a member of an affiliated group of corporations, regardless of whether the group members are filing a consolidated return or separate returns. If a Section 338(h)(10) election is made, the stock sale is treated as an asset sale by the old target to the new target—followed by the complete liquidation of the new target. In addition, any gain or loss recognized on the stock sale is ignored.

The first part of the fiction created by a Section 338(h)(10) election is that the old target is deemed to have sold all of its assets to the new target in a single transaction. If old target was a member of an affiliated group filing a consolidated return (i.e., a *selling consolidated group*), the asset sale is deemed to occur before the close of the acquisition date while old target is still a member of the selling consolidated group.

Therefore, the gain or loss is included in the selling consolidated group's federal consolidated return (Treas. Reg. §1.338(h)(10)-1(d)(3)). If the old target was a member of an affiliated group filing separate returns, the gain or loss is included in old target's separately filed final tax return. The basis of the assets that the new target is deemed to have purchased from old target gets stepped-up or stepped-down to market value.

The second part of the fiction created by a Section 338(h)(10) election is the deemed liquidation of the old target. After the deemed asset sale but before the close of the acquisition date, and while the old target is a member of the selling consolidated group (or owned by the selling affiliate), the old target is treated as having distributed the sales proceeds to the selling consolidated group or the selling affiliate as part of a complete liquidation to which Section 332 (tax-free liquidation of subsidiary) applies, and the tax attributes of the old target carry over to the selling consolidated group or selling affiliate under Section 381 (Treas. Reg. §1.338(h)(10)-1(d)(4)).

A Section 338(h)(10) election also may be made by S corporation shareholders when the stock of the S corporation is purchased by another corporation. The gain or loss from the deemed asset sale is included in old target's separately filed final tax return. The target's S corporation status continues, in effect, through the close of the acquisition date.

Therefore, the S corporation shareholders take their pro rata share of the deemed sale tax consequences into account under Code Sec. 1366, *Pass-thru of items to shareholders*, and increase or decrease their basis in the target corporation's stock under Code Sec. 1367, *Adjustments to basis of stock of shareholders, etc.* (Treas. Reg. §1.338(h)(10)-1(d)(5)).

After the deemed asset sale but before the close of the acquisition date, the old target is treated as having transferred all of its assets to the S corporation shareholders as part of a complete liquidation to which Code Sec. 331, *Gain or loss to shareholders in corporate liquidations*, applies.

> **NOTE**
>
> Unlike a Section 338(g) election, where any gains from the deemed asset sale are taxed to the stock purchaser, a Section 338(h)(10) election causes the stock seller to report and pay the tax on any gains from the deemed asset sale.
>
> As a consequence, a Section 338(h)(10) election must be made jointly on Form 8023 by both the seller and the purchaser (Treas. Reg. §1.338(h)(10)-1(c)(3)).

STUDY QUESTION

---

3. A Section 338(h)(10) election:

   a. Results in two levels of taxation

   b. Is not as popular as Section 338(g) elections

   c. Results in both gain or loss recognition and a step-up or step-down in the basis of the target's assets

---

STATE TAX TREATMENT

States generally conform to the federal income tax treatment of an election made under Section 338(g). See, for example, California Franchise Tax Board Legal Ruling 2006-03 (May 5, 2006). Accordingly, for state income tax purposes, the selling corporation recognizes gain or loss on the stock sale, and the target's deemed asset sale results in both gain or loss recognition and a step-up or step-down in the basis of the target's assets.

Most states also conform to the federal treatment of a Section 338(h)(10) election. As a consequence, for state income tax purposes, a Section 338(h)(10) election causes a deemed sale of the target corporation's assets that results in both gain or loss recognition and a step-up or step-down in the basis of the target's assets; whereas, the seller's gain or loss on the actual sale of the target's stock is ignored.

Inclusion of Gain From Deemed Asset Sale in Apportionable Income

States generally treat the gains and losses resulting from a deemed asset sale under Section 338 as apportionable *business income*. However, courts in some states have ruled that such gains are specifically allocable *nonbusiness income*.

In *Canteen Corp. v. Commonwealth of Pennsylvania*, the Pennsylvania Supreme Court ruled that the gains triggered by a Section 338(h)(10) election were *nonbusiness income*, because the transaction met neither the transactional test nor the functional test for treatment as *business income* [854 A.2d 440 (Pa. Sup. Ct., 2004)]. Referring to the standards established in *Laurel Pipe Line Comp. v. Board of Finance and Revenue*, the court noted that the transactional test was not met, because the *fictional liquidation* of assets stemming from the parent corporation's Section 338 election is not a type of transaction in which the taxpayer regularly engages [642 A.2d 472 (Pa. Sup. Ct. 1994)]. The functional test also was not met because, as in *Laurel Pipe*, the taxpayer liquidated and distributed the proceeds to its shareholders.

In 2001, the Pennsylvania Legislature broadened the definition of *business income* to include "all income which is apportionable under the Constitution of the United States." In Corporate Tax Statement of Policy 2004-01

(Nov. 9, 2004), the Pennsylvania Department of Revenue announced that, due to the statutory amendments to the definition of business income that were enacted in 2001, the ruling in **Canteen** does not apply to tax years beginning after 1998, and the taxable income generated as a result of a Section 338 election will be treated as business income.

In *ABB C-E Nuclear Power, Inc. v. Director of Revenue*, the Missouri Supreme Court ruled that a $227 million gain from the sale and liquidation of a subsidiary in a Section 338(h)(10) transaction was *nonbusiness income* that was not apportionable to Missouri [No. SC87811 (Mo. Sup. Ct., Jan. 30, 2007)]. The court concluded that the sale and liquidation was not a type of business transaction in which the subsidiary regularly engaged, nor was it a disposition of the sort that constituted an integral part of the subsidiary's ordinary business. Therefore, the transaction was a one-time, extraordinary event that did not generate business income under either the transactional test or the functional test.

In *American States Insurance Co. v. Illinois Department of Revenue*, the Illinois Appellate Court ruled that the gains arising from a Section 338(h)(10) election made in 1997 were *nonbusiness income*, because the gains were related to the complete liquidation and cessation of business operations and, therefore, the functional test was not met [No. 1-03-1646 (Ill. App. Ct., Aug. 27, 2004); *appeal denied*, No. 99589 (Ill. Jan. 26, 2005)].

In *Nicor v. Illinois Department of Revenue*, the Illinois appellate court ruled that a Section 338(h)(10) election made in 1993 gave rise to *nonbusiness income* [No. 1-07-1359 & 1-07-1591 (Ill. App. Ct., Dec. 5, 2008)]. Relying on the earlier ruling in *American States Insurance*, the appellate court held that the taxpayer's sale must be treated as a complete liquidation and cessation of business resulting in nonbusiness income.

The court also noted that, in 2004, the Illinois Legislature amended the definition of *business income* which applied to this case. As a result, the functional test no longer exists and the arguments raised in this appeal are no longer relevant. In 2004, Illinois broadened its definition of business income to include "all income that may be treated as apportionable business income under the Constitution of the United States (S.B. 2207, 2004)."

In *McKesson Water Products Company v. Division of Taxation*, the New Jersey Tax Court ruled that a gain from the sale of a corporation's stock that was part of a Section 338(h)(10) transaction was neither operational income nor investment income serving an operational function [No. 000156-2004 (N.J. Tax Ct., Aug. 13, 2007)]. As a consequence, the gain was not subject to New Jersey corporation income tax but, instead, was *non-operational income* allocable to the taxpayer's principal state of business (California).

The New Jersey Superior Court affirmed the Tax Court's determination that the gain arising from the election made under Section 338(h)(10) to treat the corporation's sale of stock as a deemed sale of all its assets was not an integral part of the corporation's trade or business and was, therefore, nonoperational income allocable to California [N.J. Super. Ct., No. A-5423 -06T3 (July 16, 2009)].

In contrast, in *General Mills, Inc. v. Commissioner of Revenue*, the taxpayer argued that the gains arising from a Section 338(h)(10) election were a federal tax fiction, and the reality of the transaction (i.e., a sale of stock) should be respected, in which case the gains were nonbusiness income [440 Mass. 154, 795 N.E.2d 552 (Mass. Sup. Jud. Ct., 2003)]. The Massachusetts Supreme Judicial Court rejected the taxpayer's argument, and ruled that the gains from the deemed asset sale were properly included in Massachusetts income tax base, consistent with the federal tax treatment of the transaction.

Likewise, in S.C. Revenue Ruling No. 09-4 (Mar. 31, 2009), the South Carolina Department of Revenue ruled that if the target subsidiary uses the assets in its trade or business, the gains triggered by a Section 338(h)(10) election are apportionable business income. An exception applies to gains from the deemed sale of real property, which are allocated to South Carolina if the real property is located in South Carolina or to the extent of depreciation previously deducted in computing South Carolina taxable income.

Also, in *Newell Window Furnishing, Inc. v. Johnson*, the Tennessee Court of Appeals ruled that where a corporation sold the stock of its subsidiary and the sale was treated as a sale of assets under Section 338(h)(10), the gain from the deemed asset sale had to be included in the subsidiary's Tennessee corporate income tax base as apportionable business income [No. M2007-02176-COA-R3-CV (Tenn. Ct. of App., Dec. 9, 2008)].

STUDY QUESTION

---

4. In which of the following cases did the state court rule that gains and losses from a deemed asset sale under Section 338 are allocable *non-business income*?

  a. *McKesson Water Products Company*
  b. *General Mills, Inc.*
  c. *Newell Window Furnishing, Inc.*

Inclusion of Gross Receipts From Deemed Asset Sale in Sales Factor

Most states apply their standard apportionment rules to the target corporation's deemed asset sale. Thus, the gross receipts from the deemed asset sale are generally included in the target corporation's sales factor.

In *Combustion Engineering, Inc. v. Commissioner of Revenue*, the Massachusetts Appellate Tax Board ruled that a parent corporation's gross receipts from the sale of a subsidiary's stock were not includible in the parent's sales factor, even though a federal Section 338(h)(10) election resulted in the stock sale being treated as a deemed asset sale, the gains from which were included in apportionable income [No. F228740 (Mass. App. Tax Bd., Mar. 29, 2000)].

Consistent with this decision, the Massachusetts Department of Revenue took the position that the receipts from a Section 338 deemed asset sale are *excluded* from the sales factor (see Technical Information Release 01-11, Aug. 28 2001). In 2004, however, the Massachusetts Legislature enacted an amendment that clarifies that—effective for tax years beginning on or after January 1, 2005—if an acquiring corporation makes a Section 338 election, the target corporation will be treated as having sold its assets for Massachusetts apportionment purposes (H.B. 4744, Aug. 9, 2004).

This amendment effectively reversed the result in *Combustion Engineering*. In response to this legislation, in Technical Information Release 04-22 (Dec. 8, 2004), the Massachusetts Department of Revenue indicated that it will amend its regulations to reflect the legislative intent to harmonize the treatment of the gains and gross receipts arising from Section 338 transactions.

Special Apportionment Rule for Section 338(h)(10) Gains

New Jersey generally requires the receipts from a deemed asset sale under Section 338(h)(10) to be allocated and sourced to New Jersey by multiplying the gain by a three-year average of the allocation factors used by a target corporation for its three tax return periods immediately prior to the sale (N.J. Admin. Code 18:7-8.12, New Jersey Division of Taxation).

STUDY QUESTION

5. In Massachusetts, when a purchasing corporation makes a Section 338 election, the target corporation is *not* treated as having sold its assets. *True or False?*

MODULE 1: CORPORATE INCOME TAXATION — CHAPTER 4

Treatment of Nonbusiness Income

This chapter discusses how states differentiate between business and nonbusiness income, and how nonbusiness income is allocated. It also explains the unitary business principle and reviews U.S. Supreme Court and state court cases that have affected the definitions of business and nonbusiness income.

LEARNING OBJECTIVES

Upon completing this chapter, the professional will be able to:

- Explain the unitary business principle
- Explain operational function test
- State UDITPA's definitions of business and nonbusiness income
- Differentiate between the transactional and functional tests for determining whether an item of income is business or nonbusiness income
- Demonstrate how nonbusiness income is allocated
- Describe the treatment of expenses attributable to nonbusiness income

CONSTITUTIONAL RESTRICTIONS ON INCLUSIONS IN APPORTIONABLE INCOME

The U.S. Constitution prohibits a state from taxing an out-of-state corporation on income derived from an unrelated activity that has nothing to do with the business activity of the corporation in the taxing state.

This principle reflects the fundamental requirement of the Due Process and Commerce Clauses that there be "some definite link, some minimum connection, between a state and the person, property or transaction it seeks to tax" [*Miller Bros. Co. v. Maryland,* 347 US 340, 1954].

Under the unitary business principle, if a corporation's interstate activities form a unitary business, a state need not isolate the corporation's in-state activities from the rest of the business in determining the corporation's taxable income. Instead, the state may tax an apportioned percentage of the income generated by the multistate unitary business.

The unitary business principle was originally developed in the 19th century to address the issues that arose when states attempted to impose property taxes on interstate railroad and telegraph companies.

EXAMPLE

To fairly determine the value of an interstate railroad's track located within a state for property tax purposes, it was necessary to apportion a share of the value of the entire multistate business rather than attempt to isolate the value of the in-state property.

In *Mobil Oil Corp. v. Commissioner of Taxes*, the Supreme Court stated that "the linchpin of apportionability in the field of state income taxation is the unitary business principle" [445 US 425 (1980)].

Mobil was an integrated petroleum company that was incorporated and commercially domiciled in New York. Mobil challenged Vermont's ability to tax dividends that the taxpayer received from its foreign subsidiaries. The essence of Mobil's argument that Vermont could not constitutionally tax the foreign dividends was that the activities of the foreign subsidiaries were "unrelated" to Mobil's activities in Vermont, which were limited to marketing petroleum products.

The Supreme Court ruled that Vermont could tax an apportioned percentage of the dividends Mobil received from its foreign subsidiaries, because those subsidiaries were part of the same integrated petroleum enterprise as the business operations conducted in Vermont. In other words, the dividends were apportionable income because they were received from unitary subsidiaries.

The Court also indicated that if the business activities of the foreign subsidiaries had "nothing to do with the activities of the recipient in the taxing state, due process considerations might well preclude apportionability, because there would be no underlying unitary business."

The two most recent Supreme Court decisions regarding apportionable income are *Allied-Signal* and *MeadWestvaco.*

Allied-Signal

In Allied-Signal, Inc. v. Director, Division of Taxation, the taxpayer was Bendix Corporation (Allied-Signal was the successor in interest to Bendix), a Delaware corporation that was commercially domiciled in Michigan and conducted business in all 50 states [504 US 768, 1992].

In 1981, Bendix realized a $211.5 million gain from the sale of 20.6 percent of the stock of ASARCO, Inc. The Supreme Court ruled that the State of New Jersey was constitutionally prohibited from including the gain in the taxpayer's apportionable income, because none of the factors that would indicate that Bendix and ASARCO were engaged in a *unitary business* (e.g., functional integration, centralized management, or economies of scale) were present.

As a result, the Court concluded that Bendix and ASARCO were "unrelated business enterprises each of whose activities had nothing to do with the other." In addition, the ownership of ASARCO stock did not serve an operational function in Bendix's business—"the mere fact that an intangible asset was acquired pursuant to a long-term corporate strategy of acquisitions and dispositions does not convert an otherwise passive investment into an integral operational one."

In arriving at its decision in *Allied-Signal,* the Supreme Court stated that "the payee and the payer need not be engaged in the same unitary business as a prerequisite to apportionment in all cases ... What is required instead is that the capital transaction serve an operational rather than an investment function."

As an example of an asset that serves an *operational function*, the Court mentions "interest earned on short-term deposits ... if that income forms part of the working capital of the corporation's unitary business." The Court's reference to an operational function in this case was widely interpreted as creating a new test for apportionable income.

Under the alleged operational function test, even if no unitary business exists between the payee (taxpayer) and payer (asset), a state may still tax an apportioned percentage of the income from an intangible asset if that asset serves an operational function rather than an investment function in the taxpayer's business.

MeadWestvaco

In *MeadWestvaco Corporation v. Illinois Department of Revenue*, the issue was whether Illinois was constitutionally prohibited from taxing an apportioned share of the $1 billion gain realized by Mead Corporation in 1994, when it sold its investment in Lexis/Nexis [128 SCt. 1498, 2008].

MeadWestvaco is the successor in interest to Mead, which was an Ohio corporation. Lexis/Nexis (Lexis) was one of Mead's business divisions. The Illinois trial court concluded that, although Mead and Lexis were not engaged in a unitary business, the gain nevertheless qualified as apportionable income, because Mead's investment in Lexis served an operational purpose. The Illinois appeals court affirmed the trial court's decision that Lexis served an *operational function* in Mead's business, but did not address the issue of whether Mead and Lexis were engaged in a unitary business.

The U.S. Supreme Court vacated the Illinois appeals court decision on the grounds that it misinterpreted the Court's references to *operational function* in *Allied-Signal* as modifying the unitary business principle to add a new basis for apportionment. The Court explained that the operational function concept described in *Allied-Signal* merely recognizes the reality that an asset can be part of a taxpayer's unitary business, even if there is no unitary relationship between the payee (taxpayer) and payer (asset).

The Court explained that its reference to *operational function* in *Allied-Signal* was "not intended to modify the unitary business principle by adding a new ground for apportionment." Instead, "[t]he concept of operational function simply recognizes that an asset can be a part of a taxpayer's unitary business even if what we may term a 'unitary relationship' does not exist between the 'payor and payee.'" Thus, whether an asset serves an operational function in the taxpayer's business is "merely instrumental to the constitutionally relevant conclusion that the asset was a unitary part of the business being conducted in the taxing State."

The Court illustrated this point using examples drawn from its earlier decisions. In *Allied-Signal,* the Supreme Court stated that *apportionable income* includes "interest earned on short-term deposits in a bank located in another State if that income forms part of the working capital of the corporation's unitary business, notwithstanding the absence of a unitary relationship between the corporation and the bank." The taxpayer is *not* unitary with the payer of the income (the bank), but the taxpayer's deposits (working capital and thus operational assets) are clearly unitary with the taxpayer's business.

Likewise, in *Container Corporation of America v. Franchise Tax Board* [463 US 159, 1983], the Supreme Court stated that "capital transactions can serve either an investment function or an operational function," and noted that it had made this distinction in another context in *Corn Products Refining Co. v. Commissioner* [350 U. S. 46, 1955].

In *Corn Products,* a manufacturer purchased commodity futures to secure supplies of raw materials at an economical price. Thus, the taxpayer was not unitary with the payer of the income (the counterparty to the futures contracts), but the taxpayer's futures contracts (hedges against the risk of a price increase for raw materials) were clearly unitary with the taxpayer's business.

Finally, the Supreme Court indicated that, because the Illinois appeals court did not rule on whether Mead and Lexis formed a unitary business, the Illinois appeals court may take up that issue on remand.

STUDY QUESTIONS

> **1.** Which statement regarding apportionable business income is *not* true?
> **a.** The payee and the payer need *not* be engaged in the same unitary business as a prerequisite to apportionment in all cases.
> **b.** To qualify as apportionable business income, a capital transaction *must* serve an investment rather than an operational function.
> **c.** The linchpin of apportionability is the unitary business principle.

> **2.** Which of the following items of income is most likely *nonbusiness* income?
>
> **a.** Gain on the sale of raw land that has *nothing* to do with the taxpayer's business activities in the taxing state.
> **b.** Dividends that a parent corporation receives from its unitary subsidiaries.
> **c.** Interest income on bank deposits that are part of the taxpayer's working capital.

STATE STATUTORY RESTRICTIONS ON INCLUSIONS IN APPORTIONABLE INCOME

The Uniform Division of Income for Tax Purposes Act (UDITPA) is a model law for apportioning the income of a corporation. The apportionment laws of most states conform, in varying degrees, to UDITPA.

Under UDITPA, *business income* is apportioned among the states in which the taxpayer has nexus; whereas, the entire amount of an item of *nonbusiness income* is specifically allocated to a *single* state. Therefore, the principal consequence of classifying an item as nonbusiness income is that the income is excluded from the tax base of every nexus state, except the state in which the nonbusiness income is taxable in full (often, the state of commercial domicile). Because the classification of an item as nonbusiness income effectively removes the income from the tax base of one or more states, the business versus nonbusiness income distinction has historically been an area of significant controversy.

UDITPA §1(e) defines *nonbusiness income* as "all income other than business income."

According to UDITPA §1(a), *business income* is:

> [I]ncome arising from transactions and activity in the regular course of the taxpayer's trade or business and includes income from tangible and intangible property if the acquisition, management, and disposition of the property constitute integral parts of the taxpayer's regular trade or business operations.

Therefore, under UDITPA, an item of income is classified as *business income* if it either arises from transactions and activity in the regular course of the taxpayer's trade or business (transactional test), or from tangible and intangible property, if the acquisition, management, and disposition of the property constitute integral parts of the taxpayer's regular trade or business operations (functional test) [MTC Reg. IV.1.(a)].

Of course, each state is free to adopt its own definition of *nonbusiness income*, subject to U.S. Constitutional constraints. This can result in the same item of income being treated differently in different states. Such inconsistent treatment can result in double taxation of the income in question.

EXAMPLE

When a grocery store chain sold its leasehold assets, the gain on the sale was held to be *nonbusiness income* in Kansas [*In re Kroger Co.,* No. 93-15316-DT (Kan. B.T.A. Feb. 13, 1997)], but *business income* in Illinois [*Kroger Co. v. Department of Revenue,* Nos. 1-95-1658, 1-95-2232 (Ill. App. Ct. Sept. 17, 1996)].

The Kansas court focused on the unusual nature of the sale transaction, whereas the Illinois court focused on the integral nature of the leasehold assets to the taxpayer's trade or business.

EXAMPLE

A Delaware law allocates the *entire* amount of a gain from the sale of property, including business property, to the state in which the asset is located [30 Del. Code §1903(b)].

In *Director of Revenue v. CNA Holdings Inc., f/k/a Hoechst Celanese Corp.,* the Delaware Supreme Court ruled that a multistate corporation must comply with this statute, and that it must allocate to Delaware 100 percent of the gain from the sale of a Delaware plant, even though other states were also taxing an apportioned percentage of the gain [No. 51, 2002 (Del. Sup. Ct. Mar. 21, 2003)].

Although Delaware's approach resulted in double taxation, the court concluded that the statute was not unreasonable because, to the extent that Delaware may be taxing more than its share of in-state property sales, it is taxing less than its share of out-of-state property sales.

STUDY QUESTION

> **3.** Which of the following is *true* of nonbusiness income?
>
> **a.** Under UDITPA, it is apportioned among the states in which the taxpayer has nexus.
> **b.** Under UDITPA, it is allocated to a *single* state.
> **c.** The definition of nonbusiness income is identical in all 50 states.

CONTROVERSY REGARDING EXISTENCE OF TWO-PART TEST

In determining whether an item of income is business or nonbusiness in nature, state courts have been divided on whether the UDITPA definition of business income includes *both* a transactional test and a functional test, or *just* a transactional test.

The *transactional test* is defined as "income arising from transactions and activity in the regular course of the taxpayer's trade or business." It looks at the frequency and regularity of the income-producing transaction in relation to the taxpayer's regular trade or business. The critical issue is whether the transaction is frequent in nature, as opposed to a rare and extraordinary event.

In contrast, the *functional test* involves "income from tangible and intangible property if the acquisition, management, and disposition of the property constitute integral parts of the taxpayer's regular trade or business operations." It looks to the relationship between the underlying income-producing asset and the taxpayer's regular trade or business. The critical issue is whether the asset is integral, as opposed to incidental, to the taxpayer's business operations.

The majority view is that the UDITPA definition of *business income* includes *both* a transactional test and a functional test, and that an item of income is properly classified as business in nature if *either* test is met.

Nevertheless, as discussed below, supreme courts in Alabama, Iowa, Kansas, Minnesota and Tennessee have held that the UDITPA definition contains *only* a transactional test. In each case, the decision has been followed by a legislative change to broaden the statute to include a functional test. In 2003, the Multistate Tax Commission amended MTC Regulation IV.1(a) to provide that *business income* means income that meets *either* the transactional test or the functional test.

Alabama

In *Uniroyal Tire Co. v. State Department of Revenue*, the Alabama Supreme Court held that the Alabama statute (adopted verbatim from UDITPA) contained *only* a transactional test [No. 1981928 (Ala. Aug. 4, 2000)].

In 1986, Uniroyal formed a 50-50 partnership with B.F. Goodrich, wherein Uniroyal transferred all of its business assets to the partnership and, thereafter, its only asset was the partnership interest.

In 1990, Uniroyal sold its entire partnership interest at a gain. Despite the fact that the partnership interest produced business income prior to its sale, the Alabama Supreme Court held that the Alabama statute contained *only* a transactional test, and that Uniroyal's complete liquidation and cessation of business did *not* give rise to business income under the transactional test.

In 2001, the Alabama Legislature broadened the statutory definition of *business income* to explicitly include a functional-type test [Ala. H.B. 7 (Dec. 28, 2001)].

California

In *Hoechst Celanese Corp. v. Franchise Tax Board*, the California Supreme Court analyzed the legislative history of the California definition of *business income*, as well as rulings in other states regarding the UDITPA definition, and concluded that the definition included *both* a transactional test and a functional test [No. S085091 (Cal. May 14, 2001), *cert. denied,* No. 01-265 (US Nov. 26, 2001)].

The court then applied the two-part definition to the taxpayer's $389 million of pension plan reversion income and ruled that, although the transactional test was not satisfied because the pension plan reversion was an extraordinary event rather than a normal trade or business activity, the functional test *was* satisfied because the pension plan assets "materially contributed" to the production of business income and therefore were integral to the taxpayer's trade or business.

In *Jim Beam Brands Co. v. Franchise Tax Board*, the California Court of Appeal ruled that there was no partial liquidation exception to the functional test, and no independent requirement that the disposition of the property be an integral part of the corporation's trade or business operations [No. A107209 (Calif. Ct. of App., Oct. 17, 2005)].

Illinois

In a case involving the sale of a pipeline, *Texaco-Cities Service Pipeline Co. v. McGaw*, the Illinois Supreme Court interpreted the applicable state statute (which was similar to the UDITPA definition) as including *both* a transactional test and a functional test [182 Ill. 2d 269 (1998)].

However, unlike the taxpayer in *Laurel Pipeline* (see Pennsylvania below), this taxpayer remained in the pipeline business after the sale, and the proceeds from the sale were immediately reinvested in the operations of the business rather than distributed as a dividend to the shareholders. Accordingly, the court ruled that the gain on the sale of pipeline assets was *business* in nature.

On the other hand, in *Blessing/White Inc. et al. v. Dept. of Revenue*, the Illinois Appellate Court for the First District ruled that the gain realized from a complete liquidation was *nonbusiness income* because the proceeds were distributed to the shareholders and not reinvested in the business [No. 1 01 0733 (Ill. App. Ct. 1st Dist., Mar. 29, 2002)].

Likewise, in *National Holdings, Inc. v. Zehnder*, the Illinois Appellate Court for the Fourth District joined the First District in recognizing a business-liquidation *exception* to the functional test, and the court concluded that the exception applied in this case [No. 4-06-0148 (Ill. App. Ct. 4th Dist., Jan. 19, 2007].

Thus, the court ruled that the gain was *nonbusiness income*, because all of the liquidation proceeds were distributed to the parent company and were not reinvested in the ongoing business.

Iowa

In *Phillips Petroleum Co. v. Iowa Department of Revenue*, the taxpayer purchased a substantial amount of its outstanding stock to stave off a hostile takeover attempt. To retire the debt incurred for this purchase, the corporation sold at a gain a significant portion of its gas and oil-producing assets, none of which were located in Iowa [511 N.W.2d 608 (Iowa 1993)]. Even though the assets in question had been used in the taxpayer's regular trade or business, the Iowa Supreme Court held that the gain was *not* business income.

The court interpreted the applicable state statute (adopted verbatim from UDITPA) as "basically transactional" in nature, stating that the so-called functional test was "added to include transactions involving disposal of fixed assets by taxpayers who emphasize the trading of assets as an integral part of regular business."

Noting that the enormity of the disposition was "unprecedented" and "clearly a once-in-a-corporate-lifetime occurrence," the court concluded that the gain *failed* the transactional test, and thus was *nonbusiness income*.

In response to this decision, the Iowa Legislature amended the Iowa statute to expressly *include* a functional test [Iowa Code Ann. §422.32].

Kansas

In 1994, the Kansas Supreme Court held that a gain on the sale of a subsidiary's stock was *nonbusiness income* because the Kansas statute contained *only* a transactional test [*In re Chief Indus., Inc., No. 69972* (Kan. June 3, 1994)].

In response to this decision, the Kansas Legislature modified the state's statute governing the treatment of nonbusiness income. In addition, to ensure that corporations that have their headquarters office (commercial domicile) in Kansas would not be at a disadvantage with regard to treatment of nonbusiness income, Kansas passed legislation that allows corporations to elect to have all income arising from the acquisition, management, use, or disposition of tangible or intangible property treated as *business income*.

Minnesota

In *Firstar Corp. v. Commissioner of Revenue*, the Minnesota Supreme Court held that the gain realized by a Wisconsin-based bank on the sale of its headquarters office in Milwaukee was *nonbusiness income* [No. CX-97-600 (Minn. Mar. 12, 1998)].

In making this determination, the court focused on two factors:

1. The frequency and regularity of similar transactions and the former business practices of the taxpayer
2. The subsequent use of the sale proceeds

With respect to the first factor, the sale of the headquarters office was an isolated transaction in the bank's history. In fact, prior to the sale of the headquarters office, Firstar had never sold a commercial office property.

With respect to the second factor, the proceeds from the sale were not reinvested in the taxpayer's ongoing business operations. Instead, they were used to retire the bonds secured by the headquarters office, pay the taxes on the gain from the sale, pay a dividend to shareholders, and redeploy the capital of Firstar into acquisitions of new banks.

In response to this decision, in 1999 the Minnesota Legislature amended the statute to define *nonbusiness income* as "income of the trade or business that cannot be apportioned to this state because of the United States Constitution ... [,] includ[ing] income that cannot constitutionally be apportioned to this state because it is derived from a capital transaction that solely serves an investment function."

Montana

In *Gannett Satellite Information Network, Inc. v. Montana Department of Revenue*, the Montana Supreme Court ruled that the state's definition of *business income*, which is based on UDITPA, contains *both* a transactional test and an independent functional test [No. DA 08-0026 (Mt. Sup. Ct., Jan. 13, 2009)].

As a result, the taxpayer's $2.54 billion gain from the sale of its cable subsidiary was apportionable *business income* because the income arose from the sale of property that was regularly used in the combined reporting group's regular course of conducting its telecommunications business.

North Carolina

In *Polaroid Corp. v. Offerman*, the North Carolina Supreme Court held that the North Carolina definition of *business income* includes *both* a transactional test and a functional test, and that "once a corporation's assets are found to constitute integral parts of the corporation's regular trade or business, income resulting from the acquisition, management, and/or disposition of those assets constitutes business income regardless of how that income is received." Under this approach, the court treated damages that the taxpayer received in a patent infringement lawsuit as business income.

In *Union Carbide Corp. v. Offerman*, the North Carolina Supreme Court ruled that income from a pension plan reversion did *not* meet the functional test because the taxpayer held only a contingent property right in the excess funds in the event of a plan termination and that contingent property right was *not* integral or essential to the taxpayer's regular trade or business [No. 453A98-2 (N.C. Feb. 4, 2000)]. Moreover, the assets of the pension plan were not used to generate income in the regular business operations, were not working capital, were not used as collateral in borrowing, and they were not relied on to purchase equipment or support research and development.

In *Lenox, Inc. v. Offerman*, the North Carolina Supreme Court held that a consumer products company's gain on the complete cessation and sale of a separate and distinct operating division (a fine jewelry business) and the distribution of the sale proceeds to the corporation's parent company satisfied *neither* the transactional test nor the functional test and, therefore, qualified as *nonbusiness income* [No. 17A01 (N.C. July 20, 2001)].

In effect, the court created an exception for dispositions of assets in a complete liquidation of a separate trade or business. Had the assets in question been disposed of under different circumstances, the sale would have given rise to business income because the assets were an integral part of the company's business.

Ohio

In *Kemppel v. Zaino*, the Ohio Supreme Court ruled that gains realized by an S corporation on the liquidating sale of its assets were *nonbusiness income* because the gains were not from a sale in the regular course of a trade or business, but rather from a liquidation of assets followed by a dissolution of the corporation [No. 00-358, Oh. Sup. Ct. May 23, 2001)].

Oregon

In *Williamette Industries, Inc. v. Oregon Department of Revenue*, the Oregon Supreme Court held that the Oregon definition of *business income* included *both* a transactional test and a functional test [331 Or. 311, 15 P.3d 18 (2000)]. The court also ruled that the royalty income received by an Oregon lumber company from oil and gas drilling performed on land it owned in Louisiana and Arkansas was *not* business income under either test.

The royalty income did not satisfy the transactional test because the taxpayer's business was growing timber and making wood products, not producing oil and gas. In addition, the court refused to apply the functional test, stating that the test applies only to the sale or disposition of *property*, and the taxpayer had not disposed of the property in question.

In *Pennzoil Co. v. Department of Revenue*, Pennzoil received a $3 billion settlement from Texaco in a lawsuit involving Texaco's alleged interference with Pennzoil's negotiations to purchase Getty Oil stock [No. S47561 (Or. Oct. 4, 2001)]. Despite the extraordinary nature of the settlement, the Oregon Supreme Court ruled that the settlement proceeds were *business income* under the transactional test because the settlement arose from Pennzoil's loss of a contract with Getty Oil and Pennzoil's attempt to gain access to Getty Oil's oil reserves was in the regular course of Pennzoil's petroleum business.

Pennsylvania

In *Laurel Pipeline Co. v. Commonwealth*, the Pennsylvania Supreme Court interpreted the applicable state statute (adopted verbatim from UDITPA) as including *both* a transactional test and a functional test [615 A.2d 841 (Pa. 1994)].

In this case, the taxpayer realized a gain on the sale of a pipeline, the use of which was discontinued three years prior to the sale. The proceeds from the sale were distributed as a dividend to the corporation's shareholders immediately after the sale. Both parties agreed that the gain on the sale of the pipeline failed the transactional test.

In addition, because the taxpayer was not in the business of buying and selling pipelines and the pipeline was not an integral part of the taxpayer's business at the time of its sale (its use had been discontinued three year earlier), the court held that the gain was *nonbusiness income*.

Tennessee

In *Associated Partnership I, Inc. v. Huddleston*, the Tennessee Supreme Court ruled that a capital gain from the sale of a partnership interest that produced business income prior to its sale was *nonbusiness income* because the sale was not a transaction in the regular course of the taxpayer's trade or business [No. 01S01-9203-CH-00045 (Tenn. Oct. 17, 1994)].

The Tennessee Legislature later amended the statute to incorporate a functional test [Tenn. Code Ann. §67-4-2004].

STUDY QUESTIONS

> **4.** Which of the following is the *functional test* for determining whether income is business or nonbusiness?
>
> **a.** Does the income arise from transactions and activity in the *regular* course of the taxpayer's trade or business?
>
> **b.** Is the income from tangible or intangible property for which the acquisition, management, and disposition of the property constitute *integral* parts of the taxpayer's regular trade or business operations?
>
> **c.** Is the transaction *frequent* in nature, as opposed to a rare and extraordinary event?

5. At present, the majority view is that the UDITPA definition of *business income* includes *both* a transactional and functional test. ***True or False?***

6. Which of the following states does ***not*** require a functional test for business income?

   a. Alabama
   b. Iowa
   c. Tennessee
   d. None of the above

7. In which of the following cases did the state court determine that there was *no* partial liquidation exception to the *functional test*?

   a. *Kemppel v. Zaino*
   b. *Phillips Petroleum Co. v. Iowa Department of Revenue*
   c. *Uniroyal Tire Co. v. State Department of Revenue*
   d. *Jim Beam Brands Co. v. Franchise Tax Board*

NONBUSINESS INCOME ALLOCATION RULES

When an item of income is determined to be *nonbusiness income*, the majority of states allocate the income to a specific state under the guidelines of §4 through §8 of UDITPA and the related MTC regulations.

The basic thrust of these rules is that nonbusiness income derived from real and tangible personal property is allocable to the state in which the property is physically located; whereas, nonbusiness income derived from intangible property is allocable to the state of commercial domicile (except for royalties, which are allocable to the state where the intangible asset is used).

Rents, Royalties, and Gains from Realty

Nonbusiness rental, royalty, and capital gain income derived from real property is generally allocable to the state in which the underlying property is located.

Rents and Gains from Tangible Personal Property

Nonbusiness rental and capital gain income derived from tangible personal property is generally allocable to the state in which the underlying property is located, if the income is taxable in that state.

If the income is not taxable in the state in which the property is located, a throwback concept applies whereby the income is allocable to the state of commercial domicile. In addition, in the case of movable property, the income is allocated based on the proportionate days of use in each state.

Interest, Dividends, and Capital Gains from Intangibles

Nonbusiness capital gains from the sale of stocks, bonds, and other intangible assets are generally allocable to the state of commercial domicile. Likewise, nonbusiness interest and dividend income is generally allocable to the state of commercial domicile.

Royalties from Patents and Copyrights

Nonbusiness royalty income derived from patents or copyrights usually is allocable to the state in which the intangible asset is used if the royalties are taxable in that state. If the royalties are not taxable in the state in which the intangible is used, a throwback concept applies whereby the income is allocable to the state of commercial domicile.

For this purpose, a patent is considered used in a state to the extent that it is employed in production, fabrication, manufacturing, or other processing in the state, or to the extent a patented product is produced in the state. If the state in which the patent is used cannot be reasonably ascertained, the income is allocable to the state of commercial domicile.

Commercial Domicile

UDITPA defines *commercial domicile* as "the principal place from which the trade or business of the taxpayer is directed or managed" [UDITPA §1(b)]. The commercial domicile of a corporation may or may not be the same as the state of incorporation.

The MTC comments to UDITPA state that the phrase directed or managed is not intended to permit both the state where the board of directors meets and the state where the company is managed to claim the commercial domicile. Instead, it is intended as two words serving the same end, not as two separate concepts.

The phrase commercial domicile was first used by the Supreme Court in Wheeling Steel Corp. v. Fox [298 US 193 (1936)]. Wheeling was a Delaware corporation that challenged the constitutionality of a West Virginia property tax imposed on its intangible assets. The tax was upheld on the basis that the taxpayer's "actual seat of corporate government" was located in West Virginia and that was where the "management functioned."

In the Matter of the Appeal of Downey Toy Company, the California State Board of Equalization ruled that an investment holding company that was incorporated in Delaware and had no employees or operating assets was commercially domiciled in California, because that was the state from which the company "was managed and controlled and from which it received its greatest benefits and protections" [No. 306793 (Calif. State Bd. of Equal., Jan. 31, 2008)].

As a consequence, the corporation's gain from the sale of a European company was subject to California corporate income tax. The taxpayer had argued that the company had a commercial domicile in Europe, because its only directors and shareholders (Chris Downey and his wife) traveled to Europe on the company's behalf and managed and controlled the company during those trips.

EXPENSES ATTRIBUTABLE TO NONBUSINESS INCOME

Generally, if a taxpayer treats an item as *nonbusiness income*, any interest expense or other expenses attributable to that nonbusiness income cannot be deducted against apportionable business income. In other words, expenses attributable to nonbusiness income may be offset only against the related nonbusiness income.

For example, California Code of Regulations Title 18, §25120(d), provides that:

> In most cases an allowable deduction of a taxpayer will be applicable only to the business income arising from a particular trade or business or to a particular item of nonbusiness income.

> In some cases an allowable deduction may be applicable to the business incomes of more than one trade or business and/or to several items of nonbusiness income.

> In such cases the deduction shall be prorated among such trades or businesses and such items of nonbusiness income in a manner which fairly distributes the deduction among the classes of income to which it is applicable.

California historically required the use of the so-called interest-offset rule to compute the amount of a taxpayer's interest expense that was attributable to nonbusiness income [Cal. Rev. & Tax. Code §24344(b)].

In *Hunt-Wesson, Inc. v. Franchise Tax Board* [120 S. Ct. 1022 (2000)], the Supreme Court ruled that California's interest-offset rule was unconstitutional. Under *California's interest-offset rule*, the amount of interest expense that a nondomiciliary corporation could deduct against apportionable business income equaled the amount by which the taxpayer's total interest expense exceeded its nonbusiness interest and dividend income.

The purpose of this rule was to prevent a nondomiciliary corporation from borrowing funds, making investments that generate nonbusiness income that is not subject to taxation in California, and then deducting the related interest expense against apportionable business income.

The California interest-offset rule effectively assumed that any borrowings were used first to make investments that produce nonbusiness income, even if there was no evidence to support this assumption. The Court concluded that it was not reasonable to expect that a rule that attributed all borrowings first to investments that produce nonbusiness income would accurately reflect the amount of interest expense related to nonbusiness income.

Because California's offset provision was not a reasonable allocation of expense deductions to nonbusiness income, it effectively resulted in taxing the underlying nonbusiness income in violation of the Due Process Clause and Commerce Clause of the U.S. Constitution. California FTB Notice 2000-9 discusses the changes in California's interest expense allocation policy in light of the *Hunt-Wesson* decision [Dec. 19, 2000].

In *Kroger Co.*, the Kansas Supreme Court held that the interest expense incurred on a loan to defend against a hostile takeover was a *nonbusiness expense* and thus could not be deducted against apportionable business income [No. 69972 (Kan. Nov. 3, 2000)].

The taxpayer, an Ohio corporation operating grocery stores in Kansas, borrowed $4.1 billion to pay a special dividend to shareholders. The borrowing resulted in large amounts of interest expense, which the taxpayer deducted on its federal income tax return.

Applying the transactional test (Kansas recognized only the transactional test during the years at issue, 1989–1992), the court determined that borrowing money to defend against a hostile takeover is not an expense in the regular course of business, but rather an extraordinary event. As a result, the interest expense was a *nonbusiness expense* allocable to Kroger's state of commercial domicile, and not apportionable to Kansas.

In *American General Realty Investment Corp., Inc.*, the California State Board of Equalization held that the taxpayer could *not* deduct interest expenses related to dividends that were not subject to the California corporation franchise tax [No. 156726 (Cal. St. Bd. of Equalization, June 25, 2003)].

STUDY QUESTIONS

---

8. Which of the following types of *nonbusiness income* is usually allocated to the state of *commercial domicile*?

   a. Royalties from realty
   b. Rents from realty
   c. Capital gains from intangibles
   d. Capital gains from real property

9. Expenses related to nonbusiness income generally can be offset against business income. *True or False?*

TREND IN STATUTORY DEFINITIONS OF BUSINESS AND NONBUSINESS INCOME

Many states have broadened their definition of *business income* during the past decade.

In 1999, Minnesota amended its definition of *nonbusiness income* to mean "income of the trade or business that cannot be apportioned to this state because of the United States Constitution ... [,] includ[ing] income that cannot constitutionally be apportioned to this state because it is derived from a capital transaction that solely serves an investment function" [Minn. Sec. 290.17].

In 2001:

- Alabama broadened its definition of nonbusiness income to explicitly include a *functional test* [H.B. 7, 2001]
- Mississippi amended its definition to include any income, other than income that *fails* both a transactional and a functional test [A.B. 1695, 2001]
- Pennsylvania broadened its definition to include "all income which is apportionable under the Constitution of the United States" [H.B. 334, 2001]

In 2002, New Jersey amended its apportionment statute to provide that "100% of the nonoperational income of a taxpayer that has its principal place from which the trade or business of the taxpayer is directed or managed in this State shall be specifically assigned to this State to the extent permitted under the Constitution and statutes of the United States" [A.B. 2501, 2002].

Also in 2002, North Carolina broadened its definition of business income to include "all income that is apportionable under the U.S. Constitution" [S.B. 1115, 2002].

In 2004, Illinois broadened its definition of business income to include "all income that may be treated as apportionable business income under the Constitution of the United States" [S.B. 2207, 2004]. This legislation also requires the recapture of expenses related to an asset or activity if income previously classified as business income from that asset or activity is determined in a later year to be nonbusiness income.

In addition, in 2004 the Oregon Department of Revenue adopted a regulation, which provides that business income includes income of any type or class, and from any activity, that meets *either* the transactional test or the functional test [OAR 150-314.610(1)-(A)(2)].

In 2005, Georgia amended its apportionment statute to provide that the state's corporate income tax applies to a corporation's income "to the extent permitted by the United States Constitution" [H.B. 488, 2005].

In 2006, the Kentucky Department of Revenue adopted a regulation which provides that the department will apply *both* the transactional test and the functional test in determining whether income is *business income* [Ky. Reg. 103 KAR 16:060E, Feb. 1, 2006].

In 2008, Kansas broadened its definition of *business income* to include *any* of the following:

- Income arising from transactions and activity in the regular course of the taxpayer's trade or business
- Income arising from transactions and activity involving tangible and intangible property or assets used in the operation of the taxpayer's trade or business
- Income of the taxpayer that may be apportioned to this state under the provisions of the Constitution of the United States and laws thereof, except that a taxpayer may elect that all income constitutes business income [H.B. 2434, May 22, 2008]

In addition, the Utah Tax Commission changed its regulatory definition of *business income* to conform to the MTC regulations, which provide that business income means income that meets either the transactional test or the functional test [Rule R865-6F-8, Utah Admin. Code, Sept. 9, 2008].

RECENT DEVELOPMENTS

Maine

In *Gannett Co., Inc. v. State Tax Assessor*, the Maine Supreme Judicial Court held that a corporation's cable, broadcast news, and newspaper affiliates constituted a single unitary business [No. Ken-07-629 (Me. Sup. Jud. Ct., Nov. 18, 2008)].

As a result, it was constitutionally permissible for Maine to tax an apportioned share of the corporation's $2.54 billion gain from the sale of its cable affiliate. In concluding that a unitary business existed, the court noted that the corporation provided intercompany services to the affiliates at cost, the affiliates shared operational expertise and legal services, centralized health and benefit plans were in place, a system of interlocking directors and officers existed, and a common pool of cash was available for capital and operating expenses.

Massachusetts

In *W.R. Grace & Co. - Conn. v. Commissioner of Revenue*, the Massachusetts Appellate Tax Board ruled that interest and dividend income received by an out-of-state parent corporation as a result of internal financing transactions undertaken to raise capital for the parent was *not* apportionable business income because the parent and the subsidiaries were not engaged in a unitary business [No. C271787 (Mass. App. Tax Bd., Apr. 6, 2009)].

In concluding that a unitary business did not exist, the court noted that there was no functional integration, centralization of management, or economies of scales between the parties. Moreover, the transactions that gave rise to the income served an investment purpose, rather than an operational function.

The board also ruled that the affiliates had no actual or expected use of the interest or dividend income for their operations within Massachusetts.

STUDY QUESTION

10. During the past decade, many states have broadened their definition of *business income.* ***True or False?***

CPE NOTE: When you have completed your study and review of chapters 1-4, which comprise Module 1, you may wish to take the Quizzer for this Module.

For your convenience, you can also take this Quizzer online at **www.cchtestingcenter.com.**

Post-Audit Strategies

This chapter explains the actions that should be taken by taxpayers during and subsequent to the final phase of a sales and use tax audit. It also discusses sales and use tax audit trends.

LEARNING OBJECTIVES

Upon completing this chapter, the professional will be able to:

- List the different types of penalties that may be assessed
- Explain common reasons for the imposition of penalties
- Describe the reasons for meeting with the auditor's supervisor
- List the different penalty defenses that may be used
- Explain what should be considered when determining whether to file an appeal
- Describe the current trends in sales and use tax audits

FINALIZING THE AUDIT

In the final phase of the audit, taxpayers have decisions to make regarding payment and appeal. Taxpayers who continuously assess the strength of their positions throughout the audit will be better prepared to make these decisions.

The following actions should be taken in the final stages of an audit:

1. Meet with auditor at a concluding conference, and verify the timetable and tasks to be completed to finalize the audit.
2. Discuss the assessment process, and clarify your rights and responsibilities. Take particular note of your appeal rights if you are planning to appeal.
3. Confirm your appeal and payment rights through analysis of the state's law.
4. If the auditor provides you with copies of the audit workpapers, verify that all agreed-upon adjustments are reflected in the final workpapers.
5. When the assessment is received, verify all amounts against the final worksheets provided by the auditor.
6. Note deadlines for payment or appeal and plan accordingly so they are not missed.

7. Discuss the probability of success with outside counsel, if an appeal or litigation is contemplated.
8. Verify that the interest calculation is correct.
9. If the state allows partial payment on agreed-upon issues, consider paying that portion of the assessment to reduce interest costs during an appeal.
10. Make sure the audit deficiency is properly accounted for on the company's books.
11. Promptly notify the auditor of any errors or discrepancies in the final audit workpapers or assessment.

The Assessment

Before making any appeal or litigation decisions, taxpayers must verify that the assessment is correct. Prior to completion of the fieldwork, taxpayers should receive copies of all audit workpapers and schedules.

These documents should be reviewed to verify that they properly reflect the agreements reached in the negotiations, particularly in the final stages of negotiations. Taxpayers should also verify that all dollar amounts have been correctly transferred from the worksheets to the assessment.

Any errors in the assessment or discrepancies from the taxpayer's final worksheets should be brought to the auditor's attention immediately. Particular attention should be paid to any last-minute adjustments that were made in final negotiations to make sure they were carried forward to the auditor's final worksheets.

After all required adjustments have been made, some states will issue a preliminary assessment while others will issue a final assessment. An *assessment* is a formal request for payment that imposes certain obligations on the taxpayer for payment or appeal of the audit results.

> **CAUTION**
>
> With the issuance of an assessment, the state has the ability to place in motion a series of events that could culminate in the placing of a lien against assets of the taxpayer or the seizure of a taxpayer's assets for failure to pay the assessment.

The issuance of either a preliminary or final assessment can take from four to 12 weeks after the fieldwork is completed. Most states issue their assessments six to eight weeks after the auditor turns in the necessary papers.

Virtually all states engage in a *review process* that the audit must pass through before an assessment can be issued. This assures that the audit results are consistent from taxpayer to taxpayer and reflect the state's current positions on key issues.

Most states rely upon the auditor's supervisor to perform the review; however, some states have a formal committee or department that reviews and processes all assessments. The level of review can vary with the amount of the assessment—larger assessments generally receive closer scrutiny.

The issuing of a *preliminary assessment* affords the taxpayer an additional opportunity to review all the details before the final assessment is issued. Some states consider the auditor's issuing of final copies of all worksheets a preliminary assessment and go directly to the final assessment.

In either case, taxpayers should carefully review all data provided as part of an assessment. All dollar amounts from the assessment should be traced to the worksheets and schedules prepared by the auditor.

States often allow the taxpayer to make a payment from the preliminary assessment to avoid incurring additional interest costs. If the audit is agreed upon, the taxpayer may wish to consider this alternative. In some states, if the audit is only partially agreed upon, the taxpayer may pay that portion to reduce interest costs on the overall settlement.

Most states allow the taxpayer 30 or 60 days from the preliminary assessment notice to call attention to any errors that require correction before the final assessment is issued. In the event they find errors, taxpayers should promptly contact the auditor.

Taxpayers should also verify the accuracy of any interest or penalty calculations that may be part of the preliminary assessment. Many states use simple interest, which makes the verification process relatively easy. If a penalty has been included in the assessment, taxpayers may wish to consider appeal of its imposition.

Taxpayers who receive a *final assessment* notice in lieu of a preliminary notice should follow the same general review procedures. Regardless of whether they receive a preliminary or final assessment notice, taxpayers need to take particular note of the deadline for appeal.

The deadline is usually 30 or 60 days after the date the notice was mailed or received. If the taxpayer fails to file an appeal or protest by the deadline, the assessment becomes final and the results cannot be appealed. If the taxpayer does not make payment or file an appeal by the deadline, an additional penalty may be assessed and additional interest will be assessed.

PLANNING POINTER

Taxpayers should consider special mailing procedures for their payments or appeals, such as certified mail with a return receipt requested. Without proof that the payment or appeal was sent prior to the due date, taxpayers may be liable for additional interest or penalty expense.

In addition, many states do not recognize overnight services, such as FedEx, until the return is received. So, care must be exercised in the use of such services.

STUDY QUESTION

> **1.** How much time from the preliminary assessment notice date do most states allow the taxpayer to report errors in the assessment?
> **a.** 90 or 120 days
> **b.** 30 or 60 days
> **c.** Most states do not impose a time limitation for the reporting of errors.

PENALTY IMPOSITION

States use penalties as a means of obtaining greater taxpayer compliance. Because penalties are nondeductible for federal income tax purposes, the after-tax cost of a penalty is substantially greater than that of a fully deductible expense.

The imposition of penalties also provides the state additional revenue. For example, a 25 percent penalty on a four percent tax base yields the equivalent of an additional one percent of tax. This does not take into account the additional income tax collections that result from the nondeductibility of the penalty expense.

A contributing factor to the states' increased use of penalties in recent years has been their efforts to make additional information available to taxpayers to assist them in compliance. In return, the states expect a higher level of compliance.

In most states, the audit supervisor has the principal authority to impose a penalty, based upon the recommendation of the auditor. A few states impose automatic penalties on any assessment after the first audit assessment. Penalties can be imposed for a number of reasons—ranging from failure to self-assess use tax on purchases from out-of-state vendors, to committing fraud in filing a false return.

Auditors are attuned to the potential for penalties in every audit they perform. They regularly amass the facts to determine if a penalty should be imposed. Taxpayers also need to be aware of the problems that could lead to the imposition of a penalty. Some of the more common reasons for imposition of a penalty include:

- Failure to file a return
- Failure to make payment of tax due
- Late filing or payment
- Failure to correct past errors in compliance
- Engaging in fraud or willful evasion of tax

Most of these reasons are fairly obvious; however, one that is frequently overlooked by taxpayers is the failure to correct past compliance problems.

The states have an arsenal of penalties to fit various circumstances. The more serious the infraction, the greater the penalty.

Following are the more common types of penalties:

- Ordinary negligence penalty
- Gross negligence penalty
- Fraud penalty
- Substantial understatement penalty

Ordinary Negligence

The penalty most commonly imposed is for ordinary negligence, which occurs when a taxpayer fails to exercise the degree of care that would be expected of a reasonable person in similar circumstances. Essentially, *ordinary negligence* means the taxpayer has not met its minimum responsibilities under the law.

For example, if the taxpayer regularly makes purchases from vendors that do not charge tax, the taxpayer would be expected to have a self-assessment procedure in place. Failure to have such a procedure in place could result in the application of penalty to the amount of tax underpaid.

> **CAUTION**
>
> Many states have extended the *ordinary care* concept to include correction of similar errors identified in prior audits. Therefore, taxpayers need to demonstrate improvement in compliance to avoid penalties in subsequent audits.

The rates for ordinary negligence penalties generally range from five percent to 15 percent of the amount of tax owed in the audit; the most common rate is 10 percent. In most states, ordinary penalties for late payment or late filing are imposed on a monthly basis up to a maximum rate or dollar amount per event.

For example, the ordinary late return filing penalty might be one percent per month of the tax due up to a maximum of 15 percent of the tax due. A minimum dollar amount often applies to penalties of this nature.

Gross Negligence

Gross negligence occurs when the taxpayer demonstrates a careless or reckless disregard for the law. Such carelessness or disregard could be manifest in several ways, many of which are subject to interpretation by the states.

For example, a careless or reckless disregard for the law could be demonstrated by a taxpayer's failure to have adequate procedures in place to meet its tax responsibilities. Many states have also interpreted gross negligence to include failure to correct errors identified in prior audits.

> **CAUTION**
>
> Many states are going to additional lengths to point out errors to taxpayers in formal communications that are part of the audit.
>
> For example, a state might inform the taxpayer in a letter that it is expected to initiate procedures to capture the tax due on certain transactions. In doing this, the state is giving the taxpayer notice and setting the stage for a future gross negligence penalty.
>
> Note that gross negligence penalties are most commonly imposed in a *subsequent audit*.

The rates for gross negligence penalties generally range from 20 to 30 percent; the most common rate is 25 percent. Many states impose additional, higher rates of interest to add to the impact of the penalty.

Fraud

Fraud occurs when the taxpayer willfully misleads or takes steps to conceal the truth about transactions as a way of evading the payment of tax. Large-scale fraud can be a criminal offense. Fraud can include filing a false return or intentionally misleading an auditor.

> **PLANNING POINTER**
>
> Written communications throughout the audit can protect the taxpayer from possible accusations at a later time.

In most jurisdictions, the penalty for fraud is generally 50 or 100 percent of the tax owed. Many jurisdictions also levy additional interest at a higher rate than otherwise might be assessed. The penalties for criminal fraud can include additional fines or imprisonment, depending on the nature and extent of the actions involved.

Substantial Understatement

The substantial understatement penalty provisions give the state authority to expand the scope of an audit and impose additional financial sanctions. Under these provisions, the amount of tax voluntarily reported throughout the audit period is compared with the amount of tax that was subsequently found to be due as a result of the audit.

If the difference exceeds a certain threshold, the state has the authority to expand the audit period and impose additional penalties. The additional time period is usually between two and four years. The substantial understatement provisions also impose greater penalty and interest rates than would otherwise be applicable on the assessment. These rates are typically greater than those imposed for ordinary negligence and are closer to the *gross negligence* rates.

Although the substantial underpayment provisions are most commonly employed in income tax audits, they can be applied in sales and use audits as well.

STUDY QUESTIONS

> **2.** Which of the following is the most common penalty imposed as the result of a *sales and use tax* audit?
>
> **a.** Ordinary negligence penalty
> **b.** Gross negligence penalty
> **c.** Fraud penalty
> **d.** Substantial understatement penalty
>
> **3.** What type of penalty would most likely be imposed if a taxpayer has shown a reckless disregard for the law?
>
> **a.** Ordinary negligence penalty
> **b.** Gross negligence penalty
> **c.** Fraud penalty
> **d.** Substantial understatement penalty

MEETING WITH THE AUDITOR'S SUPERVISOR

Near the end of the audit, the taxpayer needs to consider meeting with the auditor's supervisor. The purpose of the meeting would be to advance the potential for a settlement on certain issues. In addition, the meeting could reveal the importance of the audit supervisor in the overall audit process.

The supervisor's role varies with the nature of the audit and the auditor's level of experience. In a major audit, or if the auditor is inexperienced, the supervisor will play a more active role—at times directing the auditor through each stage of the review.

Given the field audit background of most supervisors, the supervisor may have audited the taxpayer, so the supervisor's knowledge of the taxpayer's operations could be substantial. In a routine audit, or if the auditor is experienced, the supervisor will assume a background role and only become involved in the review process or at the request of either the taxpayer or the auditor.

Occasionally, a supervisor will visit the taxpayer early in the audit process to assist the auditor in setting up certain aspects of the audit. For example, the supervisor may advise the auditor on sampling or areas to review, based on interviews with the taxpayer. Taxpayers may wish to inquire about the division of responsibility for various aspects of the audit while both parties are present to avoid confusion as the audit progresses.

To avoid conflict with taxpayers, auditors often blame their supervisors for positions that are adverse to the taxpayer. The auditor might express support for the taxpayer's position but say the supervisor insists on a different approach.

A taxpayer would request a meeting with the auditor's supervisor for the following reasons:

- To negotiate trade-offs on certain issues
- To discuss the reasons for imposition of a penalty or the abatement of a penalty that has been imposed
- To gain additional insight into the position of the state
- To discuss problems relating to the auditor

Each of these points is discussed below.

Negotiation

In the latter stages of an audit, the taxpayer may have the opportunity to negotiate settlements on certain issues. Such opportunities are more likely to arise when there are few, if any, major areas of controversy. The state's motivation may be to avoid conflict on certain issues or to achieve an agreed-upon audit settlement.

If the auditor lacks the authority to negotiate such settlements, a meeting with the auditor's supervisor will be necessary. The taxpayer may not have to initiate the meeting, as the supervisor will often plan to meet with the taxpayer anyway to finalize open issues such as the imposition of penalty.

The decision to "trade-off" issues usually comes on the last planned day of negotiations and generally involves transactions with which there is some uncertainty regarding taxability. There will usually be one or more issues favoring the taxpayer and one or more issues favoring the state. Either the taxpayer or the state can suggest that the parties agree to trade-off the issues. The state passes on a transaction that it had hoped to tax in exchange for being allowed to tax some other transaction.

PLANNING POINTER

Taxpayers should prepare for the meeting by reviewing transactions that might be eligible for trade-off. Knowing the audit impact of transactions in advance can make for more fruitful negotiations. For example, if the supervisor proposes a trade-off that is overly advantageous to the state, the taxpayer might want to counter with an additional transaction to level out the impact.

States prefer to have an agreed-upon audit settlement, so the negotiation strength of the taxpayer is the greatest when the parties are close to settlement.

If the audit process has been contentious, it is not as likely that the state will agree to any trade-offs with the taxpayer. While taxpayers should not refrain from raising legitimate issues of concern throughout the audit, they must also be realistic about the impact of doing so on other aspects of the audit.

Penalty Discussion

As previously discussed, the decision to impose a penalty is frequently made by the auditor's supervisor. Therefore, penalty issues are often the subject of discussions between a taxpayer and a supervisor.

States assign the decision to the supervisor to achieve consistency in the application of penalty and to provide for as unbiased a decision as possible. However, the auditor can play a significant role in the decision by recommending an option to the supervisor. Therefore, taxpayers should not completely discount the auditor's role in the process and should attempt to work through as many penalty issues as possible with the auditor.

> **PLANNING POINTER**
>
> Prior to meeting with the supervisor, the taxpayer should try to determine whether the state intends to impose a penalty in the audit. The taxpayer may wish to discuss the matter with the auditor. If the auditor is evasive or noncommittal, the taxpayer should be prepared for the possible imposition of a penalty.

The State's Position

Taxpayers who are considering appeal of certain issues can obtain useful information regarding the strength of the state's position from a meeting with the auditor's supervisor. In many cases, substantive discussions of issues with auditors can be difficult, if not impossible. They will frequently reply that the issue is a matter of state policy or provide vague references to the statutes as their authority to impose tax on a transaction.

To make an informed decision about an appeal or litigation, the taxpayer needs to know the strength of the state's position and whether the state is willing to contest the issue. A meeting with the supervisor will often provide this insight. In addition, the meeting will help the taxpayer focus on the strengths and merits of its own position.

Even if they do not intend to appeal or litigate, taxpayers may wish to approach the meeting with the supervisor as if they intended to do so. The supervisor may attempt to negotiate a settlement with the taxpayer to avoid a costly appeal or litigation.

Taxpayers may have to file an appeal before substantive discussions with the supervisor or other Department of Revenue official can take place.

> **CAUTION**
>
> Taxpayers need to present their argument in a comprehensive and convincing manner. Failure to do so could result in the state's discounting the taxpayer's position and being unwilling to negotiate a settlement to avoid the potential appeal or litigation. Thus, the taxpayer's position could actually worsen as a result of the meeting.

Problems with an Auditor

Serious problems with an auditor can occasionally occur in the course of an audit. When discussions with the auditor prove fruitless, the only recourse is to discuss the problems with the auditor's supervisor. This is not an action that should be taken lightly, as supervisors tend to be skeptical of taxpayer claims in this regard. In addition, the taxpayer's working relationship with the auditor can be irreparably harmed, particularly if the supervisor does not side with the taxpayer.

Generally, taxpayers should only pursue a meeting with the supervisor to remove an auditor if the auditor has:

- Been extremely unreasonable
- Displayed bias in the audit
- Engaged in inappropriate conduct

For example, if the auditor is auditing a minority-owned manufacturing company and makes statements displaying prejudice, the taxpayer would be justified in contacting the supervisor.

Before meeting with the supervisor, the taxpayer must thoroughly document the events that give rise to the concern. If the incident involves a verbal discussion, the taxpayer should carefully document whatever was said as soon as possible after the incident.

In most cases, the taxpayer should request a new auditor, but the taxpayer must recognize that the replacement auditor may be aware of what happened and, as a result, be biased against the taxpayer. Sometimes there are no easy solutions in these matters.

STUDY QUESTION

> **4.** Which of the following is **not** a reason for a taxpayer to ask a supervisor to remove an auditor?
>
> **a.** The auditor has behaved inappropriately.
> **b.** The auditor is extremely unreasonable.
> **c.** The auditor is always late to meetings.
> **d.** The auditor is biased.

VERIFYING THE CALCULATION OF INTEREST

All states impose interest on deficiencies assessed as a result of an audit. The rates vary, usually ranging from nine percent to 12 percent per year. Some states, including California, Missouri, and New York, tie their underpayment interest rates to market interest rates. The objective of the higher rates is to prevent taxpayers from using the low interest costs of underpaying their taxes to finance other activities—a practice that was once common.

Most states continue to assess simple interest, but there are several that apply compound interest rates to the underpayments (including Arizona, Arkansas, Maine, Massachusetts, New Jersey, New York, South Carolina, Washington, and West Virginia). A few states tie their interest rates to the federal interest rates plus some additional factor, while a number of other states key off the prime interest rate.

To verify the interest assessment:

1. Determine what the state statute says regarding interest
2. Estimate the amount of interest
3. Compare the estimate to the interest assessed and, if there is a significant difference, notify the auditor.

While the widespread use of computers has lessened the importance of the interest assessment review, it is still worthwhile to test the calculation along with the state's allocation assumptions underlying the computation. In an *income tax* audit, the deficiency is usually more closely related to a particular point in time. However, in a *sales and use* tax audit, that is not necessarily the case.

Because of the heavy reliance on sampling of expense purchases in sales and use tax audits, the audit deficiency may not be specifically assigned to each month under audit. In other words, the sample relates to the *entire* audit period, but not necessarily to any specific month within that period.

In order to calculate interest, the sample must be allocated across the audit period on a monthly basis. The most common allocation bases used for this purpose are sales and cost of goods sold. These indices are utilized under the assumption that they reflect the volume of business for the taxpayer.

For computational purposes, the auditor assumes that the deficiency determined by the sample was earned ratably over the audit period, and then allocates a portion of the deficiency to each month, using sales, cost of goods sold, or some other appropriate measure of business activity.

> **PLANNING POINTER**
>
> An allocation methodology that results in allocating the least amount of deficiency to the earlier years of the audit will reduce the overall interest expense. In many instances, the nature of sales volumes automatically has that effect.
>
> However, sales may not continue to increase across all audit periods. Where this is not the case, the taxpayer may wish to consider alternative methods of allocationthat will result in a more equitable interest calculation (such as volume of purchases).

In addition to regular interest, some states have penalty interest that can be assessed. *Penalty interest* is calculated in the same manner as regular interest. The only additional review that would be required for penalty interest would be to verify the reason for the additional imposition.

SUCCESSFUL PENALTY APPEALS

Taxpayers would generally be expected to appeal a penalty because of the additional financial burden it imposes, particularly when its nondeductibility for federal income tax purposes is considered. Before taxpayers can make any decisions regarding the appeal of penalties, they must establish the basis for the state's imposition of penalty.

Obtaining a specific reason for imposition of penalty from the state can be a challenge. However, an attempt to secure an explanation is in order if the taxpayer intends to appeal. In order to refute the state's position regarding a penalty, the taxpayer must understand the state's reason for imposing it.

Assuming the taxpayer obtains a satisfactory explanation for imposition of the penalty, the taxpayer must then present specific evidence to overturn its imposition. However, since the reasons cited by the state for penalty imposition are often vague, taxpayers must also be prepared to provide broad evidence to convince the state to abate the penalty.

If the state cites a specific transaction or group of transactions as giving rise to the penalty, the taxpayer will need to demonstrate that its actions with regard to the transaction(s) did not meet the penalty statute's standard for imposition.

If the state imposed a penalty because the taxpayer failed to exercise *reasonable care* in its self-assessments of tax on fixed assets, the taxpayer would want to introduce evidence to demonstrate that it had in fact exercised reasonable care.

The taxpayer would want to:

- Explain its self-assessment procedure
- Cite the dollar amounts self-assessed
- List the number of transactions reviewed
- Identify any other material fact that supports its argument for abatement of penalty

The taxpayer might also want to review department regulations, court cases, and department of revenue publications to determine if there are any guidelines that support its position.

There is a good chance that the state will not be specific in its reasons for imposing a penalty. In many instances, the state will merely indicate that the taxpayer had made errors in prior audits with self-assessments and that similar errors were found in the current audit. Or the state may cite the amount of the assessment or the number of errors in the audit as being greater than in the previous audit.

When the state provides general reasons for the imposition of penalty, the taxpayer must be prepared to respond in a broad manner. There are a number of general defenses to penalty imposition:

- Complexity in the administration of tax law
- Unsettled nature of issues
- Demonstrated level of self-compliance
- Tax voluntarily paid versus audit deficiency
- Prior audit history and compliance record (if favorable)
- Staffing issues
- Degree of cooperation with auditor

These are discussed below.

Complex and Unsettled Issues

The first two defenses would not be appropriate in situations where the penalty has been imposed on uncontroversial transactions. They are more appropriate for issues that could be resolved as either taxable or nontaxable, depending on the way the facts are interpreted. The purpose of these defenses is to establish that the issue is unclear for compliance purposes.

Self-Compliance

The purpose of the self-compliance defense is to establish that the taxpayer was making a good-faith effort to comply with the law. To demonstrate self-compliance, the taxpayer must explain its self-assessment procedures.

Voluntary Tax Payment

The reason for imposing a penalty can be diminished by comparing the amount of the deficiency with the amount of tax voluntarily paid during the audit period. For example, if the taxpayer had an audit deficiency of $50,000, but was able to show that over the entire audit period it had paid $500,000 in tax, the audit error would represent 10 percent of the amount of tax owed.

If the taxpayer has information regarding the amount of sales tax paid to vendors, that can enhance the effectiveness impact of this defense. Unfortunately, many taxpayers are unable to obtain this information because their accounts payable systems do not capture the tax paid as a separate field.

Prior History

Discussing audit history can be an effective defense, if the taxpayer has a good record. For example, if the taxpayer has had only minimal audit assessments in the past, that would be an important fact to emphasize. If the taxpayer has a consistent record of timely compliance, that should also be emphasized.

Staffing Issues

Staff turnover and other personal issues can create compliance problems that are revealed in an audit. If this has occurred, it should be highlighted in the penalty discussion. This factor bears on the intent of the taxpayer—i.e., the taxpayer intended to comply but could not due to staffing problems.

Degree of Cooperation

While it is unlikely that this defense alone will result in the abatement of penalty, it is worthwhile to raise in the appeal.

STUDY QUESTIONS

> **5.** The use of computers has made the interest assessment review unnecessary. *True or False?*
>
> **6.** Which of the following defenses should be used to establish that the taxpayer has made a *good-faith effort* to comply with the tax law?
> **a.** Prior audit history
> **b.** Staffing issues
> **c.** Degree of cooperation with the auditor
> **d.** Level of self-compliance

APPEAL AND LITIGATION DECISIONS

In the final stages of the audit, taxpayers must decide whether to appeal the audit results. A number of considerations enter into a decision to appeal or litigate. These include:

- When to involve an attorney or a CPA
- Knowledge of *local customs*
- Estimate of the probability of success
- Performance of a cost-benefit analysis
- Assessment of the intangibles of litigation
- The impact of pending challenges from other taxpayers

When to Involve an Attorney or CPA

The taxpayer can engage an attorney or a CPA either during the audit, or at the end of the audit when the appeal decision must be made. It is generally wise to engage assistance as early as possible, so the advisor can participate in the taxpayer's decision-making process regarding appeal.

The taxpayer must decide whether it would be best to hire an attorney or a CPA. Generally, taxpayers should choose the representation that is appropriate to their appeal intentions and consistent with the representative's scope, taking into consideration the representative's knowledge and skill in the area.

If the taxpayer intends to litigate the issue, it might be wise to retain an attorney at the outset to provide representation throughout the appeal process. In some instances, a CPA will be able to provide equivalent services up to the point of litigation for a lower fee.

The growth of state and local consulting services has led to the development of relationships between CPAs and attorneys that allow for cooperative efforts. It may be feasible to engage an accounting firm that has a close working relationship with a law firm that will be capable of handling the case if it goes beyond the administrative appeal level.

PLANNING POINTER

Taxpayers should determine an accounting firm's ability to provide representation beyond the administrative appeal level. Of particular concern would be any duplication of effort, and the resulting fee expense, that could result from involvement of an attorney in the case after some period of time.

Ideally, the parties should be working in concert from the outset of the engagement. Choosing an accounting firm that has a professional relationship with a law firm or vice versa should address this issue.

Once the taxpayer decides to retain an outside advisor, the advisor must be duly authorized to act on the taxpayer's behalf. The most commonly used form for this purpose is the *power-of-attorney*. Without the authorization provided by a power-of-attorney, most states will refuse to discuss any issues with a representative, unless the taxpayer is present to grant permission.

Taxpayers should be able to obtain the necessary form from their state department of revenue.

Knowledge of Local Customs

An attorney or CPA hired by a taxpayer must be familiar with local practice and procedure. There are rules, both written and unwritten, pertaining to the conduct of appeals and other administrative actions that can only be learned through experience.

The personal credibility of the representative can also be an important factor. A hearing officer will be more likely to accept the interpretation of a representative who has a reputation as a knowledgeable tax professional.

The Probability of Success

Taxpayers should estimate the probability of success before proceeding with a costly appeal. Estimating the probability of success requires an understanding of the issue and the litigation environment in the state. Estimates are most often expressed as a percentage. For example, an advisor might indicate that in his or her opinion, there is a 60 percent chance of successfully winning the appeal at the first level and an 80 percent chance if the issue goes to the next level of appeal.

Counsel's estimate of the probability of success is a key factor in the decision to appeal. The greater the probability of success, the more likely the taxpayer will want to appeal the audit and vice versa. The estimate of success is also needed to perform the cost-benefit analysis discussed below.

Cost-Benefit Analysis

Performing a cost-benefit analysis assures that the appeal, if unsuccessful, can be justified financially. In addition to counsel's estimate of the probability of success, the taxpayer will need an estimate of the appeal costs or litigation expenses. The attorney or CPA selected for the appeal should provide this estimate.

To perform the analysis, the taxpayer takes the amount that would be appealed, multiplies it by the factor for the probability of success, and compares that number to the cost of appeal. If the result is favorable, the taxpayer should proceed with the appeal. If it is unfavorable, the taxpayer may want to reconsider the appeal.

> **EXAMPLE**
>
> Assume that the issue to be appealed can have a $100,000 impact on the audit results. The CPA hired by the taxpayer estimates that it will cost $20,000 to mount an appeal, and the probability of success is 60 percent. The taxpayer would want to move forward with the appeal, since it shows a favorable cost benefit of $40,000 ($20,000 versus $60,000 (60 percent x $100,000)).

Assessment of Intangibles

If the cost-benefit analysis yields a favorable result, the *intangibles* of litigation must be assessed. These include the following:

■ **How would the public disclosure of the taxpayer's position affect the filing position in other states?** Many taxpayers are uncomfortable with the public disclosure of information that could affect filing positions in other states. For example, if the taxpayer is following the same position in another state, the taxpayer could be seriously damaged if that information was publicly disclosed in a trial or hearing with a published and identified decision. The taxpayer may wish to limit its appeal options to nonpublished decisions to avoid problems in other states.

■ **Is the taxpayer prepared for public disclosure of its practices if the appeal goes to litigation in court?** Many taxpayers are uncomfortable with disclosure of confidential tax information as part of an appeal. Taxpayers entering the appeal arena should be aware of the disclosures that will be necessary to successfully argue their position. Many taxpayers would prefer that suppliers, customers, and others not have information about their tax-filing positions.

■ **Does management support the appeal decision and understand the potential hazards of litigation?** An appeal is not wise unless it has management's financial and moral support.

Pending Challenges

One of the reasons for securing local advisors is to be able to draw upon their knowledge of pending cases. Taxpayers need to be aware of any cases that could affect their case, either favorably or unfavorably.

Taxpayers may wish to assist other taxpayers that are attempting to appeal a particular issue. It is common for a group of taxpayers to select another taxpayer with "good facts" and use that taxpayer as the lead case on a particular issue. If the case is successful, the supporting taxpayers benefit from the precedent that is set. If the case is unsuccessful, the taxpayer may still mount an appeal based on its own facts.

STUDY QUESTION

7. A taxpayer is trying to determine whether to appeal an issue that can have a $70,000 impact on the audit results. The taxpayer's CPA estimates that it will cost $20,000 to mount an appeal, and the probability of success is 70 percent. What would be the estimated cost benefit to the taxpayer?

a. $29,000
b. $49,000
c. $50,000

PREPARING FOR THE NEXT AUDIT

At the conclusion of the audit, taxpayers should begin preparing for the next audit. By addressing issues promptly, taxpayers will be able to lessen their exposure to future sales and use tax deficiencies.

Following are strategies to prepare for the next audit:

1. Identify areas requiring improvement to avoid continuation of the problem.
2. Hold training sessions and initiate procedural reviews.
3. Document all activities and procedural changes for the next audit trail.
4. Establish and maintain audit reserves for contested issues.
5. Keep abreast of accounting system and other procedural changes that could impact compliance routines.

Areas Requiring Improvement

Taxpayers often fail to correct errors that were identified in a prior audit. When a breakdown in a procedure or an error has occurred, an attempt to correct the problem should be made. As mentioned earlier, a principal reason for the imposition of penalties is the failure of taxpayers to correct past problems.

Depending on when the audit is completed, taxpayers may not be able to correct an error for all of the next audit period. However, they should be able to modify their procedures for at least a portion of the next audit period. Doing so should help the taxpayer if the penalty issue is raised in the next audit with respect to the error.

Taxpayers should carefully note the completion dates of their audits. If they need to take corrective action, they should not be subject to penalties for errors that occurred prior to a final determination in the audit.

> ### ■ EXAMPLE
>
> Assume that the taxpayer is under a four-year audit, with two years under waiver because the statute of limitations has expired. If the audit is completed in the third year of the next audit cycle, taxpayers should only be expected to demonstrate corrective action in years three and four of the next cycle.
>
> It is unlikely that the auditor will have any information to make this determination. Therefore, taxpayers must be prepared to document the timing of the cycle and conclusion of the last audit.

Training Sessions and Procedural Reviews

Following an audit, training classes should be conducted for individuals or groups that may have committed errors that affected the audit results. Training must be done in a nonconfrontational manner. Employees should feel that they are an important part of the compliance team.

> ### ■ PLANNING POINTER
>
> The purchasing and accounts payable departments often create problems in an audit. In many companies, these departments play a major role in the self-assessment and payment of sales and use tax. Making employees in these areas aware of the importance of sales and use tax compliance should be a priority.

Employees need to be educated about the multiplier effect that an audit can have on an error. For example, because of the sampling techniques used, the audit deficiency could be hundreds of times the amount of actual tax if the tax had been paid at the time it was due. And this does *not* include the interest and penalty amounts that are added to the audit deficiency.

In addition to conducting training classes, taxpayers should review their compliance procedures. All tax departments or individuals responsible for tax compliance depend on other departments to provide them the information they need to comply with the tax-reporting requirements. It is important to review old assumptions and reports to make sure they are still reliable. The period following an audit is a good time to do this because the audit issues are still fresh in everyone's mind.

Documentation

It is important to document all corrective action taken and any procedural changes made as a result of an audit. A written record of such action creates a strong defense if a negligence penalty is imposed in a subsequent audit. By initiating corrective action, the taxpayer is demonstrating concern about properly complying with the tax laws.

PLANNING POINTER

It is easy to forget that corrective actions were taken as a result of an audit. However, if the actions are thoroughly documented in a file they are less likely to be forgotten.

Audit Reserves

Financial accounting principles require that any material liabilities or potential asset impairment be recognized in financial statements. Therefore, if taxpayers have contested issues that are significant in amount, they should consider establishing audit reserves.

For issues that may be appealed, the amount of potential liability, including interest and penalty, should be recorded on the books. If the issue may extend into future years, audit reserves based on estimated amounts should be established for those periods as well.

Taxpayers with issues extending to several states may wish to consider providing for a reserve amount *less* than the entire liability, as it is unlikely that all the states will audit each year of exposure.

System Changes

Whenever an accounts payable, purchasing, fixed-asset, accounting, or feeder system is replaced or modified, the tax implications of the change should be considered. Accounts payable and purchasing systems can have a significant impact on sales and use tax compliance because of the close relationship of the transactions in those systems to the compliance function.

Taxpayers also need to be aware of changes to systems that provide the data they depend on for compliance. While the information may be reliable at the time it is first used, over time its integrity can deteriorate because of the differing uses made of it.

EXAMPLE

At the time the data is analyzed, it is determined that a particular computer field code represents purchases of delivery charges from vendors. The tax department therefore programs the accrual system to assess or not assess tax based upon that field code and each state's particular treatment of that variable.

Over time, however, a new field code is added for certain transactions, but the tax department is not notified. Without an appropriate adjustment for the change, all purchases using the new code will be incorrectly self-assessed.

PLANNING POINTER

One way for tax personnel to maintain contact with various systems is to review the systems update plan on a regular basis. Any questions that arise regarding the potential impact of a change should be directed to the individual or department initiating the change.

Another effective technique for maintaining compliance routines is to develop a network of individuals in key areas and educate them on the importance of data integrity for tax compliance. When they become aware of changes that could affect compliance, they should contact someone in the tax department to discuss the modifications that are needed to remain in compliance.

CORPORATE OFFICER AND RESPONSIBLE PERSON STATUTES

In certain circumstances, key tax personnel and corporate officers can be singled out for special penalties or held responsible for the tax liabilities of the corporation or other business entity. States use the responsible person statutes to gain greater taxpayer compliance.

These statutes impose personal liability on a *responsible person* for improperly withholding the payment of tax on transactions. Some states also impose penalties on the responsible person for negligence or fraud.

A *responsible person* is generally one who has control over compliance or the filing of returns, and who is in a position to influence payment. Individuals in this category include vice-presidents, controllers, tax directors, and tax managers. To a lesser extent, the responsible person statutes could also include the return preparers if they have substantial authority in the payment of tax.

In order to avoid personal liability, individuals in positions of tax responsibility need to demonstrate that they have made reasonable efforts to comply with the requirements of the tax law. Advisors to responsible persons should make them aware of the sanctions that can be imposed.

STUDY QUESTIONS

---

8. If an audit is completed in the third year of the next four-year audit period, the taxpayer is responsible for demonstrating corrective action only in year four of that next cycle. *True or False?*

9. Which of the following statements is *not* true?
   a. The amount of potential liability for issues that may be appealed should be recorded on the books.
   b. Being considered a *responsible person* under the tax statutes has *no* personal financial implications.
   c. Taxpayers should not be subject to penalties for errors that occurred *prior* to a final audit determination.

AUDIT TRENDS

The Streamlined Sales Tax

There is little doubt that the Streamlined Sales Tax (SST) will dramatically simplify the audit process for vendors electing one of the technology models certified by the states. Vendors opting for the one of the models certified by the states will be relieved of much of the work associated with a traditional audit and, in some cases, will not be liable for errors resulting from use of a certified system.

For sellers who do not opt to utilize one of the technology models certified by the states, the SST may still offer some relief in the form of uniform audit standards to be applied to both Certified Service Providers (CSP) and sellers.

The uniform audit standards and procedures are as follows:

- Audits will be conducted by all participating states using statistical sampling techniques in accordance with generally accepted audit standards.
- States may conduct joint audits of CSP and sellers, although Model 3 sellers (those using a proprietary system that is certified by the states) with more complex tax systems and requirements may choose to be audited by individual states.
- When joint audits are conducted and errors identified, audit information will be provided to each participating state. Each state will then determine if an assessment or refund will be required. All states will issue the assessments or refunds within 90 days of completion of the audit. States will continue to follow their own statutes of limitations.
- Each participating state will provide a matrix of all definitions (uniform definitions and definitions specific to each state) of tangible personal property and services along with the taxability of CSP, and sellers will be held harmless from errors made by the state in its matrix.
- States will provide resources to answer questions of sellers and CSP on a timely basis.

Increasing Emphasis on Sales and Use Tax

Sales and use taxation has become a major source of revenue for state government. As a result, the states are likely to place greater emphasis on audits to maximize their revenues from these taxes.

Public opinion polls identify sales and use as the preferred form of taxation. This preference stems from taxpayers' belief that they can control their level of taxation by controlling their expenditures.

Due to this preference, emphasis on sales and use tax is likely to *increase* as states seek revenue sources for new and expanded services. More intense audit scrutiny is likely to follow. In addition, litigation could increase as the states and taxpayers attempt to resolve disputes in their favor.

Change Driven by Electronic Commerce

At this point in the development of electronic commerce, nobody can be sure how the structure of transactional taxes will have to be modified. While many commentators have suggested that the traditional sales tax model may be outmoded, it is too early to make that determination.

However, it seems certain that if changes are not made, the states will face a significant erosion of revenue. Whether SST is able to bridge that divide remains to be seen.

The nature of audits and the review process will have to change to accommodate the changes brought by electronic commerce. Taxpayers and tax jurisdictions cannot assume that the traditional audit trails and techniques will continue to be relevant in a paperless business environment.

> **EXAMPLE**
>
> The definition of *tangible personal property* may come under attack as vendors and consumers have increased flexibility to download products electronically. As we have seen already, strictly electronic transactions are resulting in fewer traditional business records for the auditor to review.

Greater Use of Sampling

As state resources become increasingly stretched and audits of taxpayers become even more complicated and time-consuming, sampling should play a greater role. Reliable sampling is a viable option to increase the states' efficiency in completing audits, even though there is much room for improvement in the states' sampling procedures. Substantial efficiencies for both the taxpayer and the states could be achieved, for example, through the use of smaller and more scientifically determined sample sizes.

The states also need to be more open to the possibility of taxpayers using sampling techniques to meet their compliance obligations. Many states are becoming more flexible with larger taxpayers in this regard, but more options need to be made available. Taxpayers should not have to spend thousands or, in some cases, hundreds of thousands of dollars just to comply with the tax laws.

One option involving sampling similar to managed compliance approaches would be to allow taxpayers to estimate their tax liability based on sampling and/or prior audit results. A follow-up audit would then determine the total amount of any tax due.

Any amount due would be offset by the estimated payments that had been made during the audit period. The resulting overpayment or underpayment would be the audit adjustment. Future estimates would be adjusted for audit results and changes in business operations. Under a system of *estimated payment*, the compliance burden on taxpayers would be lessened and the states would still receive their revenue.

Database Auditing

Greater use of database programs should increase efficiency for both the taxpayer and the state. When tax information is integrated into the database, the focus of the audit can shift from a detailed review of transactions to a verification of systems logic and a review of summarized data, based on variables established by the auditor.

For example, if tax paid to vendors is a separate data field in the accounts payable computer records, a taxpayer or auditor could request a report of all tax-paid transactions by account, vendor, or some other variable. Conversely, a report of nontaxed transactions could also be prepared by account, vendor, or other appropriate sort field.

Using these two reports could eliminate the detailed review of paper transactions, once both the auditor and the taxpayer are satisfied with system controls. The ability to correctly summarize the necessary information could reduce an audit of several weeks to a few days. In addition, the quality of work is elevated from the detailed and tedious review of paper documents to a more sophisticated systems analysis.

More Audit Flexibility for Taxpayers

The states will continue to provide taxpayers options for streamlining the audit process, such as Ohio's Managed Audit Program, which allows taxpayers to perform some of the routine audit work in exchange for reduced interest and penalties.

Taxpayers considering this option should evaluate the resources they have to complete the audit. In addition, they must consider whether they are willing to highlight errors and reveal damaging information to the state. In light of these considerations, many taxpayers are choosing not to participate in this program.

Other states, such as Wisconsin, offer taxpayers the opportunity to perform the audit themselves, with state-provided guidelines for certain industries, and mail in the results of their self-review. Failure to respond or report common industry purchases can result in a field audit by the state.

Increasing Use of Penalties

States have learned that the use of penalties improves taxpayer compliance. Penalties also provide the state additional revenue. As a result, the use of penalties is likely to increase.

However, the unreasonable use of penalties can serve as a disincentive for businesses to operate in the state. Therefore, states need to develop fair and objective criteria for the imposition of penalties.

STUDY QUESTION

10. Which of the following is one of the uniform audit standards that is required under the Streamlined Sales Tax?

   a. Audits will be conducted by participating states using nonstatistical sampling.
   b. When joint audits are conducted and errors identified, all states involved will issue assessments or refunds within 30 days of completion of the audit.
   c. Each participating state will provide a matrix of all definitions of tangible personal property and services.

Nexus Issues

This chapter presents and discusses the most notable cases in the area of nexus, including the issues of physical presence and agency nexus.

LEARNING OBJECTIVES

Upon completing this chapter, the professional will be able to:

- Explain the significance of the most noteworthy court cases related to nexus
- Differentiate between the nexus requirements of the Commerce Clause and the Due Process Clause of the U.S. Constitution
- Identify how physical presence affects nexus for sales and use tax purposes
- Discuss the issues involved related to agency nexus

OVERVIEW

Over the history of sales and use taxation, the states have occasionally put forth various initiates to expand the sales tax base and impose a filing requirement on more and more vendors in order to expand the scope and reach of sales tax in their state.

However, since 1992 and the *Quill* decision, the states have been forced to live within the boundaries of *physical presence*—meaning that they cannot force a taxpayer to register to collect their sales tax, unless that taxpayer has some physical presence in the taxing jurisdiction [No. 91-194, 504 US 298, 112 SCt. 1904 (May 26, 1992)]. This physical presence can take the form of an office, an employee, a stock of merchandise, a representative, etc.

While the physical presence standard has provided a *bright line* for taxpayers and taxing jurisdiction alike, many argue that modern forms of doing business, such as e-Commerce, were not even contemplated in 1992; therefore, the standard has become outmoded. Proponents of the physical presence standard argue that selling over the Internet is fundamentally no different than selling via telemarketing or mail-order, both of which were commonplace in 1992 when the *Quill* decision was handed down.

This Chapter will explore the judicial history of the physical presence standard and agency nexus *then* and *now* with an eye toward the future of sales taxation. The cases have been redacted and edited for easier reading. Also, footnotes and some citations and references in the cases have been omitted.

PHYSICAL PRESENCE STANDARD

National Bellas Hess, Inc. v. Department of Revenue,
U.S. Supreme Court, 386 US 753, SCt. 1389 (May 8, 1967)

Author commentary. Illinois enacted a statute that required remote sellers to register and collect sales tax in Illinois if they solicited sales in Illinois via catalogues or other means from either within or without the state. The logic behind the statute was that by directing catalogues and other advertising materials to potential Illinois purchasers, the remote vendor was effectively doing business in the state—even though they were not physically present in the state.

National Bellas Hess had no office in Illinois or other physical presence. The company sold from a remote site in Missouri. Under the Illinois statute, however, they were required to register and collect Illinois sales tax on each sale.

Bellas Hess objected to the filing requirement and took the protest all the way to the U.S. Supreme Court. The Court ruled in favor of Bellas Hess, citing the unfair administrative burden that such a collection requirement would impose on a remote seller. As you read over the decision in the *Bellas Hess* case below, focus on the Court's reasons for *not* requiring Bellas Hess to register.

Mr. Justice Stewart delivered the following opinion of the Court, which reverses the decision of the Illinois Supreme Court:

Company's business activities. The appellant, National Bellas Hess (National), is a mail order house with its principal place of business in North Kansas City, Missouri. It is licensed to do business in only that State and in Delaware, where it is incorporated. Although the company has neither outlets nor sales representatives in Illinois, the appellee, the Illinois Department of Revenue, obtained a judgment from the Illinois Supreme Court that National is required to collect and pay to the State the use taxes imposed by Ill. Rev. Stat., c. 120, §439.3 (1965). Since National's constitutional objections to the imposition of this liability present a substantial federal question, we noted probable jurisdiction of its appeal.

The facts bearing upon National's relationship with Illinois are accurately set forth in the opinion of the State Supreme Court:

> [National] does not maintain in Illinois any office, distribution house, sales house, warehouse or any other place of business; it does not have in Illinois any agent, salesman, canvasser, solicitor or other type of representative to sell or take orders, to deliver merchandise, to accept payments, or to service merchandise it sells; it does not own any tangible property, real or personal, in Illinois;

it has no telephone listing in Illinois and it has not advertised its merchandise for sale in newspapers, on billboards, or by radio or television in Illinois.

All of the contacts which National does have with the State are via the U.S. mail or common carrier. Twice a year catalogues are mailed to the company's active or recent customers throughout the United States, including Illinois.

This mailing is supplemented by advertising *flyers* which are occasionally mailed to past and potential customers. Orders for merchandise are mailed by the customers to National and are accepted at its Missouri plant. The ordered goods are then sent to the customers either by mail or by common carrier.

Requirements of Illinois law. This manner of doing business is sufficient under the Illinois statute to classify National as a "[r]etailer maintaining a place of business in this State," since that term includes any retailer:

> Engaging in soliciting orders within this State from users by means of catalogues or other advertising, whether such orders are received or accepted within or without this State (Ill. Rev. Stat. c. 120, §439.2 (1965).

Accordingly, the statute requires National to collect and pay to the appellee Department the tax imposed by Illinois upon consumers who purchase the company's goods for use within the State.

State's power to tax. National argues that the liabilities that Illinois has imposed violate the Due Process Clause of the Fourteenth Amendment and create an unconstitutional burden upon interstate commerce. These two claims are closely related.

The test of whether a particular state's demand for payment of taxes invades the exclusive authority of Congress to regulate trade between the States, and the test for a State's compliance with the requirements of due process in this area are similar.

As to the former, the Court has held that "State taxation falling on interstate commerce ... can only be justified as designed to make such commerce bear a fair share of the cost of the local government whose protection it enjoys [*Freeman v. Hewit*, 329 US 249, 253]." And in determining whether a state tax falls within the confines of the Due Process Clause, the Court has said that the "simple but controlling question is whether the state has given anything for which it can ask return [*Wisconsin v. J. C. Penney Co.*, 311 U. S. 435, 444]."

The same principles have been held applicable in determining the power of a State to impose the burdens of collecting use taxes upon interstate sales. Here, too, the Constitution requires "some definite link, some minimum connection, between a state and the person, property or transaction it seeks to tax [*Miller Bros. Co. v. Maryland,* 347 US 340, 344-345; *Scripto, Inc. v. Carson,* 362 US 207, 210-211]."

In applying these principles, the Court has upheld the power of a State to impose liability upon an out-of-state seller to collect a local use tax in a variety of circumstances. Where the sales were arranged by local agents in the taxing State, the Court has upheld such power [*Felt & Tarrant Co. v. Gallagher,* 306 US 62; *General Trading Co. v. Tax Comm'n,* 322 US 335]. The Court reached the same result where the mail order seller maintained local retail stores [*Nelson v. Sears, Roebuck & Co.,* 312 US 359; *Nelson v. Montgomery Ward,* 312 US 373].

In those situations, the out-of-state seller was plainly accorded the protection and services of the taxing State. The *Scripto* case represents the furthest constitutional reach to date of a State's power to deputize an out-of-state retailer as its collection agent for a use tax. In this case, the Court held that Florida *could* constitutionally impose upon a Georgia seller the duty of collecting a state use tax upon the sale of goods shipped to customers in Florida. The seller had "10 wholesalers, jobbers, or 'salesmen' conducting continuous local solicitation in Florida and forwarding the resulting orders from that State to Atlanta for shipment of the ordered goods [362 U. S., at 211]."

But the Court has never held that a State may impose the duty of use tax collection and payment upon a seller whose *only* connection with customers in the State is by common carrier or the U.S. mail. Indeed, in the *Sears, Roebuck* case the Court sharply differentiated such a situation from one where the seller had local retail outlets, pointing out that "those other concerns ... are not receiving benefits from Iowa for which it has the power to exact a price [312 U. S., at 365]."

In *Miller Bros.,* the Court held that Maryland could *not* constitutionally impose a use tax obligation upon a Delaware seller who had no retail outlets or sales solicitors in Maryland. The seller advertised its wares to Maryland residents through newspaper and radio advertising, in addition to mailing circulars four times a year. As a result, it made substantial sales to Maryland customers and made deliveries to them by its own trucks and drivers [347 US 340, 344-345].

Effect of decisions on taxing powers. In order to uphold the power of Illinois to impose use tax burdens on National in this case, we would have to repudiate completely the sharp distinction which these and other decisions have drawn between:

- Mail order sellers with retail outlets, solicitors, or property within a State
- Those who do no more than communicate with customers in the State by mail or common carrier as part of a general interstate business

This basic distinction, which until now has been generally recognized by the state taxing authorities, is a valid one, and we decline to obliterate it.

We need not rest on the broad foundation of all that was said in the *Miller Bros.* opinion, for here there was neither local advertising nor local household deliveries, upon which the dissenters in *Miller Bros.* so largely relied. Indeed, it is difficult to conceive of commercial transactions more exclusively interstate in character than the mail order transactions involved here.

And if the power of Illinois to impose use tax burdens upon National were upheld, the resulting impediments upon the free conduct of its interstate business would be neither imaginary nor remote. For if Illinois can impose such burdens, so can every other State, and so, indeed, can every municipality, every school district, and every other political subdivision throughout the United States with power to impose sales and use taxes.

The many variations in rates of tax, in allowable exemptions, and in administrative and recordkeeping requirements, could entangle National's interstate business in a virtual welter of complicated obligations to local jurisdictions with no legitimate claim to impose "a fair share of the cost of the local government."

The very purpose of the Commerce Clause was to ensure a national economy free from such unjustifiable local entanglements. Under the Constitution, this is a domain where Congress alone has the power of regulation and control.

The judgment is reversed.

Dissenting Opinion. J. Fortas provided the following dissenting opinion. Mr. Justice Black and Mr. Justice Douglas joined in the dissent.

In their opinion, the Court's decision in *Scripto* as well as a realistic approach to the facts of appellant's business, dictates that the judgment of the Supreme Court of Illinois should be affirmed.

Facts. National Bellas Hess is a large retail establishment specializing in wearing apparel. Directly and through subsidiaries, it operates a national retail mail order business with headquarters in Missouri, and its wholly owned subsidiaries operate a large number of retail stores in various states. In 1961, appellant's net sales were in the neighborhood of $60 million and its accounts receivable amounted to about $15.5 million.

Its sales in Illinois amounted to $2,174,744 for the approximately 15 months for which the taxes in issue in this case were assessed. This substantial volume is obtained by twice-a-year catalogue mailings, supplemented by intermediate smaller *sales books* or *flyers*. The catalogue contains about 4,000 items of merchandise. The company's mailing list includes over 5 million names. The *flyers* are sent to an even larger list than the catalogues and are occasionally mailed in bulk addressed to *occupant*.

A substantial part of Bellas Hess' sales is on credit. Its catalogue features *NBH Budget Aid Credit*—which requires no money down but requires the purchaser to make monthly payments which include a service fee or interest charge, and which also incorporates an agreement, unless expressly rejected by the purchaser, for *Budget Aid Family Insurance*. The company also offers *charge account* services—payable monthly including a *service charge* if the account is not fully paid within 30 days. Merchandise can also be bought c.o.d. or by sending a check or money order with the order for goods.

Exploitation of market. There should be no doubt that this large-scale, systematic, continuous solicitation and exploitation of the Illinois consumer market is a sufficient *nexus* to require Bellas Hess to collect from Illinois customers and to remit the use tax, especially when coupled with the use of the credit resources of residents of Illinois, dependent as that mechanism is upon the State's banking and credit institutions.

Bellas Hess is not simply using the facilities of interstate commerce to serve customers in Illinois. It regularly and continuously engaged in *exploitation of the consumer market* of Illinois (*Miller Bros.*) by soliciting residents of Illinois who live and work there and have homes and banking connections there, and who, absent the solicitation of Bellas Hess, might buy locally and pay the sales tax to support their state.

Bellas Hess could not carry on its business in Illinois, and particularly its substantial credit business, without utilizing Illinois banking and credit facilities. Since the case was tried on affidavits, we are not informed as to the details of the company's credit operations in Illinois. We do not know whether it utilizes credit information or collection agencies, or similar institutions. The company states that it has "brought no suits in the State of Illinois."

Accepting this as true, it would nevertheless be unreasonable to assume that the company does not either sell or assign its accounts or otherwise take measures to collect its delinquent accounts, or that collection does not include local activities by the company or its assignees or representatives.

State-conferred benefits. Bellas Hess enjoys the benefits of, and profits from the facilities nurtured by, the State of Illinois as fully as if it were a retail store or maintained salesmen therein. Indeed, if it did either, the benefit that it received from the State of Illinois would be no more than it now has—the ability to make sales of its merchandise, to utilize credit facilities, and to realize a profit; and, at the same time, it would be required to pay additional taxes.

Under the present arrangement, it conducts its substantial, regular, and systematic business in Illinois and the State demands only that it collect from its customer-users—and remit to the State—the use tax which is merely equal to the sales tax which resident merchants must collect and remit. To excuse Bellas Hess from this obligation is to burden and penalize retailers located in Illinois who must collect the sales tax from their customers.

In Illinois the rate is 3.5 percent, and when it is realized that in some communities the sales tax requires, in effect, that as much as five percent be added to the amount that customers of local, tax-paying stores must pay, the importance of the competitive discrimination becomes apparent. While this advantage to out-of-state sellers is tolerable and a necessary constitutional consequence where the sales are occasional, minor and sporadic and not the result of a calculated, systematic exploitation of the market, it certainly should not be extended to instances where the out-of-state company is engaged in exploiting the local market on a regular, systematic, large-scale basis. In such cases, the difference between the nature of the business conducted by the mail order house and by the local enterprise is not entitled to constitutional significance. The national mail order business amounts to over $2.4 billion a year.

Some of this is undoubtedly subject to the full range of taxes because of the location of stores in the various States, and some of it is and should be exempt from state use tax because of its sporadic or minor nature. But the volume which, under the present decision, will be placed in a favored position and exempted from bearing its fair burden of the collection of state taxes certainly will be substantial, and as state sales taxes increase, this haven of immunity may well increase in size and importance.

Prior Court decisions. In *Scripto,* this Court applied a sensible, practical conception of the Commerce Clause. The interstate seller which, in that case, claimed constitutional immunity from the collection of the Florida use tax had, like Bellas Hess, no office or place of business in the State, and had no property or employees there. It solicited orders in Florida through local *independent contractors* or brokers paid on a commission basis. These brokers were furnished catalogues and samples, and forwarded orders to Scripto, out of state.

The Court noted that the seller was "charged with no tax—save when ... he fails or refuses to collect it" and that the State "reimburse[d] [the seller] ... for its service" as tax collector. The same is true in the present case. I do not see how *Scripto* is meaningfully distinguishable from this case. In fact, *Scripto* involved the sale of a single article of commerce. The "exploitation" of the State's market was by no means as pervasive or comprehensive as it is here, nor was there any reference to the company's use of the State's credit institutions.

The present case is, of course, not at all controlled by *Miller Bros.* In that case, as this Court said, the company sold its merchandise at its store in Delaware; there was "no solicitation other than the incidental effects of general advertising ... no invasion or exploitation of the consumer market ...." As the Court noted in *Scripto, Miller Bros.* was a case in which there was "no regular, systematic displaying of its products by catalogs, samples or the like." On the contrary, in the present case, appellant regularly sends not only its catalogue, but even bulk mailings soliciting business addressed to *occupant,* and it offers and extends credit to residents of Illinois based on their local financial references.

Summary. As the Court says, the test whether an out-of-state business must comply with a state levy is variously formulated:
- "Whether the state has given anything for which it can ask return"
- Whether the out-of-state business enjoys the protection or benefits of the State
- Whether there is a sufficient nexus: "Some definite link, some minimum connection, between a state and the person, property or transaction it seeks to tax."

However this is formulated, it seems to me entirely clear that a mail order house engaged in the business of regularly, systematically, and on a large scale offering merchandise for sale in a State in competition with local retailers, and soliciting deferred payment-credit accounts from the State's residents, is not excused from compliance with the State's use tax obligations by the Commerce Clause or the Due Process Clause of the Constitution.

It is hardly worth remarking that Bellas Hess's expressions of consternation and alarm at the burden which the mechanics of compliance with use tax obligations would place upon it and others similarly situated should not give us pause. The burden is no greater than that placed upon local retailers by comparable sales tax obligations; and the Court's response that these administrative and recordkeeping requirements could *entangle* appellant's interstate business in a welter of complicated obligations vastly underestimates the skill of contemporary man and his machines.

There is no doubt that the collection of taxes from consumers is a burden; but it is no more of a burden on a mail order house such as appellant located in another State than on an enterprise in the same State which accepts orders by mail; and it is, indeed, hardly more of a burden than it is on any ordinary retail store in the taxing State.

I would affirm.

Author Commentary. In the dissenting opinion in the **Bellas Hess** case, Justice Fortas noted that where there was systematic, large-scale solicitation of sales in a state via catalogues or other marketing materials, and that his opinion was that the distribution of those items constituted a nexus-creating activity. His logic was that at some level of activity the taxpayer has an obligation to collect the tax for the state, regardless of whether the taxpayer is located within or without the tax jurisdiction, since the taxpayer is reaping the benefits of doing business in the state.

Several jurisdictions incorporated that language into their statutes, indicating that nexus was created by the "systematic, large-scale solicitation of sales"—regardless of whether or not the taxpayer was physically present. These statutes became known as "anti-*Bellas Hess*" statutes since their intent was to overturn the decision in that case.

North Dakota adopted this language, which ultimately led to another Supreme Court case in 1992, *Quill v. North Dakota*, which is covered in the next section. North Dakota's statute required vendors with no physical presence in the state to register and collect their sales tax.

STUDY QUESTIONS

1. Which of the following was **not** an argument *in favor* of requiring National Bellas Hess to collect sales tax?

   a. National Bellas Hess solicited and exploited the Illinois consumer market.

   b. National Bellas Hess fully enjoyed the benefits of, and profits from the facilities nurtured by, the State of Illinois.

   c. National Bellas Hess had physical presence in Illinois.

2. The dissenting opinion in **National Bellas Hess** was based primarily on the previous decision in which of the following cases?

   a. *Miller Bros.*

   b. *Scripto*

   c. *Quill*

3. Which of the following was a reason why the Court **reversed** the Illinois Supreme Court decision in **National Bellas Hess?**

   a. The tax liability imposed by Illinois did *not* create an unconstitutional burden upon interstate commerce.

   b. The only connection National Bellas Hess had with customers in Illinois was by common carrier or U.S. mail.

   c. The facts of the case were similar to those in *Scripto.*

4. The U.S. Supreme Court decision in **National Bellas Hess** basically acknowledged that there is a physical presence requirement for the imposition of sales and use taxes. **True or False?**

Quill Corporation v. North Dakota, by and through its Tax Commissioner, Heitkamp, U.S. Supreme Court, 504 US 298, 112 SCt. 1904 (May 26, 1992)

Author Commentary. In *Quill* the Supreme Court retrenched its position in *Bellas Hess;* however, the Court identified two different thresholds for nexus under the Due Process Clause and the Commerce Clause of the U.S. Constitution. As you read through the case, note the differing levels of activity required to create nexus under each of the two operative sections of the U.S. Constitution, along with the Court's invitation for the U.S. Congress to enact legislation to clarify when nexus is triggered by remote sellers operating in the state.

Opinion. The following opinion, written by Justice Stevens, reverses the North Dakota Supreme Court.

This case, like *National Bellas Hess,* involves a State's attempt to require an out-of-state mail-order house that has neither outlets nor sales representatives in the State to collect and pay a use tax on goods purchased for use within the State. In *Bellas Hess* we held that a similar Illinois statute violated the Due Process Clause of the Fourteenth Amendment and created an unconstitutional burden on interstate commerce. In particular, we ruled that a "seller whose only connection with customers in the State is by common carrier or the United States mail" lacked the requisite minimum contacts with the State.

In this case the Supreme Court of North Dakota declined to follow *Bellas Hess* because "the tremendous social, economic, commercial, and legal innovations" of the past quarter-century have rendered its holding "obsole[te]." [470 N.W.2d 203, 208 (1991).] Having granted certiorari, we must either reverse the State Supreme Court or overrule *Bellas Hess.* While we agree with much of the State Court's reasoning, we take the former course.

I. Facts. Quill is a Delaware corporation with offices and warehouses in Illinois, California, and Georgia. None of its employees work or reside in North Dakota and its ownership of tangible property in that State is either insignificant or nonexistent.

Quill sells office equipment and supplies; it solicits business through catalogs and flyers, advertisements in national periodicals, and telephone calls. Its annual national sales exceed $200 million, of which almost $1 million are made to about 3,000 customers in North Dakota. It is the sixth largest vendor of office supplies in the State. It delivers all of its merchandise to its North Dakota customers by mail or common carrier from out-of-state locations.

As a corollary to its sales tax, North Dakota imposes a use tax upon property purchased for storage, use or consumption within the State. North Dakota requires every "retailer maintaining a place of business in" the State to collect the tax from the consumer and remit it to the State. [N.D. Cent. Code §57-40.2-07 (Supp. 1991)]. In 1987 North Dakota amended the statutory definition of the term *retailer* to include "every person who engages in regular or systematic solicitation of a consumer market in th[e] state [§57-40.2-01(6)]."

State regulations in turn define *regular or systematic solicitation* to mean three or more advertisements within a 12-month period [N.D. Admin. Code §81-04.1-01-03.1 (1988)]. Thus, since 1987, mail-order companies that engage in such solicitation have been subject to the tax even if they maintain no property or personnel in North Dakota.

Quill has taken the position that North Dakota does not have the power to compel it to collect a use tax from its North Dakota customers. Consequently, the State, through its Tax Commissioner, filed this action to require Quill to pay taxes (as well as interest and penalties) on all such sales made after July 1, 1987. The trial court ruled in Quill's favor, finding the case indistinguishable from *Bellas Hess;* specifically, it found that because the State had not shown that it had spent tax revenues for the benefit of the mail-order business, there was no "nexus to allow the state to define retailer in the manner it chose [App. to Pet. for Cert. A41]."

The North Dakota Supreme Court reversed the decision, concluding that *wholesale changes* in both the economy and the law made it inappropriate to follow *Bellas Hess* today. The principal economic change noted by the court was the remarkable growth of the mail-order business "from a relatively inconsequential market niche" in 1967 to a "goliath" with annual sales that reached "the staggering figure of $183.3 billion in 1989." Moreover, the court observed, advances in computer technology greatly eased the burden of compliance with a "welter of complicated obligations" imposed by state and local taxing authorities.

Equally important, in the court's view, were the changes in the *legal landscape.* With respect to the Commerce Clause, the court emphasized that *Complete Auto Transit, Inc. v. Brady* [430 US 274 (1977)], rejected the line of cases holding that the direct taxation of interstate commerce was impermissible and adopted instead a "consistent and rational method of inquiry [that focused on] the practical effect of [the] challenged tax [*Mobil Oil Corp. v. Commissioner of Taxes of Vt.,* 445 US 425, 443 (1980)]." This and subsequent rulings, the court maintained, indicated that the Commerce Clause no longer mandated the sort of physical-presence nexus suggested in *Bellas Hess.*

Similarly, with respect to the Due Process Clause, the North Dakota court observed that cases following *Bellas Hess* had not construed *minimum contacts* to require physical presence within a State as a prerequisite to the legitimate exercise of state power. The State Court then concluded that "the Due Process requirement of a 'minimal connection' to establish nexus is encompassed within the *Complete Auto* test" and that the relevant inquiry under the latter test was whether "the state has provided some protection, opportunities, or benefit for which it can expect a return."

Turning to the case at hand, the State Court emphasized that North Dakota had created "an economic climate that fosters demand for" Quill's products, maintained a legal infrastructure that protected that market, and disposed of 24 tons of catalogs and flyers mailed by Quill into the State every year.

Based on these facts, the court concluded that Quill's *economic presence* in North Dakota depended on services and benefits provided by the State and therefore generated "a constitutionally sufficient nexus to justify imposition of the purely administrative duty of collecting and remitting the use tax."

II. Prior cases. As in a number of other cases involving the application of state taxing statutes to out-of-state sellers, our holding in ***Bellas Hess*** relied on both the Due Process Clause and the Commerce Clause. Although the "two claims are closely related [***Bellas Hess***, 386 US, at 756]," the clauses pose distinct limits on the taxing powers of the States. Accordingly, while a State may, consistent with the Due Process Clause, have the authority to tax a particular taxpayer, imposition of the tax may nonetheless violate the Commerce Clause.

The two constitutional requirements differ fundamentally, in several ways. As discussed at greater length below, the Due Process Clause and the Commerce Clause reflect different constitutional concerns. Moreover, while Congress has complete power to regulate commerce among the States and thus may authorize state actions that burden interstate commerce, it does not similarly have the power to authorize violations of the Due Process Clause.

Thus, although we have not always been precise in distinguishing between the two, the Due Process Clause and the Commerce Clause are analytically distinct.

"'Due process' and 'commerce clause' conceptions are not always sharply separable in dealing with these problems. ... To some extent they overlap. If there is a want of due process to sustain the tax, by that fact alone any burden the tax imposes on the commerce among the states becomes 'undue.' But, though overlapping, the two conceptions are not identical. There may be more than sufficient factual connections, with economic and legal effects, between the transaction and the taxing state to sustain the tax as against due process objections. Yet it may fall because of its burdening effect upon the commerce. And, although the two notions cannot always be separated, clarity of consideration and of decision would be promoted if the two issues are approached, where they are presented, at least tentatively as if they were separate and distinct, not intermingled ones." [***International Harvester Co. v. Department of Treasury***, 322 US 340, 353 (1944) (Rutledge, J., concurring in part and dissenting in part).]

Heeding Justice Rutledge's counsel, we consider each constitutional limit in turn.

III. Due Process Clause. The Due Process Clause "requires some definite link, some minimum connection, between a state and the person, property or transaction it seeks to tax," [*Miller Bros. Co. v. Maryland,* 347 US 340, 344-345 (1954)] and that the "income attributed to the State for tax purposes must be rationally related to 'values connected with the taxing State.'" [*Moorman Mfg. Co. v. Bair,* 437 US 267, 273 (1978) (citation omitted)]. Here, we are concerned primarily with the first of these requirements.

Prior to *Bellas Hess,* we had held that that requirement was satisfied in a variety of circumstances involving use taxes. For example, the presence of sales personnel in the State, or the maintenance of local retail stores in the State, justified the exercise of that power because the seller's local activities were "plainly accorded the protection and services of the taxing State." [*Bellas Hess,* 386 US, at 757.]

The furthest extension of that power was recognized in *Scripto,* in which the Court upheld a use tax despite the fact that all of the seller's in-state solicitation was performed by independent contractors. These cases all involved some sort of physical presence within the State, and in *Bellas Hess* the Court suggested that such presence was not only sufficient for jurisdiction under the Due Process Clause, but also necessary. We expressly declined to obliterate the "sharp distinction ... between mail order sellers with retail outlets, solicitors, or property within a State, and those who do no more than communicate with customers in the State by mail or common carrier as a part of a general interstate business."

Our due process jurisprudence has evolved substantially in the 25 years since *Bellas Hess,* particularly in the area of judicial jurisdiction. Building on the seminal case of *International Shoe Co. v. Washington* [326 US 310 (1945)], we have framed the relevant inquiry as whether a defendant had minimum contacts with the jurisdiction "such that the maintenance of the suit does not offend 'traditional notions of fair play and substantial justice.'"

In that spirit, we have abandoned more formalistic tests that focused on a defendant's *presence* within a State in favor of a more flexible inquiry into whether a defendant's contacts with the forum made it reasonable, in the context of our federal system of government, to require it to defend the suit in that State. In *Shaffer v. Heitner* [433 US 186, 212 (1977)], the Court extended the flexible approach that *International Shoe* had prescribed for purposes of *in personam* jurisdiction to *in rem* jurisdiction, concluding that "all assertions of state-court jurisdiction must be evaluated according to the standards set forth in *International Shoe* and its progeny."

Applying these principles, we have held that if a foreign corporation purposefully avails itself of the benefits of an economic market in the forum State, it may subject itself to the State's *in personam* jurisdiction even if it has no physical presence in the State. As we explained in ***Burger King Corp. v. Rudzewicz*** [471 US 462 (1985)]:

> Jurisdiction in these circumstances may not be avoided merely because the defendant did not *physically* enter the forum State. Although territorial presence frequently will enhance a potential defendant's affiliation with a State and reinforce the reasonable foreseeability of suit there, it is an inescapable fact of modern commercial life that a substantial amount of business is transacted solely by mail and wire communications across state lines, thus obviating the need for physical presence within a State in which business is conducted. So long as a commercial actor's efforts are 'purposefully directed' toward residents of another State, we have consistently rejected the notion that an absence of physical contacts can defeat personal jurisdiction there [*Id.*, at 476 (emphasis in original)].

Comparable reasoning justifies the imposition of the collection duty on a mail-order house that is engaged in continuous and widespread solicitation of business within a State. Such a corporation clearly has "fair warning that [its] activity may subject [it] to the jurisdiction of a foreign sovereign." [***Shaffer v. Heitner***, 433 US, at 218 (Stevens, J., concurring in judgment).]

In *modern commercial life* it matters little that such solicitation is accomplished by a deluge of catalogs rather than a phalanx of drummers: the requirements of due process are met irrespective of a corporation's lack of physical presence in the taxing State. We therefore agree with the North Dakota Supreme Court's conclusion that the Due Process Clause does not bar enforcement of that State's use tax against Quill.

IV. Commerce Clause. Article I, §8, cl. 3 of the Constitution expressly authorizes Congress to "regulate Commerce with foreign Nations, and among the several States." It says nothing about the protection of interstate commerce in the absence of any action by Congress. Nevertheless, as Justice Johnson suggested in his concurring opinion in ***Gibbons v. Ogden*** [9 Wheat. 1, 231-232, 239 (1824)], the Commerce Clause is more than an affirmative grant of power; it has a negative sweep as well. The clause, in Justice Stone's phrasing, "by its own force" prohibits certain state actions that interfere with interstate commerce [***South Carolina State Highway Dept. v. Barnwell Bros., Inc.***, 303 US 177, 185 (1938)].

Our interpretation of the *negative* or *dormant* Commerce Clause has evolved substantially over the years, particularly as that clause concerns limitations on state taxation powers. Our early cases swept broadly, beginning with **Brown v. Maryland** [12 Wheat. 419 (1827)]. And, in **Leloup v. Port of Mobile** [127 US 640, 648 (1888)], we declared that "no State has the right to lay a tax on interstate commerce in any form." We later narrowed that rule and distinguished between direct burdens on interstate commerce, which were prohibited, and indirect burdens, which generally were not.

However, in **Freeman v. Hewit** [329 US 249, 256 (1946)], we embraced again the formal distinction between direct and indirect taxation, invalidating Indiana's imposition of a gross receipts tax on a particular transaction because that application would "impos[e] a direct tax on interstate sales." Most recently, in **Complete Auto Transit**, we renounced the **Freeman** approach as "attaching constitutional significance to a semantic difference." **Complete Auto** emphasized the importance of looking past "the formal language of the tax statute [to] its practical effect," and set forth a four-part test that continues to govern the validity of state taxes under the Commerce Clause.

Bellas Hess was decided in 1967, in the middle of this latest rally between formalism and pragmatism. Contrary to the suggestion of the North Dakota Supreme Court, this timing does not mean that **Complete Auto** rendered **Bellas Hess** *obsolete*. **Complete Auto** rejected **Freeman**'s formal distinction between *direct* and *indirect* taxes on interstate commerce because that formalism allowed the validity of statutes to hinge on *legal terminology, draftsmanship and phraseology*. **Bellas Hess** did not rely on any such labeling of taxes and therefore did not automatically fall with **Freeman.**

While contemporary Commerce Clause jurisprudence might not dictate the same result were the issue to arise for the first time today, **Bellas Hess** is not inconsistent with **Complete Auto** and our recent cases. Under **Complete Auto**'s four-part test, we will sustain a tax against a Commerce Clause challenge so long as the tax:

1. Is applied to an activity with a substantial nexus with the taxing State
2. Is fairly apportioned
3. Does not discriminate against interstate commerce
4. Is fairly related to the services provided by the State

Bellas Hess concerns the first of these tests and stands for the proposition that a vendor whose only contacts with the taxing State are by mail or common carrier lacks the *substantial nexus* required by the Commerce Clause.

Thus, three weeks after *Complete Auto* was handed down, we cited *Bellas Hess* for this proposition and discussed the case at some length. In *National Geographic Society v. California Bd. of Equalization* [430 US 551, 559 (1977)], we affirmed the continuing vitality of *Bellas Hess'* "sharp distinction ... between mail-order sellers with [a physical presence in the taxing] State and those ... who do no more than communicate with customers in the State by mail or common carrier as part of a general interstate business." We have continued to cite *Bellas Hess* with approval ever since. For these reasons, we disagree with the State Supreme Court's conclusion that our decision in *Complete Auto* undercut the *Bellas Hess* rule.

The State of North Dakota relies less on *Complete Auto* and more on the evolution of our due process jurisprudence. The State contends that the nexus requirements imposed by the Due Process and Commerce Clauses are equivalent and that if, as we concluded above, a mail-order house that lacks a physical presence in the taxing State nonetheless satisfies the due process *minimum contacts* test, then that corporation also meets the Commerce Clause *substantial nexus* test. We disagree. Despite the similarity in phrasing, the nexus requirements of the Due Process and Commerce Clauses are *not* identical. The two standards are animated by different constitutional concerns and policies.

Due process centrally concerns the fundamental fairness of governmental activity. Thus, at the most general level, the due process nexus analysis requires that we ask whether an individual's connections with a State are substantial enough to legitimate the State's exercise of power over him. We have, therefore, often identified *notice* or *fair warning* as the analytic touchstone of due process nexus analysis.

In contrast, the *Commerce Clause* and its nexus requirement are informed not so much by concerns about fairness for the individual defendant as by structural concerns about the effects of state regulation on the national economy. Under the Articles of Confederation, State taxes and duties hindered and suppressed interstate commerce; the Framers intended the Commerce Clause as a cure for these structural ills. It is in this light that we have interpreted the negative implication of the Commerce Clause. Accordingly, we have ruled that that Clause prohibits discrimination against interstate commerce, and bars state regulations that unduly burden interstate commerce.

The *Complete Auto* analysis reflects these concerns about the national economy. The second and third parts of that analysis, which require fair apportionment and non-discrimination, prohibit taxes that pass an unfair share of the tax burden onto interstate commerce. The first and fourth prongs, which require a substantial nexus and a relationship between the tax and State-provided services, limit the reach of State taxing authority so as to ensure that State taxation does not unduly burden interstate commerce. Accordingly, contrary to the State's suggestion, a corporation may have the *minimum contacts* with a taxing State as required by the Due Process Clause, and yet lack the *substantial nexus* with that State as required by the Commerce Clause.

The State Supreme Court reviewed our recent Commerce Clause decisions and concluded that those rulings signaled a "retreat from the formalistic constrictions of a stringent physical presence test in favor of a more flexible substantive approach" and thus supported its decision not to apply *Bellas Hess.* Although we agree with the State Court's assessment of the evolution of our cases, we do not share its conclusion that this evolution indicates that the Commerce Clause ruling of *Bellas Hess* is no longer good law.

First, as the State Court itself noted, all of these cases involved taxpayers who had a physical presence in the taxing State and therefore do not directly conflict with the rule of *Bellas Hess* or compel that it be overruled. Second, and more importantly, although our Commerce Clause jurisprudence now favors more flexible balancing analyses, we have never intimated a desire to reject all established *bright-line* tests. Although we have not, in our review of other types of taxes, articulated the same *physical presence* requirement that *Bellas Hess* established for sales and use taxes, that silence does not imply repudiation of the *Bellas Hess* rule.

Like other bright-line tests, the *Bellas Hess* rule appears artificial at its edges: whether or not a State may compel a vendor to collect a sales or use tax may turn on the presence in the taxing State of a small sales force, plant, or office. This artificiality, however, is more than offset by the benefits of a clear rule. Such a rule firmly establishes the boundaries of legitimate state authority to impose a duty to collect sales and use taxes and reduces litigation concerning those taxes.

This benefit is important, for, as we have so frequently noted, our law in this area is something of a "quagmire" and the "application of constitutional principles to specific state statutes leaves much room for controversy and confusion and little in the way of precise guides to the States in the exercise of their indispensable power of taxation." [***Northwestern States Portland Cement Co. v. Minnesota,*** 358 U.S. 450, 457-458 (1959).]

Moreover, a bright-line rule in the area of sales and use taxes also encourages settled expectations and, in doing so, fosters investment by businesses and individuals. Indeed, it is not unlikely that the mail-order industry's dramatic growth over the last quarter-century is due in part to the bright-line exemption from state taxation created in *Bellas Hess.*

In sum, although in our cases subsequent to *Bellas Hess* and concerning other types of taxes we have not adopted a similar bright-line, physical-presence requirement, our reasoning in those cases does not compel that we now reject the rule that *Bellas Hess* established in the area of sales and use taxes. To the contrary, the continuing value of a bright-line rule in this area and the doctrine and principles of *stare decisis* indicate that the *Bellas Hess* rule remains good law. For these reasons, we disagree with the North Dakota Supreme Court's conclusion that the time has come to renounce the bright-line test of *Bellas Hess.*

This aspect of our decision is made easier by the fact that the underlying issue is not only one that Congress may be better qualified to resolve, but also one that Congress has the ultimate power to resolve. No matter how we evaluate the burdens that use taxes impose on interstate commerce, Congress remains free to disagree with our conclusions.

Indeed, in recent years Congress has considered legislation that would *overrule* the *Bellas Hess* rule. Its decision not to take action in this direction may, of course, have been dictated by respect for our holding in *Bellas Hess* that the Due Process Clause prohibits States from imposing such taxes, but today we have put that problem to rest. Accordingly, Congress is now free to decide whether, when, and to what extent the States may burden interstate mail-order concerns with a duty to collect use taxes.

The judgment of the Supreme Court of North Dakota is reversed and the case is remanded for further proceedings not inconsistent with this opinion.

It is so ordered.

Dissenting opinion. Justice White concurred in part but dissented regarding Part IV.

In summary, he noted that although Congress can and should address itself to this area of law, the Court "should not adhere to a decision, however right it was at the time, that by reason of later cases and economic reality can no longer be rationally justified. The Commerce Clause aspect of *Bellas Hess*, along with its due process holding, should be overruled."

Other justices. Justice Scalia, with whom Justice Kennedy and Justice Thomas joined, concurring in part and concurring in the judgment. A section of their opinion follows:

I do not share Justice White's view that we may disregard these reliance interests because it has become unreasonable to rely upon *Bellas Hess*,. Even assuming for the sake of argument (I do not consider the point) that later decisions in related areas are inconsistent with the principles upon which *Bellas Hess* rested, we have never acknowledged that, but have instead carefully distinguished the case on its facts.

It seems to me important that we retain our ability—and, what comes to the same thing, that we maintain public confidence in our ability—sometimes to adopt new principles for the resolution of new issues without abandoning clear holdings of the past that those principles contradict. We seemed to be doing that in this area. Having affirmatively suggested that the *physical presence* rule could be reconciled with our new jurisprudence, we ought not visit economic hardship upon those who took us at our word.

It is strangely incompatible with this to demand that private parties anticipate our overrulings. It is my view, in short, that reliance upon a square, unabandoned holding of the Supreme Court is *always* justifiable reliance (though reliance alone may not always carry the day). Finally, the *physical presence* rule established in **Bellas Hess** is not unworkable; to the contrary, whatever else may be the substantive pros and cons of the rule, the *bright-line* regime that it establishes is unqualifiedly in its favor. Justice White's concern that reaffirmance of **Bellas Hess** will lead to a flurry of litigation over the meaning of *physical presence*, seems to me contradicted by 25 years of experience under the decision.

For these reasons, I concur in the judgment of the Court and join Parts I, II, and III of its opinion.

STUDY QUESTIONS

> **5.** According to the **Quill** Court, which of the following is true concerning the Commerce Clause and/or Due Process Clause?
>
> **a.** The Commerce Clause requires substantial nexus.
> **b.** The Due Process Clause concerns the effects of state regulation on the national economy.
> **c.** The Commerce Clause concerns the fairness of governmental activity.
>
> **6.** Following the majority decision in **Quill,** which of the following companies would most likely have nexus in State A for sales and use tax purposes?
>
> **a.** A company sells products from its store in State B to State A residents who visit there.
> **b.** A company located in State B sells and delivers products to customers in State A through its salesmen who reside in State A.
> **c.** A company located in State B sells products over the Internet to customers in State A.
>
> **7.** The majority opinion in **Quill** concluded that **National Bellas Hess:**
>
> **a.** Is inconsistent with **Complete Auto Transit**
> **b.** Is no longer good law
> **c.** Established a continuing bright-line rule
>
> **8.** While a State may have authority consistent with the Due Process Clause to tax a taxpayer, imposition of the tax may still violate the Commerce Clause. **True or False?**

AGENCY NEXUS

Scripto, Inc. v. Carson, **U.S. Supreme Court, 362 US 207, 80 SCt. 619 (Mar. 21, 1960)**

Author commentary. The *Scripto* case was an early sales tax case that established that the efforts of an agent or representative in a state had the same nexus implications for the taxpayer as the taxpayer engaging in those activities on their own. The Court reasoned that the level of representation in the state was fundamentally the same regardless of whether the representation was done by an employee or independent sales representative at least to the extent it related to the execution of a sale. Therefore, the Court held they had equal nexus-creating impact.

Opinion. Mr. Justice Clark delivered the opinion of the Court.

Florida, by statute, requires appellant, a Georgia corporation, to be responsible for the collection of a use tax on certain mechanical writing instruments which appellant sells and ships from its place of business in Atlanta to residents of Florida for use and enjoyment there. Upon Scripto's failure to collect the tax, the appellee comptroller levied a use tax liability of $5,150.66 against it.

Appellant then brought this suit to test the validity of the imposition, contending that the requirement of Florida's statute places a burden on interstate commerce and violates the Due Process Clause of the Fourteenth Amendment to the Constitution. It claimed, in effect, that the nature of its operations in Florida does not form a sufficient nexus to subject it to the Statute's exactions. Both the Trial Court and the Supreme Court of Florida held that appellant does have sufficient jurisdictional contacts in Florida and, therefore, must register as a dealer under the statute and collect and remit to the State the use tax imposed on its aforesaid sales. We agree with the result reached by Florida's Courts.

Facts. Appellant operates in Atlanta an advertising specialty division trading under the name of Adgif Company. Through it, appellant is engaged in the business of selling mechanical writing instruments which are adapted to advertising purposes by the placing of printed material thereon. In the state of Florida, the appellant's Adgif operation does *not*:

1. Own, lease, or maintain any office, distributing house, warehouse or other place of business
2. Have any regular employee or agent
3. Own or maintain any bank account or stock of merchandise

Orders for its products are solicited by advertising specialty brokers or, as the Supreme Court of Florida called them, wholesalers or jobbers, who are residents of Florida. At the time of suit, there were 10 such brokers—each having a written contract and a specific territory. The somewhat detailed contract provides, *inter alia,* that all compensation is to be on a commission basis on the sales made, provided they are accepted by appellant; repeat orders, even if not solicited, also carry a commission if the salesman has not become inactive through failure to secure acceptable orders during the previous 60 days.

The contract specifically provides that it is the intention of the parties "to create the relationship of independent contractor." Each order is to be signed by the solicitor as a *salesman*; however, he has no authority to make collections or incur debts involving appellant. Each salesman is furnished catalogs, samples, and advertising material, and is actively engaged in Florida as a representative "of Scripto for the purpose of attracting, soliciting and obtaining Florida customers" for its mechanical advertising specialties.

Orders for such products are sent by these salesmen directly to the Atlanta office for acceptance or refusal. If accepted, the sale is consummated there and the salesman is paid his commission directly. No money passes between the purchaser and the salesman—although the latter does occasionally accept a check payable to the appellant, in which event he is required to forward it to appellant with the order.

Statute construed. As construed by Florida's highest court, the impost levied by the statute is a tax on the privilege of using personal property which has come to rest and has become a part of the mass of property within the State. It is not a sales tax, but was developed as a device to complement such a tax in order to prevent evasion by the completion of purchases in a non-taxing State and shipment by interstate commerce into a taxing forum. The tax is collectible from *dealers* and is to be added to the purchase price of the merchandise "as far as practicable." In the event that a dealer fails to collect the tax, he himself is liable for its payment. Florida held appellant to be a dealer under its statute.

The question remaining is whether Florida, in the light of appellant's operations there, may collect the State's use tax from it on the basis of property bought from appellant and shipped from its home office to purchasers in Florida for use there.

Sufficient nexus. Florida has well stated the course of this Court's decisions governing such levies, and we need but drive home its clear understanding. There must be, as our brother Jackson stated in *Miller Bros.,* "some definite link, some minimum connection, between a state and the person, property or transaction it seeks to tax." We believe that such a nexus is present here.

First, the tax is a nondiscriminatory exaction levied for the use and enjoyment of property which has been purchased by Florida residents and which has actually entered into and become a part of the mass of property in that State. The burden of the tax is placed on the ultimate purchaser in Florida and it is he who enjoys the use of the property, regardless of its source. We note that the appellant is charged with no tax—save when, as here, he fails or refuses to collect it from the Florida customer.

Next, as Florida points out, appellant has 10 wholesalers, jobbers, or *salesmen* conducting continuous local solicitation in Florida and forwarding the resulting orders from that State to Atlanta for shipment of the ordered goods. The only incidence of this sales transaction that is nonlocal is the acceptance of the order. True, the *salesmen* are not regular employees of appellant devoting full time to its service, but we concluded that such a fine distinction is without constitutional significance.

The formal shift in the contractual tagging of the salesman as *independent* neither results in changing his local function of solicitation nor bears upon its effectiveness in securing a substantial flow of goods into Florida. This is evidenced by the amount assessed against appellant on the statute's three percent basis over a period of but four years. To permit such formal *contractual shifts* to make a constitutional difference would open the gates to a stampede of tax avoidance. Moreover, we cannot see, from a constitutional standpoint, "that it was important that the agent worked for several principals." [Chief Judge Learned Hand, in ***Bomze v. Nardis Sportswear,*** 165 F. 2d 33, 36.] The test is simply the nature and extent of the activities of the appellant in Florida.

In short, we conclude that this case is controlled by ***General Trading Co.*** As was said there, "all these differentiations are without constitutional significance. Of course, no State can tax the privilege of doing interstate business. ... That is within the protection of the Commerce Clause and subject to the power of Congress. On the other hand, the mere fact that property is used for interstate commerce or has come into an owner's possession as a result of interstate commerce does not diminish the protection which he may draw from a state to the upkeep of which he may be asked to bear his fair share."

Nor do we believe that Florida's requirement that appellant be its tax collector on such orders from its residents changes the situation. As was pointed out in ***General Trading Co.,*** this is "a familiar and sanctioned device." Moreover, we note that Florida reimburses appellant for its service in this regard.

Miller Bros. **distinguished.** Appellant earnestly contends that *Miller Bros.* is to the contrary. We think not. Miller had no solicitors in Maryland; there was no "exploitation of the consumer market"; no regular, systematic displaying of its products by catalogs, samples or the like. But, on the contrary, the goods on which Maryland sought to force Miller to collect its tax were sold to residents of Maryland when personally present at Miller's store in Delaware.

True, there was an *occasional* delivery of such purchases by Miller into Maryland, and it did occasionally mail notices of special sales to former customers; but Marylanders went to Delaware to make purchases—Miller did not go to Maryland for sales. Moreover, it was impossible for Miller to determine that goods sold for cash to a customer over the counter at its store in Delaware were to be used and enjoyed in Maryland. This led the Court to conclude that Miller would be made "more vulnerable to liability for another's tax than to a tax on itself." In view of these considerations, we conclude that the *minimum connections* not present in *Miller* are more than sufficient here.

The judgment is therefore affirmed.

STUDY QUESTIONS

9. In **Scripto,** the U.S. Supreme Court reasoned that which of the following had the same nexus implications in a state as the taxpayer engaging in the same activities?

   a. An employee but not an independent sales representative
   b. An independent sales representative but not an employee
   c. Both an employee and an independent sales representative

10. According to the **Scripto** Court, which of the following is required for an agent to create sufficient nexus?

    a. The agent must work for only one principal.
    b. The agent must be a salesman and not an independent contractor.
    c. The agent must create a minimum connection between the state and the transaction.

11. The **Scripto** Court found that, unlike Miller Bros., Scripto had nexus. *True or False?*

Borders Online, LLC v. State Board of Equalization., ¶403-800, (May 31, 2005)

(California Court of Appeal, First Appellate District, No. A105488, 129 Cal. App. 4th 1179, 29 Cal. Rptr. 3d 176, May 31, 2005. Appeal from San Francisco County Superior Court, No. 414210.)

Author commentary. The *Borders Online* case outlines the 21st Century equivalent of an agency relationship and the impact on tax collection responsibilities when such a relationship exists. While one could read the *Borders Online* case as a rebuke of typical online relationships, one could also read the case as an enumeration of what not to do if you want to shield a related-party remote seller from the tax collection responsibility.

As you read through the case, note the emphasis on the two entities operating as independently as possible to avoid being characterized as the agent of the other for sales tax purposes. Maintaining as much autonomy as possible will protect the remote seller from having a sales tax collection responsibility because of their relationship with the in-state vendor.

Opinion. We face with increasing frequency issues at the junction of Internet technology and constitutional principles. This is another such case.

Borders Online, LLC (Online), a Delaware company, sold more than $1.5 million in merchandise over the Internet to California consumers in 1998 and 1999. Online's website included a notice that any goods purchased from Online could be returned to any Borders Books and Music store (Borders store). Under the policy of Borders, Inc. (the owner of Borders stores), customers could exchange the items or receive a credit card refund. Numerous Borders stores are located all over California. Borders, Inc. (Borders) and Online also engaged in incidental cross-marketing practices to benefit the Borders brand. Online and Borders are affiliated through a common parent company but are distinct corporate entities.

The State Board of Equalization (Board) determined that Borders was Online's representative operating in the state "for the purpose of selling" Online's goods, and therefore Online was required to collect and remit a use tax from its California customers for the period April 1, 1998, through September 30, 1999 (the disputed period). The primary questions posed by this appeal are whether Borders's activities on behalf of Online were "for the purpose of selling" Online's goods and whether, through Borders, Online had a sufficient presence in the state to justify the imposition of the tax collection burden. The trial court, on summary judgment, ruled in favor of the Board. Online challenges the ruling on the merits and argues the case should have gone to trial. We conclude the trial court's determination was correct, and affirm.

I. Factual and procedural background. Online is a limited liability corporation formed under Delaware law in 2001 with headquarters in Michigan. From April 1998 to September 1999, Online sold books, book accessories, magazines, compact discs, videotapes, and similar tangible goods over the Internet to customers, including customers in California.

It did not own or lease property in California during the disputed period and did not have any employees or bank accounts in the state. Online employees located outside California received and processed all orders placed through Online's website, Borders.com. Online neither collected tax from its California purchasers nor paid sales or use taxes to the Board for its sales to California purchasers during the disputed period.

Online was wholly owned by Borders Group, Inc. Borders Group, Inc., also owns Borders, which, in turn, owns Borders stores. Numerous Borders stores are located throughout California and in other states. Borders stores sell merchandise that is comparable to the goods sold by Online over the Internet. Receipts at Borders stores sometimes contained the phrase "Visit us online at www.Borders.com." Although Borders stores did not have facilities to assist customers wishing to place orders with Online, Borders's employees were encouraged to refer customers to Online. Visitors to Online's website could access a *link* to Borders's website (www.BordersStores.com) which provided advertising and promotional information for Borders stores, including a list of store locations.

Two people who served on Online's board of directors also served on Borders's three-person board of directors during the disputed period. All but two of the nine people who served as officers of Online during the disputed period, including the two people who served as president in 1998 and 1999, also served as officers of Borders at some point during the disputed period. Borders and Online shared a similar logo. They also shared some financial and market data but did not intermingle their corporate assets. Borders and Online filed their tax returns on the combined report basis pursuant to Revenue and Taxation Code §25101 et seq.

Online's California sales increased each quarter during the disputed period:

Period	California Sales
2d Quarter 1998	$40,176.92
3d Quarter 1998	$139,897.16
4th Quarter 1998	$248,294.13
1st Quarter 1999	$361,205.97
2d Quarter 1999	$365,988.29
3d Quarter 1999	$500,451.29

From September 30, 1998, to August 11, 1999, Online posted the following return policy on its website: "You may return items purchased at Borders. Com to any Borders Books and Music store within 30 days of the date the item was shipped.

All returns must be accompanied by a valid packing slip (your online receipt and shipping notification are not valid substitutes for a packing slip on returns to stores). Gift items may be returned or exchanged if they are accompanied by a valid gift packing slip. You may not return opened music or video items, unless they are defective."

Any merchandise returned to Borders pursuant to this policy was either absorbed into Borders's own inventory or disposed of. Borders did not charge Online for accepting returns of Online's merchandise. Borders also accepted returns of saleable merchandise presented without a receipt (including merchandise purchased from competitor retailers) for store credit, provided that Borders carried the returned items. However, exchanges or credit card refunds for returned items were routinely provided only to Borders and Online customers with receipts or packing slips.

On July 29, 1999, the Board sent a letter to Online stating the company was required to collect and remit use taxes on all sales to California purchasers because Online's affiliate Borders acted as Online's agent by accepting return merchandise. In stating its opinion that Online was required to pay a use tax, the Board relied on §6203(c)(2), which defines the term *retailer engaged in business in this state* as "[a]ny retailer having any representative, agent, salesperson, canvasser, independent contractor, or solicitor operating in this state under the authority of the retailer or its subsidiary for the purpose of selling, delivering, installing, assembling, or the taking of orders for any tangible personal property." The Board reasoned that Online was "engaged in business in California" because Borders was "acting as an agent by accepting return merchandise on behalf of [Online] as defined in [the company's] Web site return policy."

Online removed its return policy message from its website on August 11, 1999. The Board continued to regard Online as a retailer engaged in business in California, however, and again wrote to the company on October 25, 1999, stating Online was required to collect and pay state use tax. On January 27, 2000, the Board issued a notice of determination to Online for unpaid use taxes, plus interest and penalties, for Online's sales to California purchasers during the disputed period.

Online filed a petition for redetermination, which the Board denied in a memorandum opinion. The Board found that Online was covered by §6203(c)(2) because:

1. Borders was Online's authorized representative in California for the purpose of accepting returns from Online's California customers
2. The taking of returns constituted *selling* for purposes of the statute.

In so ruling, the Board held that the term *selling* includes "all activities that are an integral part of making sales." The Board reasoned that Online's favorable return policy was designed to induce potential customers who might otherwise not make an online purchase to place orders, and thus the policy was *integral* to selling in e-commerce transactions. The Board also ruled that Online had a sufficient physical presence in California (through Borders) to satisfy the commerce clause of the United States Constitution.

On November 5, 2001, the Board issued a notice of redetermination to Online for unpaid use taxes, plus interest (but not penalties) for the company's sales to California purchasers. Online paid $167,667.78 to the Board and then timely submitted a claim for refund, which the Board denied. After exhausting its administrative remedies, Online filed a complaint in San Francisco Superior Court seeking a refund. Its complaint alleged it was not a California retailer and therefore was not required to pay taxes under state law and claimed the Commerce Clause prohibited imposing taxes on the company.

The Board filed a motion for summary judgment, and the trial court granted the motion. The court held that:

1. Online was covered by section 6203(c)(2) because of Online's policy providing for returns at Borders stores.
2. The imposition of a tax on Online did not violate the Commerce Clause.
3. The fact that Online's return policy was not posted on its website during the entire disputed period did not affect the conclusion that Online had a sufficient physical presence in California to support a finding of *substantial nexus*.

Online timely appealed.

Borders acted under Online's authority as its agent. The trial court found that Online's return policy posted on its website provided *undisputed evidence* "confirm[ing] that Borders was [Online's] authorized agent or representative for the purpose of accepting returns of online merchandise from California purchasers."

It held this finding was supported by the fact that:

1. Each Borders store in the state would accept returns and provide a refund, store credit or exchange of Online's merchandise.
2. Borders encouraged its store employees to refer customers to Online's website.
3. Receipts at Borders stores sometimes invited patrons to "Visit us online at www.Borders.com."

The trial court concluded, "Borders' practice of providing unique and preferential services to Online purchasers by offering cash refunds to any purchaser of Online merchandise who wanted one, when it could refuse to do so for customers of Online's competitors, indicates that Borders provided such preferential services because it was Online's authorized agent or representative."

Online claims the trial court erred in ruling as a matter of law that Borders was Online's agent because issues of agency typically are questions of fact. It is true that "[t]he existence of an agency relationship is usually a question of fact, *unless the evidence is susceptible of but a single inference.*" [*Violette v. Shoup* (1993) 16 Cal.App.4th 611, 619, italics added.] Here, the undisputed evidence is susceptible of but one inference—that Borders was acting as Online's authorized agent or representative.

The term *representative* is defined as "[o]ne who stands for or acts on behalf of another." (Black's Law Dict. (7th ed. 1999) p. 1304, col. 2.) "An *agent* is one who represents another, called the *principal*, in dealings with third persons (Civ. Code, §2295)" [*Scholastic Book Clubs, Inc. v. State Bd. of Equalization* (1989) 207 Cal.App.3d 734, 737.] An agency relationship "may be implied based on conduct and circumstances." (*Id.* at pp. 737-738.)

In *Scholastic,* cited by the trial court, the appellant was an out-of-state mail order book seller that had no physical presence in California. It mailed catalogs to teachers, who distributed offer sheets to students and then forwarded orders to the appellant. The appellant claimed, as Online does in this case, that it was not subject to California's use tax because the teachers were not acting as its agents or representatives.

The court *disagreed* and held the teachers were acting under the appellant's authority, based on the fact that "[b]y accepting the orders, the payment and shipping the merchandise, appellant clearly and unequivocally ratified the acts of the teachers and confirmed their authority as appellant's agents or representatives." Likewise here, there is no dispute either that Online announced on its website that Borders was authorized to accept Online's merchandise for return, or that Borders would provide customers with an exchange, store credit, or a credit card credit. By accepting Online's merchandise for return, Borders acted on behalf of Online as its *agent* or *representative* in California.

Online claims the trial court erred in holding Borders was Online's agent because it failed to apply what it refers to as California's *four-factor test* to review the agency issue. It insists an agency relationship exists only all of the following are true:

1. The agent has power to alter legal relationships of the principal.
2. The agent acts as the fiduciary of the principal.
3. The principal can control the agent.
4. The agent consents to act as the principal's agent.

While it is true courts consider these factors when considering agency issues in various contexts, there is no bright-line *four-factor test* in determining agency. Online overstates its position in claiming the trial court erred by "failing to apply" such a test.

Indeed, the cases Online relies on to advocate the existence of the so-called *four-factor test* were decided in other contexts, analyzed far different factual situations, and did not necessarily apply each of the four factors cited by Online.

Online also claims that, although the trial court relied on a quotation from **Scholastic,** it disregarded the *four-factor test* that was applied in that case. On the contrary, **Scholastic** addressed only the appellant's authority over the teachers who took orders because of their *power* and *authority* to solicit orders. The court did not refer to a *four-factor test* but, instead, analyzed the particular facts of that case.

Online claims it had no *control* over Borders's action, but it does not dispute that Borders implemented the return policy posted on Online's website. Online also notes there was no written agreement between Online and Borders, but "[t]he creation of an agency relationship is not dependent upon the existence of a written agreement." In fact, "[t]he relationship may be implied based on conduct and circumstances, as well as by ratification." [*Scholastic, supra,* 207 Cal.App.3d at p. 737-738.]

It therefore does not matter, as Online claims, that Borders did not have the subjective belief it was Online's agent. By accepting Online's merchandise under the terms of Online's return policy, Borders was effectuating Online's policy— even if it was also Borders' own policy. The undisputed facts show Borders acted as Online's agent or representative and, therefore, Online meets the first part of §6203(c)(2)'s definition of a *retailer engaged in business* in California—as a retailer having a *representative* or *agent* operating in California.

Online contends, however, that the trial court denied it "an opportunity" to present evidence that there was no agency relationship between Online and Borders during the period in controversy. But Online does not explain why it declined to present such evidence to the trial court in connection with its opposition after the Board had shown that Borders stores accepted returns of Online's merchandise and that Borders referred customers to Online.

Specifically, Online claims there is no evidence regarding several "issues of material fact relating to the agency analysis." It argues there was no evidence regarding the extent of returns of Online merchandise to Borders during the disputed period, no evidence that Borders employees ever referred customers to Online's website, and no evidence that Online's sales in California were benefited by the return policy or by the printing of "Visit us online at www. Borders.com" on customer receipts.

Again, however, Online cannot simply point to an absence of evidence to avoid summary judgment. This is especially true where, as in this case, Borders did not track the extent of returns of Online merchandise, thereby making it impossible for the Board to provide evidence that Online claims should have been produced. Thus, we conclude the trial court correctly determined Borders acted as Online's agent.

Borders was *selling* for purposes of §6203(c)(2). The trial court concluded that by providing refunds and exchanges to Online's customers pursuant to Online's return policy, Borders was engaged in *selling* as that term is used in §6203(c)(2). The court reasoned that "the term *selling* may properly be defined to include all activities that constitute an integral part of inducing sales."

The term *selling* is not defined in the statute. The Board construed the term to include "all activities that are an integral part of making sales," and concluded that this interpretation accords with its "common usage." The Board reasoned:

> When out-of-state retailers that make offers of sale to potential customers in California authorize in-state representatives to take returns, these retailers acknowledge that the taking of returns is an integral part of their selling efforts. Such an acknowledgement comports with common sense because the provision of convenient and trustworthy return procedures can be crucial to an out-of-state retailer's ability to make sales. This is especially evident in the realm of e-commerce.

Online, by contrast, proposes the term *selling* be narrowly defined as "the act of making a sales transaction."

Although this court independently determines the meaning of a statute, if an agency charged with administering the statute issues its own interpretation, we will give due consideration to that construction. Here, the Board is responsible for administering the applicable statutes.

We think the Board's interpretation of the term *selling* is persuasive. In contrast, Online's narrow interpretation would mean that even if a local representative were to provide dramatic incentives to California customers to purchase the out-of-state retailer's goods, no tax could be imposed unless the representative is actually involved in the solicitation of the sale or the sale transaction itself.

We agree with the Board that Online's return policy undoubtedly made purchasing merchandise on its website more attractive to California customers, as they would know that returning or exchanging any unwanted items would be far simpler than if they purchased items from an e-commerce retailer with no presence in California.

Online contends this conclusion is a "theory of marketing without evidentiary support from the record" and that, as a factual matter, the policy was meant to benefit Borders, not Online. It also claims there was no evidence in the record that the return policy actually induced customers to purchase from Online. In effect, Online is contending the Board did not present a *prima facie* case that the returns-to-Borders-stores policy was an integral part of Online's sales activities. We disagree.

The Board concedes it bears the initial burden of demonstrating that Online's return policy was implemented for the purpose of selling goods in California. It argues, however, that it need not prove the buyers' motives because it is the intent of the seller that is relevant. The return policy manifestly was not put in place to maximize *returns* of Online's merchandise, and Online does not contend otherwise.

Therefore, the Board concludes, the only reasonable inference is that the policy was created for the purpose of inducing *sales* in California. This conclusion rests on the logical inferences that at least some online consumers will not place orders if the retailer does not provide a return policy "worthy of confidence" and, therefore, Online's ability to offer these potential customers convenient returns and exchanges at nearby reputable brick-and-mortar stores would definitely help promote confidence.

We think these compelling inferences, drawn from the undisputed facts, are sufficient to present a *prima facie* case—shifting the burden to Online to present evidence (or to argue contrary inferences) and, thus, creating a triable issue of fact. Online did not do so.

Instead, it merely argued that the Board's definition of *selling* was overbroad, and that Border's actions on Online's behalf did not constitute selling. Online now contends that the trial court denied it the opportunity to present evidence that its return policy was not a cause of sales increases in 1998. But the time to present such evidence was at the summary judgment motion.

As to the merits, Online cannot seriously dispute that its return policy made its website more appealing to potential customers. One of the documents Online produced to the Board—apparently an information sheet prepared for Borders's employees—described Online as "an extension of the Borders brand" and touted the reciprocal benefits of cross-referrals:

> If we don't refer customers to Borders.com, those interested in purchasing online will go to Amazon or barnesandnoble.com. Additionally, well under five percent of visitors to the site purchase online, but 100 percent receive a message about the Borders brand and will experience our active promotion of Borders stores. Even if the return policy also benefited Borders, that does not mean the policy was any less attractive to Online's customers.

Whatever the subjective intent of Online or its individual customers, the Board's conclusion that Online's return policy is integral to making sales because of its attractiveness, convenience, and trustworthiness is persuasive—especially in the context of e-commerce.

Our analysis is reinforced by the fact that Online's return policy contemplates that "sales" may take place pursuant to the policy. Borders was authorized to provide Online's customers with store credit that could be used for the future purchase of Borders merchandise. Borders also would exchange Online's merchandise for its own merchandise.

Either transaction certainly falls within the Legislature's definition of the term *sale*, under §6006, subdivision (a). When considered in tandem with other cross-selling techniques, such as Borders's employees referring customers to Online and Borders's receipts printed with the message "Visit us online at www.Borders.com," the Board's conclusion that Borders was Online's representative *for the purpose of selling* Online's goods is a correct application of the law.

The Trial Court's ruling is consistent with the Commerce Clause. It is well settled that under the Commerce Clause, there must be a sufficient connection between a state and a retailer in order for the state to impose a use tax on the seller's goods. This nexus prevents states from otherwise imposing impermissible burdens on interstate commerce. A tax passes Constitutional muster only if it is applied to an activity with a substantial nexus with the taxing State.

In *Quill*, the U.S. Supreme Court reversed an opinion of the North Dakota Supreme Court that permitted a tax on a mail-order business with no physical presence in the state. Confirming the *bright-line* rule articulated in *National Bellas Hess*, the *Quill* court held that a use tax is impermissible where a seller's only connection with a particular state is orders placed and merchandise delivered through a common carrier or the U.S. mail.

A seller must have a *physical presence* in a state to satisfy the Commerce Clause. As the U.S. Supreme Court has observed, the crucial factor governing nexus is whether the activities performed in the state on behalf of the taxpayer are significantly associated with the taxpayer's ability to establish and maintain a market in the state for the sales. Online does not dispute it established and maintained a robust market for sales in California. The question is whether the record satisfies the remainder of the test—i.e., that the activities performed by Borders on its behalf were significantly associated with Online's ability to establish and maintain its California market. We conclude that they were.

As an initial matter, we address Online's position that a state has no authority to impose a tax collection duty on an out-of-state retailer unless its in-state representative is actually making sales, as was the case in *Scripto*. Online's formulation of the test is too constricted. The key question when testing a state's taxing authority against the dormant Commerce Clause is not whether the foreign company has agents soliciting sales in the state. The question, rather, is whether the activities of the retailer's in-state representatives are significantly associated with its ability to *establish and maintain* a market in the state for the sales. While the cases assess a combination of activities that often include solicitation or sales, the analysis turns on the totality of the activities undertaken to maintain a successful market.

Of particular interest is the clarification of this issue by New York's highest court in ***Orvis Co. v. Tax Tribunal*** [(1995) 86 N.Y.2d 165]. After conducting an in-depth review of Commerce Clause jurisprudence before and after ***Quill***, the Court concluded that the Supreme Court in ***Quill*** had reluctantly reaffirmed the *bright-line **Bellas Hess*** rule requiring *some* physical presence to support taxation, while at the same time endorsing a more flexible approach of later commerce clause jurisprudence in which "the *quid pro quo* for State taxation could be found in the benefits and protections the State confers in providing for a stable and secure legal-economic environment for a mail-order vendor's substantial marketing efforts aimed at the taxing State."

> Accordingly, the New York court articulated the Commerce Clause standard in this way: While a physical presence of the vendor is required, it need not be substantial. Rather, it must be demonstrably more than a 'slightest presence'. And it may be manifested by the presence in the taxing State of the vendor's property or the conduct of economic activities in the taxing State performed by the vendor's personnel or on its behalf.

Although other courts have disagreed with this interpretation of ***Quill***, we think ***Orvis*** is more in keeping with the realities of 21st century marketing and technology, which increasingly affords opportunities for out-of-state vendors to establish a strong economic presence in California, utilizing California's *legal-economic environment*, while maintaining only a minimal or vicarious presence here.

Thus, in ***Orvis***, an out-of-state seller of computer hardware and software included in its sales agreement a promise to provide one on-site visit should problems arise within 60 days of the sale. The taxing authority's audit revealed that there had been 41 such trouble-shooting trips made to New York during a three-year period in which 154 sales transactions had been made to New York customers.

The court concluded that this provided ample support for the tax tribunal's findings that the "trouble-shooting visits to New York vendees and its assurances to prospective customers that it would make such visits enhanced sales and significantly contributed to [the vendor's] ability to establish and maintain a market for the computer hardware and software it sold in New York. [The vendor's] activities in New York were, thus, definite and of greater significance than merely a slightest presence [citation]."

In sum, there is no requirement that the out-of-state retailer's in-state representative be engaged in the *solicitation of sales* or in *sales transactions* to satisfy the substantial *nexus* required by the Commerce Clause. We turn now to application of the nexus requirement to the undisputed facts before us.

We have already determined that Online's return policy was part of its strategy to build a market in California. We further note that Borders's efforts on Online's behalf were *not* limited to accepting returns from and providing exchanges and credit card refunds to Online customers. Borders's receipts were sometimes imprinted with "Visit us online at www.Borders.com," and Borders's employees were encouraged to refer customers to Online to find merchandise not available at Borders stores.

The cross-selling synergy was also maintained by the use of similar logos, by the link to Borders' website from Online's website, and by the sharing of some market and financial data between the two entities. Online generated more than $1.5 million in sales in California in 18 months. These facts amply support the conclusion that Online had a *representative* with a *physical presence* in the State, and that the representative's activities were significantly associated with Online's ability to establish and maintain a market in California for the sales.

Online contends the trial court's conclusion is inconsistent with *SFA Folio Collections, Inc. v. Tracy* [(Ohio 1995) 652 N.E.2d 693, 697] and *Bloomingdale's v. Dept. of Revenue* [(Pa.Cmmw.Ct. 1989) 567 A.2d 773, 778], which held that a department store's acceptance of returns from an affiliated out-of-state mail-order business was insufficient to create a substantial *nexus* between the mail-order company and the state.

But in *SFA Folio Collections,* the mail-order house did not formulate or initiate the return policy. Rather, the returns were accepted according to the department store's own policy for its own benefit and for the convenience of its customers. And in *Bloomingdale's* the acceptance of two returns from mail-order customers was considered an aberration from the normal practice.

Online also contends that the Board must present evidence that quantifies the activities actually undertaken by Borders on behalf of Online establishing that those activities had more than a de minimis effect on Online's sales. Here, Borders did not keep records of the returns from Online customers and, presumably, also did not either record each instance in which an employee referred a customer to Online or keep track of how many receipts were imprinted with "Visit us online at www.Borders.com."

Accordingly, we cannot see how such evidence would be assembled. We do agree that evidence of *de minimis* local activities or proof that the local activities do not generate any significant proportion of local sales would create an issue of fact that would have to be resolved at trial. No such evidence was introduced by Online, other than a declaration by Borders's former tax manager that Borders "expected" only a small amount of returns.

Our holding is not affected by the fact Online's return policy was not posted on its website during the entire disputed period. The trial court held that its finding Online had a substantial nexus with California was not affected by evidence that the company's return policy was not in effect during the entire disputed period. Quoting *Scripto,* the trial court's order stated, "[e] vidence that an out-of-state retailer's physical presence in the taxing state was not continuous throughout the *entire* tax period in controversy is 'without constitutional significance.'" The trial court also cited *Scholastic.* The trial court's reliance on these cases was somewhat misplaced.

In *Scripto,* the Supreme Court upheld the imposition of Florida's use tax on a Georgia company that used jobbers in Florida to sell its goods. The Court concluded that although the jobbers were not regular employees of the taxpayer and did not work full time for the company, "such a fine distinction is without constitutional significance." This conclusion was based on the fact that the 10 jobbers working in Florida provided "continuous local solicitation" in the state and secured a "substantial flow of goods" into the state. The fact the jobbers worked for several principals did not change the fact they provided the taxpayer with its sales in the state.

Similarly, in *Scholastic,* the Court held that the fact teachers did not work exclusively for the appellant book company did not affect whether they provided a substantial *nexus* with California, because the company depended on them for all its revenues in California. In both *Scripto* and *Scholastic,* the courts looked at the extent of the *actions* of the taxpayers' agents and did not consider the issue presented here—whether a lack of temporal continuity in advertising a policy designed to induce sales affected the constitutional analysis.

We conclude that the fact Online's return policy was posted for less than 11 months during the 18-month disputed period does not alter the Constitutional analysis. As Online itself notes, the question for purposes of the Commerce Clause is the "nature and extent" of the activities in the taxing state. Here, Borders stood ready to accept returns and issue refunds for all Online merchandise purchased in California, whether or not this policy was actually posted on Online's website. All the while, Borders and Online were involved in cross-promotional activities, promoting the Borders "brand."

Were we to accept Online's argument that a substantial nexus did not exist during the entire time period, the company would be free to simply promote the policy through its in-state agent and reap the benefits of that policy while avoiding the state's use tax by promoting, and then by simply removing, the policy on its website.

In short, we conclude that the imposition of a use tax on Online during the entire disputed period does *not* violate the Commerce Clause of the U.S. Constitution.

The judgment is affirmed.

CONCLUSION

As is the case with most tax issues, the courts have played an important role in helping to define the limits for taxpayers and taxing jurisdictions alike. Understanding the judicial boundaries of nexus is important, since there are clearly opportunities to leverage and hazards to avoid in the nexus area. While sales tax is currently governed by the *physical presence* standard, states and taxpayers alike are continuing to push the limits of that decision.

Recent decisions, such as in the ***Borders Online*** case, provide guidance on what to avoid so that a remote online entity can avoid a tax collection responsibility. For many taxpayers, business needs will dictate the activities undertaken and will generally take precedence over tax filing requirements. In such an instance, care must be exercised in making nexus determinations to avoid exposing the remote selling entity to uncollected taxes.

> **CAUTION**
>
> The statute of limitations does not begin to toll until a return is *filed*. So, if a taxpayer has never filed a return and has nexus, a state can force collection of tax as far back as the state can establish a connection without limitation on the number of years.
>
> For example, if a taxpayer has been doing business for 10 years and never filed a tax return and gets picked up in a nexus audit, the state can force that taxpayer to pay all 10 years of tax, plus interest, and likely a substantial penalty.

So, when it comes to nexus determinations, caution should be the guiding principle to avoid future potential liabilities. Taxpayers who continuously assess the strength of their positions throughout the audit will be better prepared to make these decisions.

STUDY QUESTIONS

12. The ***Borders Online*** case is significant to taxpayers because:

a. It shows that filing requirements should take precedence over business needs.

b. It shows what to do to so that a remote entity can avoid a tax collection responsibility.

c. It shows that two entities must operate as independently as possible to avoid one being viewed as the agent for the other.

13. What was a primary reason why Borders was considered an *agent* of Online by the court?

a. Border's consent to act as Online's principal

b. Online's return policy

c. Online's control of Borders

14. Based on the decision in **Borders Online,** which facts below would most likely cause Company A to be considered Company B's *agent?*

a. Company A belongs to the same parent company as Company B.

b. Company A refers customers to Company B's online site for purchases.

c. Company A accepts a return from an out-of-state affiliated mail-order business.

15. There is a *bright-line*, four-factor test that must be used to determine agency. *True or False?*

MODULE 2: SALES AND USE TAXES — CHAPTER 7

Constitutional Issues

This chapter presents and discusses the most influential cases challenging the U.S. Constitution's Commerce Clause and Equal Protection Clause.

LEARNING OBJECTIVES

Upon completing this chapter, the professional will be able to:

- State the prohibitions covered under the Commerce Clause and the Equal Protection Clause
- List and state the origin of the four essential elements necessary for a tax to be considered unconstitutional under the Commerce Clause
- Explain the significance, arguments, and findings in each of the three cases dealing with constitutional issues discussed in this course

OVERVIEW

The U.S. Constitution provides a framework that any taxing jurisdiction must follow if it intends to impose a tax upon a taxpayer. The key constitutional provisions that will be reviewed in this chapter are the Commerce Clause and the Equal Protection Clause. The Due Process Clause, another important clause, is addressed in *Nexus Issues*—chapter 6 of this course.

In general terms, the Commerce Clause prohibits states from interfering with interstate commerce as that is the exclusive domain of the U.S. Congress.

Under the Equal Protection Clause, taxing jurisdictions are prohibited from making laws that single out specific taxpayers and impose tax on their activities in a discriminatory manner. The state imposing the tax must be able to show that there is a rational basis for imposing tax on a specific group of taxpayers for the tax to be considered constitutional.

Lastly, the Due Process Clause requires that the taxing jurisdiction only impose tax upon activities that have a substantial nexus or level of activity in the taxing jurisdiction.

One important consideration involving the constitutionality of a taxing statute is that it will not be deemed to be unconstitutional unless or until it is challenged by a taxpayer in the courts. Therefore, taxpayers need to be attuned to potential problems that may mean a tax is unconstitutional. The purpose of this chapter is to make you aware of some of the more common constitutional issues that may arise in the administration of sales and use tax compliance.

This chapter will explore the judicial history of the Commerce Clause and Equal Protection Clause. The cases that are included have been redacted and edited for easier reading. Also, footnotes and some citations and references in the cases have been omitted.

COMMERCE CLAUSE

The Commerce Clause states that "Congress shall have the power ... to regulate commerce with foreign nations, and among the several states, and with the Indian Tribes" (U.S. Constitution, Art. 1). Therefore, only Congress may impose laws and regulations that regulate or impact interstate commerce. Where states typically overstep their authority regarding the Commerce Clause is in enacting tax laws that give in-state taxpayers some advantage over out-of-state taxpayers.

For example, in-state taxpayers may be given a credit that is only available to taxpayers performing certain activities within the state and not available to out-of-state taxpayers performing the same or similar activities from outside the state.

Another common example of a discriminatory tax structure is to impose tax on goods coming from outside the state, but not impose a comparable tax on goods coming from within the state. While these over-reaches in authority are frequently intended as a way to stimulate local economic development in a state, they occur more often than you might expect.

> **PLANNING POINTER**
>
> Taxpayers need to be alert to potentially unconstitutional taxes, as it may affect the way the taxpayer complies. If substantial tax amounts are involved, it also may be worthwhile to challenge the state's authority to impose the tax in court.

Complete Auto Transit, Inc. v. Brady, Chairman, Mississippi State Tax Commission, U.S. Supreme Court, 430 US 274, (Mar. 7, 1977)

Author commentary. The *Complete Auto Transit* case is a landmark case in state and local taxation and provides a guideline for states to follow in enacting taxes that are within a constitutional safe harbor. As you read through the case, focus on the four essential elements that the Court identified for a tax to be constitutional:

1. There must be a substantial nexus with the taxing state.
2. The tax must be fairly apportioned.
3. The tax must not discriminate against interstate commerce.
4. The tax must be fairly related to the services provided by the state.

A redacted version of the case follows:

The Mississippi tax imposed on the taxpayer was a sales tax levied for the privilege of engaging or continuing in business or doing business in the state and was imposed as a percentage of gross income.

The taxpayer, a Michigan corporation, was a transporter of motor vehicles. The vehicles were shipped into Jackson, Mississippi, and were then transported by the taxpayer to Mississippi dealers—usually within 48 hours. The taxpayer argued that its transportation was a part of an interstate movement, and that the tax was unconstitutional as applied to operations in interstate commerce.

The Court emphasized that the taxpayer did *not* allege that:

● Its activity taxed by Mississippi did not have a sufficient nexus with the state to subject it to taxation

● The tax discriminated against interstate commerce, OR

● The tax was unfairly apportioned or that the tax was unrelated to services provided by the state

Rather, the attack on the Mississippi tax was based *solely* on prior U.S. Supreme Court's *Spector* rule. The *Spector* rule states that a tax on the privilege of engaging in an activity in a state may not be applied to an activity that is part of interstate commerce.

The Court noted that the *Spector* rule, which reflects the philosophy that interstate commerce should enjoy a sort of free trade immunity from state taxation, looks only to the fact that the incidence of a tax is the privilege of doing business, with no consideration of the practical effect of the tax.

Many other decisions, however, have sustained state taxation of companies doing exclusively interstate business:

● When the tax was related to local activities

● When the tax was nondiscriminatory and properly apportioned, AND

● When the state had provided benefits and protection for the activities for which it was justified in asking fair and reasonable compensation

The Court concluded that while the view of the Commerce Clause that gave rise to the *Spector* rule was not without substance, later decisions had rejected the proposition that interstate commerce is immune from state taxation.

Thus, the *Spector* rule has been stripped of any practical significance and has become merely a hazard for unwary draftsmen of tax laws. Because economic realities, not labels or phraseology, should determine whether a tax on interstate activities is constitutional, the Court *overruled* the *Spector* decision. Since the only challenge to the Mississippi tax was that it was imposed on nothing more than the privilege of doing business that was interstate, the tax is *constitutional*. Mr. Justice Blackmun delivered the unanimous opinion of the Court:

Opinion. A Mississippi tax on the privilege of doing business in the State held *not* to violate the Commerce Clause when (*Spector Motor Service v. O'Connor,* 340 US 602, overruled. Pp. 6-15. 330 So. 2d 268, affirmed):

- It is applied to an interstate activity (here the transportation by motor carrier in Mississippi to Mississippi dealers of cars manufactured outside the State) with a substantial nexus with the taxing State.
- It is fairly apportioned.
- It does not discriminate against interstate commerce.
- It is fairly related to the services provided by the State.

Issue. Once again we are presented with "'the perennial problem of the validity of a state tax for the privilege of carrying on, within a state, certain activities' relating to a corporation's operation of an interstate business" [*Colonial Pipeline Co. v. Traigle,* 421 US 100, 101 (1975), quoting *Memphis Gas Co. v. Stone,* 335 US 80, 85 (1948)].

The issue in this case is whether Mississippi runs afoul of the Commerce Clause (Const., Art. I, § 8, cl. 3) when it applies the tax it imposes on "the privilege of ... doing business" within the State to appellant's activity in interstate commerce. The Supreme Court of Mississippi unanimously sustained the tax *against* appellant's constitutional challenge [330 So. 2d 268 (1976)].

The Mississippi Tax

The taxes in question are sales taxes assessed by the Mississippi State Tax Commission against the appellant, Complete Auto Transit, Inc., for the period from August 1, 1968, through July 31, 1972. The assessments were made pursuant to the following Mississippi statutes:

> There is hereby levied and assessed and shall be collected privilege taxes for the privilege of engaging or continuing in business or doing business within this state to be determined by the application of rates against gross proceeds of sales or gross income or values, as the case may be, as provided in the following sections (Miss. Code Ann. §10105 (1942), as amended).

> Upon every person operating a pipeline, railroad, airplane, bus, truck, or any other transportation business for the transportation of persons or property for compensation or hire between points within this State, there is hereby levied, assessed, and shall be collected, a tax equal to five per cent (5%) of the gross income of such business ..." (Miss. Code Ann. §10109(2), as amended).

Facts. Appellant is a Michigan corporation engaged in the business of transporting motor vehicles by motor carrier for General Motors Corporation. General Motors assembles outside Mississippi vehicles that are destined for dealers within the State. The vehicles are then shipped by rail to Jackson, Miss., where they are loaded onto appellant's trucks and transported by appellant to the Mississippi dealers—usually within 48 hours. Appellant is paid on a contract basis for the transportation from the railhead to the dealers.

By letter dated October 5, 1971, the Mississippi Tax Commission informed appellant that it was being assessed taxes and interest totaling $122,160.59 for the sales of transportation services during the three-year period from August 1, 1968, through July 31, 1971. Remittance within 10 days was requested.

By similar letter dated December 28, 1972, the Commission advised appellant of an assessment of $42,990.89 for the period from August 1, 1971, through July 31, 1972. Appellant paid the assessments under protest and, in April 1973, pursuant to §10121.1, as amended, of the 1942 Code (now §27-65-47 of the 1972 Code), instituted the present refund action in the Chancery Court of the First Judicial District of Hinds County.

Appellant claimed that its transportation was but one part of an interstate movement, and that the taxes assessed and paid were unconstitutional as applied to operations in interstate commerce. The Chancery Court, in an unreported opinion, sustained the assessments.

Mississippi Supreme Court's decision. The Mississippi Supreme Court affirmed. It concluded:

> It will be noted that Taxpayer has a large operation in this State. It is dependent upon the State for police protection and other State services the same as other citizens. It should pay its fair share of taxes so long, but only so long, as the tax does not discriminate against interstate commerce, and there is no danger of interstate commerce being smothered by cumulative taxes of several states. There is no possibility of any other state duplicating the tax involved in this case (330 So. 2d, at 272).

Taxpayer's contention. Appellant, in its complaint in Chancery Court, did *not* allege that:
- Its activity which Mississippi taxes does not have a sufficient nexus with the State
- The tax discriminates against interstate commerce
- The tax is unfairly apportioned, OR
- It is unrelated to services provided by the State

No such claims were made before the Mississippi Supreme Court and, although the appellant argues here that a tax on "the privilege of doing interstate commerce" creates an unacceptable risk of discrimination and undue burdens, it does not claim that discrimination or undue burdens exist in fact.

Appellant's attack is based solely on decisions of this Court holding that a tax on the "privilege" of engaging in an activity in the State may not be applied to an activity that is part of interstate commerce. This rule looks only to the fact that the incidence of the tax is the "privilege of doing business;" it deems irrelevant any consideration of the practical effect of the tax. The rule reflects an underlying philosophy that interstate commerce should enjoy a sort of "free trade" immunity from state taxation.

Tax Commission's contention. Appellee, in its turn, relies on decisions of this Court stating that, "[i]t was not the purpose of the commerce clause to relieve those engaged in interstate commerce from their just share of state tax burden even though it increases the cost of doing the business" [*Western Live Stock v. Bureau of Revenue,* 303 US 250, 254 (1938)].

These decisions have considered not the formal language of the tax statute but, rather, its practical effect, and they have sustained a tax against Commerce Clause challenge when the tax:

- Is applied to an activity with a substantial nexus with the taxing state
- Is fairly apportioned
- Does not discriminate against interstate commerce, and
- Is fairly related to the services provided by the State

Over the years, the Court has applied this practical analysis in approving many types of tax that avoided running afoul of the prohibition against taxing the "privilege of doing business," but in each instance it has refused to overrule the prohibition.

Under the present state of the law, the *Spector* rule has no relationship to economic realities. Rather, it stands only as a trap for the unwary draftsman.

Case Law

The modern origin of the *Spector* rule may be found in *Freeman v. Hewit, supra.* At issue in *Freeman* was the application of an Indiana tax upon "the receipt of the entire gross income" of residents and domiciliaries. Indiana sought to impose this tax on income generated when a trustee of an Indiana estate instructed his local stockbroker to sell certain securities.

The broker arranged with correspondents in New York to sell the securities on the New [York] Stock Exchange. The securities were sold and the New York brokers, after deducting expense and commission, transmitted the proceeds to the Indiana broker who in turn delivered them (less his commission) to the trustee. The Indiana Supreme Court sustained the tax, but this Court reversed it.

Justice Frankfurter, speaking for five Members of the Court, announced a blanket prohibition against any state taxation imposed directly on an interstate transaction. He explicitly deemed unnecessary to the decision of the case any showing of discrimination against interstate commerce or error in apportionment of the tax.

He recognized that a State could constitutionally:

- Tax local manufacture
- Impose license taxes on corporations doing business in the State
- Tax property within the State, and
- Tax the privilege of residence in the State and measure the privilege by net income, including that derived from interstate commerce

Nevertheless, a direct tax on interstate sales, even if fairly apportioned and nondiscriminatory, was held to be unconstitutional *per se.*

Justice Rutledge, in a lengthy concurring opinion, argued that the tax should be judged by its economic effects rather than by its formal phrasing. After reviewing the Court's prior decisions, he concluded that, "The fact is that 'direct incidence' of a state tax or regulation ... has long since been discarded as being itself sufficient to outlaw state legislation." In his view, a state tax is unconstitutional *only* if the:

- Activity lacks the necessary connection with the taxing state to give *jurisdiction to tax*
- Tax discriminates against interstate commerce, or
- Activity is subject to multiple taxation

Although the rule announced in **Freeman** might have been utilized as the keystone of a movement toward absolute immunity of interstate commerce from state taxation, the Court consistently has indicated that "interstate commerce may be made to pay its way," and has moved toward a standard of permissibility of state taxation based upon its actual effect rather than its legal terminology.

The Court recognized that "where a taxpayer is engaged both in intrastate and interstate commerce, a state may tax the privilege of carrying on intrastate business and, within reasonable limits, may compute the amount of the charge by applying the tax rate to a fair proportion of the taxpayer's business done within the state, including both interstate and intrastate."

It held, nevertheless, that a tax on the "privilege" of doing business is unconstitutional if applied against what is *exclusively interstate* commerce. The dissenters argued, on the other hand, that there is no constitutional difference between an *exclusively interstate* business and a *mixed* business, and that a fairly apportioned and nondiscriminatory tax on either type is not prohibited by the Commerce Clause.

Spector **Case Overruled**

In this case, of course, we are confronted with a situation like that presented in *Spector*. The tax is labeled a privilege tax "for the privilege of ... doing business" in Mississippi (§10105 of the State's 1942 Code, as amended), and the activity taxed is, or has been assumed to be, interstate commerce. We note again that no claim is made that the activity is not sufficiently connected to the State to justify a tax, or that the tax is not fairly related to benefits provided the taxpayer, or that the tax discriminates against interstate commerce, or that the tax is not fairly apportioned.

The view of the Commerce Clause that gave rise to the rule of *Spector* perhaps was not without some substance. Nonetheless, the possibility of defending it in the abstract does not alter the fact that the Court has rejected the proposition that interstate commerce is immune from state taxation:

> It is a truism that the mere act of carrying on business in interstate commerce does not exempt a corporation from state taxation. 'It was not the purpose of the commerce clause to relieve those engaged in interstate commerce from their just share of state tax burden even though it increases the cost of doing business' [***Western Live Stock v. Bureau of Revenue,*** 303 US 250, 254 (1938)] (***Colonial Pipeline Co. v. Traigle,*** 421 US, at 108).

Not only has the philosophy underlying the rule been rejected, but the rule itself has been stripped of any practical significance.

If Mississippi had called its tax one on *net income* or on the *going concern value* of appellant's business, the ***Spector*** rule could not invalidate it. There is no economic consequence that follows necessarily from the use of the particular words, *privilege of doing business*, and a focus on that formalism merely obscures the question whether the tax produces a forbidden effect.

Simply put, the ***Spector*** rule does not address the problems with which the Commerce Clause is concerned. Accordingly, we now reject the rule of ***Spector,*** that a state tax on the *privilege of doing business* is *per se* unconstitutional when it is applied to interstate commerce, and that case is overruled.

There being no objection to Mississippi's tax on appellant except that it was imposed on nothing other than the "privilege of doing business" that is interstate, the judgment of the Supreme Court of Mississippi is affirmed.

It is so ordered.

STUDY QUESTIONS

1. Which clause of the U.S. Constitution *prohibits* jurisdictions from passing laws that impose tax on specific taxpayers' activities in a discriminatory manner?
   a. Commerce Clause
   b. Equal Protection Clause
   c. Due Process Clause

2. The opinion in **Complete Auto Transit** did all **except** which of the following?
   a. Overruled the **Spector** decision
   b. Identified specific elements necessary for a tax to be considered unconstitutional
   c. Held that a Mississippi tax on the privilege of doing business in the state was unconstitutional

3. Which of the following is a *requirement* for a tax to be considered constitutional under the Commerce Clause?
   a. The tax must be fairly related to services provided by the state.
   b. The tax must be applied to an activity that has at least a minimal nexus connection with the taxing state.
   c. The tax must be apportioned primarily to the taxing state.

West Lynn Creamery, Inc. et al. v. Jonathan Healy, Commissioner of Massachusetts Department of Food and Agriculture, U.S. Supreme Court, 512 US 186, (Jun. 17, 1994)

Author Commentary. The *West Lynn Creamery* case in Massachusetts provides an example of a tax that was held to be discriminatory because it imposed a greater burden on interstate than intrastate commerce. As you read through the case, focus on the discussion of what constitutes a *discriminatory tax* and why this particular tax was held to be discriminatory.

Opinion. Justice Stevens delivered the opinion of the Court.

A Massachusetts pricing order imposes an assessment on all fluid milk sold by dealers to Massachusetts retailers. About two-thirds of that milk is produced out of State. The entire assessment, however, is distributed to Massachusetts dairy farmers. The question presented is whether the pricing order unconstitutionally discriminates against interstate commerce. We hold that it does.

Background. Petitioner West Lynn Creamery, Inc., is a milk dealer licensed to do business in Massachusetts. It purchases raw milk, which it processes, packages, and sells to wholesalers, retailers, and other milk dealers. About 97 percent of the raw milk it purchases is produced by out-of-state farmers. Petitioner LeComte's Dairy, Inc., is also a licensed Massachusetts milk dealer. It purchases all of its milk from West Lynn and distributes it to retail outlets in Massachusetts.

Since 1937, the Agricultural Marketing Agreement Act has authorized the Secretary of Agriculture to regulate the minimum prices paid to producers of raw milk by issuing marketing orders for particular geographic areas (50 Stat. 246, as amended, 7 U.S.C. §601 *et seq.*).

While the Federal Government sets minimum prices based on local conditions, those prices have not been so high as to prevent substantial competition among producers in different States. In the 1980's and early 1990's, Massachusetts dairy farmers began to lose market share to lower cost producers in neighboring States. In response, the Governor of Massachusetts appointed a Special Commission to study the dairy industry.

The Commission found that many producers had sold their dairy farms during the past decade and that, if prices paid to farmers for their milk were not significantly increased, a majority of the remaining farmers in Massachusetts would be "forced out of business within the year." On January 28, 1992, relying on the Commission's Report, the Commissioner of the Massachusetts Department of Food and Agriculture (respondent) declared a State of Emergency.

In his declaration he noted that the average federal blend price had declined from $14.67 per hundred pounds (cwt) of raw milk in 1990 to $12.64/cwt in 1991, while costs of production for Massachusetts farmers had risen to an estimated average of $15.50/cwt. He concluded:

> Regionally, the industry is in serious trouble and ultimately, a federal solution will be required. In the meantime, we must act on the state level to preserve our local industry, maintain reasonable minimum prices for the dairy farmers, thereby ensure a continuous and adequate supply of fresh milk for our market, and protect the public health.

Promptly after his declaration of emergency, respondent issued the pricing order that is challenged in this proceeding.

The order requires every *dealer* in Massachusetts to make a monthly *premium payment* into the Massachusetts Dairy Equalization Fund. Each month the fund is distributed to Massachusetts producers. Each Massachusetts producer receives a share of the total fund equal to his proportionate contribution to the State's total production of raw milk.

Petitioners West Lynn and LeComte's complied with the pricing order for two months, paying almost $200,000 into the Massachusetts Dairy Equalization Fund. Starting in July 1992, however, petitioners refused to make the premium payments, and the respondent commenced license revocation proceedings. Petitioners then filed an action in state court seeking an injunction against enforcement of the order on the ground that it violated the Commerce Clause of the Federal Constitution. The state court denied relief and respondent conditionally revoked their licenses.

The parties agreed to an expedited appellate procedure, and the Supreme Judicial Court of Massachusetts transferred the cases to its own docket. It affirmed, because it concluded that "the pricing order does not discriminate on its face, is evenhanded in its application, and only incidentally burdens interstate commerce" [*West Lynn Creamery, Inc. v. Commissioner of Dept. of Food and Agriculture*, 415 Mass. 8, 15, 611 N.E.2d 239, 243 (1993)].

The Court noted that the "pricing order was designed to aid only Massachusetts producers." It conceded that "[c]ommon sense" indicated that the plan has an "adverse impact on interstate commerce" and that "the fund distribution scheme does burden out-of-State producers." Nevertheless, the Court asserted that "the burden is incidental given the purpose and design of the program." Because it found that the "local benefits" provided to the Commonwealth's dairy industry "outweigh any incidental burden on interstate commerce," it sustained the constitutionality of the pricing order. We granted certiorari and now reverse.

The Commerce Clause. The Commerce Clause vests Congress with ample power to enact legislation providing for the regulation of prices paid to farmers for their products. An affirmative exercise of that power led to the promulgation of the federal order setting minimum milk prices.

The Commerce Clause also limits the power of the Commonwealth of Massachusetts to adopt regulations that discriminate against interstate commerce.

> "This 'negative' aspect of the Commerce Clause prohibits economic protectionism—that is, regulatory measures designed to benefit in-state economic interests by burdening out-of-state competitors. … Thus, state statutes that clearly discriminate against interstate commerce are routinely struck down … unless the discrimination is demonstrably justified by a valid factor unrelated to economic protectionism" [*New Energy Co. of Indiana v. Limbach*, 486 US 269, 273-274 (1988)].

The paradigmatic example of a law discriminating against interstate commerce is the protective tariff or customs duty, which taxes goods imported from other States, but does not tax similar products produced in State.

A *tariff* is an attractive measure because it simultaneously raises revenue and benefits local producers by burdening their out-of-state competitors. Nevertheless, it violates the principle of the unitary national market by handicapping out-of-state competitors, thus artificially encouraging in-state production even when the same goods could be produced at lower cost in other States.

Because of their distorting effects on the geography of production, tariffs have long been recognized as violative of the Commerce Clause. In fact, tariffs against the products of other States are so patently unconstitutional that our cases do not reveal a single attempt by any State to enact one.

Instead, the cases are filled with state laws that aspire to reap some of the benefits of tariffs by other means. In *Baldwin v. G.A.F. Seelig, Inc.,* the State of New York attempted to protect its dairy farmers from the adverse effects of Vermont competition by establishing a single minimum price for all milk, whether produced in New York or elsewhere [294 US 511 (1935)]. This Court did not hesitate, however, to strike it down. Writing for a unanimous Court, Justice Cardozo reasoned:

> Neither the power to tax nor the police power may be used by the state of destination with the aim and effect of establishing an economic barrier against competition with the products of another state or the labor of its residents. Restrictions so contrived are an unreasonable clog upon the mobility of commerce. They set up what is equivalent to a rampart of customs duties designed to neutralize advantages belonging to the place of origin.

Thus, because the minimum price regulation had the same effect as a tariff or customs duty—neutralizing the advantage possessed by lower cost out-of-state producers—it was held unconstitutional.

Similarly, in *Bacchus Imports, Ltd. v. Dias,* this Court invalidated a law which advantaged local production by granting a tax exemption to certain liquors produced in Hawaii. There are a multitude of other cases of this kind [468 US 263 (1984)]. Under these cases, Massachusetts' pricing order is clearly *unconstitutional.* Its avowed purpose and its undisputed effect are to enable higher cost Massachusetts dairy farmers to compete with lower cost dairy farmers in other States.

The *premium payments* are effectively a tax which makes milk produced out of State more expensive. Although the tax also applies to milk produced in Massachusetts, its effect on Massachusetts producers is entirely (indeed more than) offset by the subsidy provided exclusively to Massachusetts dairy farmers. Like an ordinary tariff, the tax is thus effectively imposed only on out-of-state products.

The pricing order thus allows Massachusetts dairy farmers who produce at higher cost to sell at or below the price charged by lower cost out-of-state producers. If there were no federal minimum prices for milk, out-of-state producers might still be able to retain their market share by lowering their prices. Nevertheless, out-of-staters' ability to remain competitive by lowering their prices would not immunize a discriminatory measure.

In this case, because the Federal Government sets minimum prices, out-of-state producers may not even have the option of reducing prices in order to retain market share. The Massachusetts pricing order thus will almost certainly "cause local goods to constitute a larger share, and goods with an out-of-state source to constitute a smaller share, of the total sales in the market" [***Exxon Corp. v. Governor of Maryland***, 437 US 117, 126, n. 16 (1978)].

In fact, this effect was the motive behind the promulgation of the pricing order. This effect renders the program unconstitutional, because it, like a tariff, "neutralize[s] advantages belonging to the place of origin" [***Baldwin***, 294 US, at 527].

In some ways, the Massachusetts pricing order is most similar to the law at issue in Bacchus Imports [U.S. Supreme Court, ¶400-100, 468 US 263, (Jun. 29, 1984)]. Both involve a broad-based tax on a single kind of good and special provisions for in-state producers. ***Bacchus*** involved a 20 percent excise tax on *all* liquor sales, coupled with an exemption for fruit wine manufactured in Hawaii and for okolehao, a brandy distilled from the root of a shrub indigenous to Hawaii.

The Court held that Hawaii's law was *unconstitutional* because it "had both the purpose and effect of discriminating in favor of local products." By granting a tax exemption for local products, Hawaii in effect created a protective tariff. Goods produced out of State were taxed, but those produced in State were subject to no net tax.

The result in ***Bacchus*** would have been the same if, instead of exempting certain Hawaiian liquors from tax, Hawaii had rebated the amount of tax collected from the sale of those liquors. And if a discriminatory tax rebate is unconstitutional, then Massachusetts' pricing order is surely invalid; for Massachusetts offers rebates to domestic milk producers for both the tax paid on the sale of Massachusetts milk to domestic milk producers and the tax paid on the sale of milk produced elsewhere.

The additional rebate of the tax paid on the sale of milk produced elsewhere in no way reduces the danger to the national market posed by tariff-like barriers; instead, it exacerbates the danger by giving domestic producers an additional tool with which to shore up their competitive position.

The State's Arguments. Respondent advances four arguments against the conclusion that its pricing order imposes an unconstitutional burden on interstate commerce:

1. Because each component of the program—a local subsidy and a non-discriminatory tax—is valid, the combination of the two is equally valid.
2. The dealers who pay the order premiums (the tax) are not competitors of the farmers who receive disbursements from the Dairy Equalization Fund, so the pricing order is not discriminatory.
3. The pricing order is not protectionist, because the costs of the program are borne only by Massachusetts dealers and consumers, and the benefits are distributed exclusively to Massachusetts farmers.
4. The order's incidental burden on commerce is justified by the local benefit of saving the dairy industry from collapse.

State's First Argument

Respondent's principal argument is that, because "the milk order achieves its goals through lawful means," the order as a whole is constitutional. He argues that the payments to Massachusetts dairy farmers from the Dairy Equalization Fund are valid, because subsidies are constitutional exercises of state power, and that the order premium which provides money for the Fund is valid, because it is a nondiscriminatory tax.

Therefore, the pricing order is constitutional, because it is merely the combination of two independently lawful regulations. In effect, respondent argues that:

- If the State may impose a valid tax on dealers, then it is free to use the proceeds of the tax as it chooses, AND
- If it may independently subsidize its farmers, it is free to finance the subsidy by means of any legitimate tax

Even granting respondent's assertion that both components of the pricing order would be constitutional standing alone, the pricing order nevertheless must fall. A pure subsidy funded out of general revenue ordinarily imposes no burden on interstate commerce, but merely assists local business.

The pricing order in this case, however, is funded principally from taxes on the sale of milk produced in other States. By so funding the subsidy, respondent not only assists local farmers, but burdens interstate commerce. The pricing order thus violates the cardinal principle that a State may not "benefit in-state economic interests by burdening out-of-state competitors" [*New Energy Co. of Indiana v. Limbach,* 486 US, at 273-274].

More fundamentally, respondent errs in assuming that the constitutionality of the pricing order follows logically from the constitutionality of its component parts. By conjoining a tax and a subsidy, Massachusetts has created a program more dangerous to interstate commerce than either part alone. Nondiscriminatory measures, like the evenhanded tax at issue here, are generally upheld, in spite of any adverse effects on interstate commerce, in part because "[t]he existence of major in-state interests adversely affected ... is a powerful safeguard against legislative abuse" [*Minnesota v. Clover Leaf Creamery Co.,* 449 US 456, 473, n. 17 (1981)].

However, when a nondiscriminatory tax is coupled with a subsidy to one of the groups hurt by the tax, a state's political processes can no longer be relied upon to prevent legislative abuse, because one of the in-state interests which would otherwise lobby against the tax has been mollified by the subsidy. So, in this case, one would ordinarily have expected at least three groups to lobby *against* the order premium, which, as a tax, raises the price (and hence lowers demand) for milk, dairy farmers, milk dealers, and consumers. But because the tax was coupled with a subsidy Massachusetts dairy farmers, one of the most powerful of these groups, were its primary supporters.

Respondent's argument would require us to analyze separately two parts of an integrated regulation, but we cannot divorce the premium payments from the use to which the payments are put. It is the entire program, not just the contributions to the fund or the distributions from that fund, that simultaneously burdens interstate commerce and discriminates in favor of local producers.

The choice of constitutional means, nondiscriminatory tax and local subsidy, cannot guarantee the constitutionality of the program as a whole. New York's minimum price order also used constitutional means (a State's power to regulate prices), but was held unconstitutional because of its deleterious effects [*Baldwin v. G.A.F. Seelig, Inc.,* 294 US 511 (1935)]. Similarly, the law held unconstitutional in *Bacchus* involved the exercise of Hawaii's undisputed power to tax and to grant tax exemptions.

Our Commerce Clause jurisprudence is not so rigid as to be controlled by the form by which a State erects barriers to commerce. Rather our cases have avoided formalism for a sensitive, case-by-case analysis of purposes and effects. As the Court declared over 50 years ago:

> The Commerce Clause forbids discrimination, whether forthright or ingenious. In each case it is our duty to determine whether the statute under attack, whatever its name may be, will in its practical operation work discrimination against interstate commerce [*Best & Co. v. Maxwell,* 311 US 454, 455-456 (1940); *Maryland v. Louisiana,* 451 US 725, 756 (1981); *Exxon Corp. v. Governor of Maryland,* 437 US, at 147 (1978)].

State's Second Argument

Respondent also argues that since the Massachusetts milk dealers who pay the order premiums are not competitors of the Massachusetts farmers, the pricing order imposes no discriminatory burden on commerce. This argument cannot withstand scrutiny.

Is it possible to doubt that if Massachusetts imposed a higher sales tax on milk produced in Maine than milk produced in Massachusetts, then the tax would be struck down—despite the fact that the sales tax was imposed on consumers, and consumers do not compete with dairy farmers? For over 150 years, our cases have rightly concluded that the imposition of a differential burden on any part of the stream of commerce from wholesaler to retailer to consumer is *invalid*, because a burden placed at any point will result in a disadvantage to the out-of-state producer.

State's Third Argument

Respondent also argues that "the operation of the Order disproves any claim of protectionism," because "*only* in-state consumers feel the effect of any retail price increase … [and] [t]he dealers themselves … have a substantial in-state presence." If accepted, this argument would undermine almost every discriminatory tax case.

State taxes are ordinarily paid by in-state businesses and consumers, but they are unconstitutional if they discriminate against out-of-state products. The idea that a discriminatory tax does not interfere with interstate commerce "merely because the burden of the tax was borne by consumers" in the taxing State was thoroughly repudiated in ***Bacchus Imports***. The cost of a tariff is also borne primarily by local consumers, yet a tariff is the typical Commerce Clause violation. More fundamentally, respondent ignores the fact that Massachusetts dairy farmers are part of an integrated interstate market.

As noted above, the purpose and effect of the pricing order are to divert market share to Massachusetts dairy farmers. This diversion necessarily injures the dairy farmers in neighboring States. Furthermore, the Massachusetts order regulates a portion of the same interstate market in milk that is more broadly regulated by a federal milk marketing order which covers most of New England.

The Massachusetts producers who deliver milk to dealers in that regulated market are participants in the same interstate milk market as the out-of-state producers who sell in the same market and are guaranteed the same minimum blend price by the federal order. The fact that the Massachusetts order imposes assessments only on Massachusetts sales and distributes them only to Massachusetts producers does not exclude either the assessments or the payments from the interstate market.

To the extent that those assessments affect the relative volume of Class I milk products sold in the marketing area as compared to other classes of milk products, they necessarily affect the blend price payable even to out-of-state producers who sell only in non-Massachusetts markets. The obvious impact of the order on out-of-state production demonstrates that it is simply wrong to assume that the pricing order burdens only Massachusetts consumers and dealers.

State's Fourth Argument

Finally, respondent argues that any incidental burden on interstate commerce "is outweighed by the 'local benefits' of preserving the Massachusetts dairy industry." In a closely related argument, respondent urges that "the purpose of the order, to save an industry from collapse, is not protectionist." If we were to accept these arguments, we would make a virtue of the vice that the rule against discrimination condemns.

Preservation of local industry by protecting it from the rigors of interstate competition is the hallmark of the economic protectionism that the Commerce Clause prohibits. In *Bacchus Imports,* we explicitly rejected any distinction "between thriving and struggling enterprises." Whether a State is attempting to "enhance thriving and substantial business enterprises" or to "subsidize ... financially troubled" ones is irrelevant to Commerce Clause analysis. With his characteristic eloquence, Justice Cardozo responded to an argument that respondent echoes today:

> The argument is pressed upon us, however, that the end to be served by the Milk Control Act is something more than the economic welfare of the farmers or of any other class or classes. The end to be served is the maintenance of a regular and adequate supply of pure and wholesome milk, the supply being put in jeopardy when the farmers of the state are unable to earn a living income (*Nebbia v. New York, supra*) ...

> Let such an exception be admitted, and all that a state will have to do in times of stress and strain is to say that its farmers and merchants and workmen must be protected against competition from without, lest they go upon the poor relief lists or perish altogether. To give entrance to that excuse would be to invite a speedy end of our national solidarity.

> The Constitution was framed under the dominion of a political philosophy less parochial in range. It was framed upon the theory that the peoples of the several states must sink or swim together, and that in the long run prosperity and salvation are in union and not division [*Baldwin v. G.A.F. Seelig,* 294 US, at 522-523.]

In a later case, also involving the welfare of Massachusetts dairy farmers, Justice Jackson described the same overriding interest in the free flow of commerce across state lines:

> Our system, fostered by the Commerce Clause, is that every farmer and every craftsman shall be encouraged to produce by the certainty that he will have free access to every market in the Nation, that no home embargoes will withhold his exports, and no foreign state will by customs duties or regulations exclude them.

> Likewise, every consumer may look to the free competition from every producing area in the Nation to protect him from exploitation by any. Such was the vision of the Founders; such has been the doctrine of this Court which has given it reality" [***H.P. Hood & Sons, Inc. v. Du Mond,*** 336 US 525, 539 (1949)].

The judgment of the Supreme Judicial Court of Massachusetts is reversed. *It is so ordered.*

STUDY QUESTIONS

4. In ***West Lynn Creamery,*** the U.S. Supreme Court found that Massachusetts' milk pricing order was *constitutional* because the milk dealers that paid the order premiums were not competitors of Massachusetts farmers. ***True or False?***

5. In ***West Lynn Creamery,*** the State's argument that the order as a whole was constitutional, since the milk pricing order achieved its goal through lawful means, was *repudiated* by the U.S. Supreme Court because:
   a. Pure subsidies funded out of general revenue impose a burden on interstate commerce.
   b. The pricing order benefitted in-state economic interests by burdening out-of-state competitors.
   c. It was a combination of two independently unlawful regulations.

6. In ***West Lynn Creamery,*** the State's argument that the milk pricing order did not cause protectionism because only in-state consumers felt the effect of any price increase was:
   a. Repudiated by the Supreme Court
   b. Supported by ***Bacchus Imports***
   c. Based on previous U.S. Supreme Court decisions

---

7. Which of the following was the U.S. Supreme Court's response to the State's argument in **West Lynn Creamery** that any incidental burden on interstate commerce "is outweighed by the 'local benefits' of preserving the Massachusetts dairy industry?"

    a. It is not protectionist to save an industry from collapse.
    b. There is a distinction between thriving and struggling enterprises.
    c. Preserving a local industry by protecting it from the difficulties of interstate competition is economic protectionism.

Concurring Opinion

Justice Scalia, with whom Justice Thomas joins, concurring in judgment.

In my view the challenged Massachusetts pricing order is invalid under our negative-Commerce-Clause jurisprudence, for the reasons explained in Part II below. I do not agree with the reasons assigned by the Court, which seem to me, as explained in Part I, a broad expansion of current law.

Accordingly, I concur only in the judgment of the Court.

Part I. The purpose of the negative Commerce Clause, we have often said, is to create a national market. However, it does not follow from that, and we have never held, that every state law which obstructs a national market violates the Commerce Clause. Yet that is what the Court says today.

It seems to have canvassed the entire corpus of negative-Commerce-Clause opinions, culled out every free-market snippet of reasoning, and melded them into the sweeping principle that the Constitution is violated by any state law or regulation that "artificially encourag[es] in-state production even when the same goods could be produced at lower cost in other States."

As the Court seems to appreciate by its eagerness expressly to reserve the question of the constitutionality of subsidies for in-state industry, this expansive view of the Commerce Clause calls into question a wide variety of state laws that have hitherto been thought permissible. It seems to me that a State subsidy would *clearly* be invalid under any formulation of the Court's guiding principle identified above.

The Court guardedly asserts that a "pure subsidy funded out of general revenue *ordinarily* imposes no burden on interstate commerce, but merely assists local business." That must be taken to be true only because most local businesses (*e.g.*, the local hardware store) are not competing with businesses out of State.

The Court notes that, in funding this subsidy, Massachusetts has taxed milk produced in other States, and thus "not only assists local farmers, but burdens interstate commerce." But the same could be said of almost all subsidies funded from general state revenues, which almost invariably include monies from use taxes on out-of-state products.

And, even where the funding does not come in any part from taxes on out-of-state goods, "merely assist[ing]" in-state businesses unquestionably neutralizes advantages possessed by out-of-state enterprises. Such subsidies, particularly when they are in the form of cash or (what comes to the same thing) tax forgiveness, are often admitted to have as the purpose—*indeed, are nationally advertised as having as their purpose*—of making it more profitable to conduct business in-state than elsewhere—i.e., distorting normal market incentives.

The Court's guiding principle also appears to call into question many garden-variety state laws heretofore permissible under the negative Commerce Clause. For example, a state law which (contrary to industry practice) requires the use of recyclable packaging materials, *favors* local non-exporting producers who do not have to establish an additional, separate packaging operation for in-state sales.

If the Court's analysis is to be believed, such a law would be unconstitutional without regard to whether disruption of the "national market" is the real purpose of the restriction, and without the need to "balance" the importance of the state interests thereby pursued [see *Pike v. Bruce Church, Inc.*, 397 US 137 (1970)]. These results would greatly extend the negative Commerce Clause beyond its current scope. If the Court does not intend these consequences and does not want to foster needless litigation concerning them, it should not have adopted its expansive rationale. Another basis for deciding the case is available, which I will proceed to discuss.

Part II. "The historical record provides no grounds for reading the Commerce Clause to be other than what it says—an authorization for Congress to regulate commerce" [*Tyler Pipe Industries, Inc. v. Washington State Dept. of Revenue*, 483 US 232, 263 (1987) (Scalia, J., concurring in part and dissenting in part)]. Nonetheless, we formally adopted the doctrine of the negative Commerce Clause 121 years ago and, since then, have decided a vast number of negative-Commerce-Clause cases engendering considerable reliance interests [see *Case of the State Freight Tax*, 15 Wall. 232 (1873)].

As a result, I will, on *stare decisis* grounds, enforce a self-executing "negative" Commerce Clause in two situations:

1. Against a state law that facially discriminates against interstate commerce
2. Against a state law that is indistinguishable from a type of law previously held unconstitutional by this Court.

Applying this approach—or at least the second part of it—is not always easy, since once one gets beyond facial discrimination, our negative-Commerce-Clause jurisprudence becomes (and long has been) a "quagmire" [*Northwestern States Portland Cement Co. v. Minnesota*, 358 US 450, 458 (1959)].

The object should be, however, to produce a clear rule that honors the holdings of our past decisions but declines to extend the rationale that produced those decisions any further.

There at least four possible devices that would enable a State to produce the economic effect that Massachusetts has produced here:

1. A discriminatory tax upon the industry, imposing a higher liability on out-of-state members than on their in-state competitors
2. A tax upon the industry that is nondiscriminatory in its assessment, but that has an "exemption" or "credit" for in-state members
3. A nondiscriminatory tax upon the industry, the revenues from which are placed into a segregated fund, which fund is disbursed as "rebates" or "subsidies" to in-state members of the industry (the situation at issue in this case)
4. With or without nondiscriminatory taxation of the industry, a subsidy for the in-state members of the industry, funded from the State's general revenues.

It is long settled that the first of these methodologies is unconstitutional under the negative Commerce Clause. The second of them, "exemption" from or "credit" against a "neutral" tax, is no different in principle from the first, and has likewise been held invalid.

The fourth methodology, application of a state subsidy from general revenues, is so far removed from what we have hitherto held to be unconstitutional, that prohibiting it must be regarded as an extension of our negative-Commerce-Clause jurisprudence and, therefore, unacceptable to me. Indeed, in my view, our negative-Commerce-Clause cases have already approved the use of such subsidies.

The issue before us in the present case is whether the third of these methodologies must fall. Although the question is close, I conclude it would not be a principled point at which to disembark from the negative-Commerce-Clause train. The only difference between methodologies (2) (discriminatory "exemption" from nondiscriminatory tax) and (3) (discriminatory refund of nondiscriminatory tax) is that the money is taken and returned rather than simply left with the favored in-state taxpayer in the first place. The difference between (3) and (4), on the other hand, is the difference between assisting in-state industry through discriminatory taxation, and assisting in-state industry by other means.

I would, therefore, allow a State to subsidize its domestic industry, so long as it does so from nondiscriminatory taxes that go into the State's general revenue fund. Perhaps, as some commentators contend, that line comports with an important economic reality: a State is less likely to maintain a subsidy when its citizens perceive that the money (in the general fund) is available for any number of competing, non-protectionist, purposes.

That is not, however, the basis for my position, for, as The Chief Justice explains, "[a]nalysis of interest group participation in the political process may serve many useful purposes, but serving as a basis for interpreting the dormant Commerce Clause is not one of them" [*Post*, at 4 (dissenting opinion)].

I draw the line where I do because it is a clear, rational line at the limits of our extant negative-Commerce-Clause jurisprudence.

Dissenting Opinion

Chief Justice Rehnquist, with whom Justice Blackmun joins, dissenting.

The Court is less than just in its description of the reasons which lay behind the Massachusetts law which it strikes down. The law undoubtedly sought to aid struggling Massachusetts dairy farmers, beset by steady or declining prices and escalating costs. This situation is apparently not unique to Massachusetts; New Jersey has filed an *amicus* brief in support of respondent because New Jersey has enacted a similar law.

Both States lie in the northeastern metropolitan corridor, which is the most urbanized area in the United States and has every prospect of becoming more so. The value of agricultural land located near metropolitan areas is driven up by the demand for housing and similar urban uses; distressed farmers eventually sell out to developers. Not only is farm produce is lost (milk production in this case), but, as the Massachusetts Special Commission whose report was the basis for the order in question here found:

> Without the continued existence of dairy farmers, the Commonwealth will lose its supply of locally produced fresh milk, together with the open lands that are used as wildlife refuges, for recreation, hunting, fishing, tourism, and education.

Massachusetts has dealt with this problem by providing a subsidy to aid its beleaguered dairy farmers. In case after case, we have approved the validity under the Commerce Clause of such enactments. "No one disputes that a State may enact laws pursuant to its police powers that have the purpose and effect of encouraging domestic industry" [*Bacchus Imports, Ltd. v. Dias,* 468 US 263, 271 (1984)].

"Direct subsidization of domestic industry does not ordinarily run afoul of the [dormant Commerce Clause]; discriminatory taxation of out-of-state manufacturers does" [*New Energy Co. of Indiana v. Limbach,* 486 US 269, 278 (1988)]. But today the Court relegates these well-established principles to a footnote and, at the same time, gratuitously casts doubt on the validity of state subsidies, observing that "[w]e have never squarely confronted" their constitutionality.

But in *Milk Control Bd. v. Eisenberg Farm Products,* the Court upheld a Pennsylvania statute establishing minimum prices to be paid to Pennsylvania dairy farmers against a Commerce Clause challenge by a Pennsylvania milk dealer which shipped all of its milk purchased in Pennsylvania to New York to be sold there [306 US 346 (1939)]. The Court observed that "[t]he purpose of the statute ... is to reach a domestic situation in the interest of the welfare of the producers and consumers of milk in Pennsylvania." It went on to say:

> One of the commonest forms of state action is the exercise of police power directed to the control of local conditions and exerted in the interest of the welfare of the state's citizens. Every state police statute necessarily will affect interstate commerce in some degree, but such a statute does not run counter to the grant of Congressional power merely because it incidentally or indirectly involves or burdens interstate commerce ... These principles have guided judicial decision for more than a century.

The Massachusetts subsidy under consideration is similar in many respects to the Pennsylvania statute described in *Eisenberg, supra.* Massachusetts taxes all dealers of milk within its borders. The tax is even-handed on its face—*i.e.,* it affects all dealers, regardless of the point of origin of the milk. The State has not acted to strong-arm sister States as in *Limbach*; rather, its motives are purely local. As the Supreme Judicial Court of Massachusetts aptly described it, "[T]he premiums represent one of the costs of doing business in the Commonwealth, a cost all milk dealers must pay."

Consistent with precedent, the Court observes: "A pure subsidy funded out of general revenue ordinarily imposes no burden on interstate commerce, but merely assists local business." And the Court correctly recognizes that "[n]ondiscriminatory measures, like the evenhanded tax at issue here, are generally upheld" due to the deference normally accorded to a State's political process in passing legislation in light of various competing interest groups.

But the Court strikes down this method of state subsidization because the non-discriminatory tax levied against all milk *dealers* is coupled with a subsidy to milk *producers.* The Court does this because of its view that the method of imposing the tax and subsidy distorts the State's political process— the dairy farmers, who would otherwise lobby against the tax, have been mollified by the subsidy.

As the Court itself points out, there are still at least two strong interest groups opposed to the milk order—consumers and milk dealers. More importantly, nothing in the dormant Commerce Clause suggests that the fate of state regulation should turn upon the particular lawful manner in which the state subsidy is enacted or promulgated. Analysis of interest group participation in the political process may serve many useful purposes, but serving as a basis for interpreting the dormant Commerce Clause is not one of them.

The Court concludes that the combined effect of the milk order "simultaneously burdens interstate commerce and discriminates in favor of local producers." In support of this conclusion, the Court cites *Baldwin* and *Bacchus Imports* as two examples in which constitutional means were held to have unconstitutional effects on interstate commerce. But both *Baldwin* and *Bacchus* are a far cry from this case.

In *Baldwin,* to sell bottled milk in New York, milk dealers were required to pay a minimum price for milk—even though they could have purchased milk from Vermont farmers at a lower price. This scheme was found to be an effort to prevent Vermont milk producers from selling to New York dealers at their lower market price. As Justice Cardozo explained, under the New York statute, "the importer ... may keep his milk or drink it, but sell it he may not."

Such a scheme clearly made it less attractive for New York dealers to purchase milk from Vermont farmers, for the disputed law negated any economic advantage in so doing. Under the Massachusetts milk order, there is no such adverse effect. Milk dealers have the same incentives to purchase lower priced milk from out-of-state farmers; dealers of all milk are taxed equally. To borrow Justice Cardozo's description, milk dealers in Massachusetts are free to keep their milk, drink their milk, and sell it, on equal terms as local milk.

In *Bacchus,* the State of Hawaii combined its undisputed power to tax and grant exemptions in a manner that the Court found violative of the Commerce Clause. There, the State exempted a local wine from the burdens of an excise tax levied on all other liquor sales. Despite the Court's strained attempt to compare the scheme in *Bacchus* to the milk order, in this case it is clear that the milk order does not produce the same effect on interstate commerce as the tax exemption in *Bacchus.*

I agree with the Court's statement that *Bacchus* can be distinguished "by noting that the rebate in this case goes not to the entity which pays the tax (milk dealers) but to the dairy farmers themselves." This is not only a distinction, but a significant difference. No decided case supports the Court's conclusion that the negative Commerce Clause prohibits the State from using money that it has lawfully obtained through a neutral tax on milk dealers and distributing it as a subsidy to dairy farmers. Indeed, the case which comes closest to supporting the result the Court reaches is the ill-starred opinion in *United States v. Butler,* 297 US 1 (1936), in which the Court held unconstitutional what would have been an otherwise valid tax on the processing of agricultural products because of the use to which the revenue raised by the tax was put.

More than half a century ago, Justice Brandeis said in his dissenting opinion in *New State Ice Co. v. Liebmann,* 285 US 262, 311 (1932):

> To stay experimentation in things social and economic is a grave responsibility. Denial of the right to experiment may be fraught with serious consequences to the Nation. It is one of the happy incidents of the federal system that a single courageous State may, if its citizens choose, serve as a laboratory; and try novel social and economic experiments without risk to the rest of the country.

Justice Brandeis' statement has been cited more than once in subsequent majority opinions of the Court. His observation bears heeding today, as it did when he made it.

The wisdom of a messianic insistence on a grim sink-or-swim policy of laissez-faire economics would be debatable had Congress chosen to enact it, but Congress has done nothing of the kind. It is the Court which has imposed the policy under the dormant Commerce Clause—a policy which bodes ill for the values of federalism which have long animated our constitutional jurisprudence.

STUDY QUESTIONS

---

8. Chief Judge Rehnquist's dissenting opinion in **West Lynn Creamery** *disagreed* with the U.S. Supreme Court that **Bacchus** can be distinguished "by noting that the rebate in this case goes not to the entity which pays the tax (milk dealers) but to the dairy farmers themselves." **True or False?**

9. Justice Scalia's concurring opinion in **West Lynn Creamery** listed devices that could by used by a state to produce an economic effect similar to what Massachusetts was attempting to achieve. Which of those did he consider to be *constitutional* under the negative Commerce Clause?

   a. A state subsidy from general revenues with or without nondiscriminatory taxation of the industry
   b. A tax on the industry that is nondiscriminatory in assessment, but that has a credit for in-state businesses in the same industry
   c. A discriminatory tax on the industry, imposing a higher liability on out-of-state members than on their in-state competitors

---

EQUAL PROTECTION CLAUSE

Taxing jurisdictions are not prohibited from drawing necessary distinctions between individuals as part of a tax structure that provides a rational basis for the distinctions. The Equal Protection Clause requires that any distinctions drawn be based upon a legitimate state interest. Therefore, there must be a plausible reason for any classification system provided by a tax statute.

Income levels are a typical classification that would have a rational basis in an income tax system. A taxpayer being an in-state resident versus an out-of-state resident would not provide a rational basis for discrimination. In seeking relief from unwarranted discrimination, many out-of-state taxpayers have elected to appeal their cases under the Equal Protection Clause, rather than the Commerce Clause.

Williams et al. v. Vermont et al, U.S. Supreme Court, 472 US 14, (Jun. 4, 1985)

Author Commentary. In the *Williams v Vermont* case, the taxpayer was denied a credit offset against Vermont Use Tax for sales taxes paid on the purchase of a vehicle outside Vermont when the individual was not a resident of Vermont. As you read through this case, notice that many of the same issues raised against discrimination in the Commerce Clause cases emerge in this case as well.

Facts. Vermont collects a use tax when cars are registered with it, but the tax is not imposed if the car was purchased in Vermont and a sales tax has been paid. The tax is also reduced by the amount of any sales or use tax paid to another State, if that State would afford a credit for taxes paid to Vermont in similar circumstances.

The credit is available, however, *only* if the registrant was a Vermont resident at the time he paid the taxes. Appellants who bought and registered cars outside of Vermont before becoming Vermont residents were required to pay the *full* use tax in order to register their cars in Vermont.

In proceedings in the Vermont Superior Court, appellants alleged that Vermont's failure to afford them credit for the out-of-state sales taxes they had paid violated, *inter alia,* the Equal Protection Clause of the Fourteenth Amendment, because the credit was provided in the case of vehicles acquired outside the State by Vermont residents. Rejecting appellants' contention, the court dismissed the complaint.

The Vermont Supreme Court affirmed by citation to another decision handed down the same day, *Leverson v. Conway,* 144 Vt. 523, 481 A.2d 1029, in which it rejected a similar equal protection challenge to the tax credit, concluding that the Vermont statute was rationally related to the legitimate state interest in raising revenue to maintain and improve the highways, and that it rationally placed the burden on those who used them.

When the Vermont statute is viewed on its face, appellants have stated a claim of discrimination prohibited by the Equal Protection Clause.

While the State asserts that the tax credit applies only to Vermont residents who register their cars in Vermont without first having registered them elsewhere, and that a resident who purchases, pays a sales or use tax on, and registers a car in another State must also pay the Vermont use tax upon his return, it does not appear that the Vermont Supreme Court, in ruling on the equal protection claim in *Leverson*, construed the exemption in such a manner. Instead, every indication is that a Vermont resident enjoys a credit for any sales taxes paid to a reciprocating State—even if he registered and used the car there before registering it in Vermont.

An exemption such as the one challenged here will be sustained if the legislature could have reasonably concluded that the challenged classification would promote a legitimate state purpose. No legitimate purpose is furthered by the discriminatory exemption here. Residence at the time of purchase is a wholly arbitrary basis on which to distinguish among present Vermont registrants—at least among those who used their cars elsewhere before coming to Vermont. The distinction between them bears no relation to the statutory purpose of raising revenue for the maintenance and improvement of Vermont roads.

The customary rationale for a use tax—relating to protecting local merchants from out-of-state competition which, because of its lower or nonexistent tax burdens, can offer lower prices—has no application to purchases made out-of-state by those who were not residents of the taxing State at the time of purchase. Nor can the distinction here be justified by a state policy of making those who use the highways contribute to their maintenance and improvement, or as encouraging interstate commerce by enabling Vermont residents, faced with limited automobile offerings at home, to shop outside the State without penalty (144 Vt. 649, 478 A. 2d 993, reversed and remanded).

Opinion. White, J., delivered the opinion of the Court, in which three other justices concurred:

The State of Vermont collects a use tax when cars are registered with it. The tax is not imposed if the car was purchased in Vermont and a sales tax has been paid. The tax is also reduced by the amount of any sales or use tax paid to another State if that State would afford a credit for taxes paid to Vermont in similar circumstances. The credit is available, however, only if the registrant was a Vermont resident at the time he paid the taxes. Appellants, who bought cars outside of Vermont before becoming residents of that State, challenge the failure to grant them a similar credit. We agree that this failure *denies* them the equal protection of the law.

Appellants' complaint. Appellants' complaint, which was dismissed before an answer was filed, sets out the following facts.

In December 1980, appellant Norman Williams purchased a new car in Illinois, paying a five percent sales tax. Three months later, he moved to Vermont, bringing the car with him. He subsequently attempted to register the car in Vermont without paying the required use tax. The Vermont Department of Motor Vehicles refused to register the car.

Williams responded by suing in the Federal District Court for the District of Vermont, which, relying on 28 U.S.C. §1341, dismissed his complaint. Williams then paid the tax, which came to $172, unsuccessfully sought a refund from the Department of Motor Vehicles, and filed the present suit in Vermont Superior Court.

The complaint alleged a number of constitutional defects in the State's failure to afford appellants credit for the sales taxes they had paid. One of them was that the Equal Protection Clause of the Fourteenth Amendment forbade the State to deny the credit to them, while providing it in the case of vehicles "acquired outside the state by a resident of Vermont" [Vt. Stat. Ann., Tit. 32, §8911(9) (1981)].

The Superior Court dismissed the complaint. Acknowledging that the use tax "does not afford, on its face, equal treatment to residents and non-residents who purchase cars out-of-state," the court considered the relevant inquiry to be "whether discrimination occurs within the state."

It saw no such discrimination, reasoning that, in practice, Vermont residents always pay the use tax, because reciprocal States excuse payment of the sales tax and, therefore, there is no out-of-state payment to credit the use tax against. The court also found no burden on the right to travel, no violation of the Privileges and Immunities Clause, and no interference with interstate commerce.

The Vermont Supreme Court affirmed by citation to the ***Leverson*** decision, handed down the same day. ***Leverson*** was an essentially identical case brought by a former Wisconsin resident who, like appellants, had purchased a car in his home State and paid a sales tax, then moved to Vermont and been obliged to pay the use tax.

The Vermont Supreme Court upheld the tax. First, it rejected the argument that denying a credit for sales tax paid to another State infringed the right to travel. The use tax did not impose a penalty for moving to Vermont—the obligation was incurred only by registering one's car there. Absent such a penalty, and given that there is no fundamental right to have or to register a car, the Equal Protection Clause required only minimal scrutiny. The statute was rationally related to the legitimate state interest in raising revenue to maintain and improve the highways, and rationally placed the burden on those who used them.

The exemption for residents who purchased cars in reciprocal States encouraged purchases within Vermont by residents of those States. This goal would not be furthered by granting an exemption to new residents who have already purchased cars elsewhere. The court went on to hold that the Privileges and Immunities Clause did not come into play because no right, such as the right to travel, qualifying as a privilege or immunity was involved. It also rejected a Commerce Clause challenge, viewing this as a straightforward use tax, imposed only on goods that had come to rest in Vermont.

The Vermont Supreme Court denied rehearing, and appellants brought this appeal. We now reverse.

The Vermont tax. The Vermont Motor Vehicle Purchase and Use Tax, is distinct from the State's general sales and use taxes [Vt. Stat. Ann., Tit. 32, ch. 219 (1981)]. Its purpose includes the improvement and maintenance of the state and interstate highway systems and to pay the principal and interest on bonds issued for the improvement and maintenance of those systems (§8901). The revenue from the tax goes into a distinct transportation fund. The tax is of two sorts:

1.   A four percent sales tax imposed at the time of purchase of a motor vehicle in Vermont by a Vermont resident [§8903(a)]
2.   A four percent use tax imposed upon registration of a motor vehicle in Vermont, unless the Vermont sales tax was paid [§8903(b)]

A number of vehicles are exempt—including, for example, those owned by a State, the United States, or charitable institutions, and those transferred within a family. (See generally §8911.)

One other exemption is critical to this case. Section 8911(9) provides that the tax does *not* apply to:

> ... pleasure cars acquired outside the state by a resident of Vermont on which a state sales or use tax has been paid by the person applying for a registration in Vermont, providing that the state or province collecting such tax would grant the same pro-rata credit for Vermont tax paid under similar circumstances. If the tax paid in another state is less than the Vermont tax the tax due shall be the difference.

There is some dispute as to the reach of this provision. Appellants assert that, in light of this provision, had they been residents when they purchased their cars, they would now be exempt from the use tax.

The State disagrees, asserting that the exemption applies only to Vermont residents who register their cars in Vermont without first having registered them elsewhere. According to it, a resident who purchases, pays a sales or use tax on, and registers a car in another State must also pay the Vermont use tax upon his return, bearing the same obligation as appellants.

The State's submission, if it is to be accepted, would negate any claim that appellants were treated differently than Vermont residents in similar circumstances. For several reasons, however, we do *not* believe that in ruling on the equal protection claim the Vermont Supreme Court construed the exemption in this manner.

The exemption contained in §8911(9) refers to "pleasure cars acquired outside the state by a resident of Vermont." That language, on its face, exempts Vermont residents who register in another State.

In *Leverson*, the Vermont Supreme Court appears to have proceeded on this basis. The court set out a comprehensive list of who must pay the tax, from which the Vermont resident who first registers the car in another State is conspicuously absent. The opinion also points out several times that residents who pay a tax in a nonreciprocal State do not enjoy the credit upon registering their cars in Vermont.

Had the court believed that those purchasing and registering a car in a reciprocal State are also not exempt, one would have expected it to have said so. Similarly, the court noted that someone in appellants' position "is treated in exactly the same manner as all non-exempt persons, including the resident who purchases his vehicle in a nonreciprocal state." If the court had understood the statute as do appellees, it would also have noted that appellants were treated just like any resident who had previously registered a car elsewhere—not just one who purchased in a nonreciprocal State.

More fundamentally, had the Vermont Supreme Court accepted the narrow construction of the exemption that the State urges, it surely would have stated that the new resident suffers no unequal treatment under the statute at all and would have found no necessity to justify any discriminatory impact of the tax. This would have been a simple and straightforward answer to the equal protection claim, and there would have been no occasion to address the level of scrutiny to be applied to the discrimination or to identify the State's interest in imposing the differential treatment of the nonresident. Instead, the court concluded that the State need have only a rational basis for the discrimination, and proceeded to hold that there was adequate justification for not extending the exemption to nonresidents.

In short, every indication is that a Vermont resident who, like appellants, bought a car in another State, paid a sales or use tax, and used the car there for a period of time before coming to Vermont, would receive the credit. Appellees offer only their own say-so to the contrary. Pointing to nothing in the statute or in the opinion below to support their narrow reading, they would have us essentially add a clause that is not there. We cannot do so without stronger authority. We, therefore, proceed on the understanding that a Vermonter enjoys a credit for *any* sales taxes paid to a reciprocating State, even if he registered and used the car there before registering the car in Vermont.

Sales tax credits. This Court has expressly reserved the question of whether a State must credit a sales tax paid to another State against its own use tax. The District of Columbia and all but three states with sales and use taxes provide such a credit, although reciprocity may be required.

As noted above, Vermont provides a credit with regard to its general use tax. Such a requirement:

- Has been endorsed by at least one state court [*Montgomery Ward & Co. v. State Board of Equalization,* 272 Cal. App. 2d 728, 78 Cal. Rptr. 373 (1969), *cert. denied,* 396 US 1040 (1970)]
- Was advocated 20 years ago in the much-cited Report of the Willis Subcommittee [H. R. Rep. No. 565, 89th Cong., 1st Sess., 1136, 1177-1178 (1965)]
- Is adopted in the Multistate Tax Compact [Art. V, §1], and
- Has significant support in the commentary

Appellants urge us to hold that it is a constitutional requirement. Once again, however, we find it unnecessary to reach this question.

Whatever the general rule may be, to provide a credit only to those who were residents at the time they paid the sales tax to another State is an arbitrary distinction that *violates* the Equal Protection Clause.

This Court has many times pointed out that in structuring internal taxation schemes "the States have large leeway in making classifications and drawing lines which in their judgment produce reasonable systems of taxation" [*Lehnhausen v. Lake Shore Auto Parts Co.,* 410 US 356, 359 (1973)]. It has been reluctant to interfere with legislative policy decisions in this area. An exemption such as the one challenged here "will be sustained if the legislature could have reasonably concluded that the challenged classification would promote a legitimate state purpose" [*Exxon Corp. v. Eagerton,* 462 US 176, 196 (1983)].

We perceive no legitimate purpose, however, that is furthered by this discriminatory exemption. As we said in holding that the use tax base cannot be broader than the sales tax base, "equal treatment for in-state and out-of-state taxpayers similarly situated is the condition precedent for a valid use tax on goods imported from out-of-state" [*Halliburton Oil Well Co. v. Reily,* 373 US 64, 70 (1963)]. A State may not treat those within its borders unequally solely on the basis of their different residences or States of incorporation [*Wheeling Steel Corp. v. Glandar,* 337 US 562, 571-572 (1949)].

In the present case, residence at the time of purchase is a wholly arbitrary basis on which to distinguish among present Vermont registrants—at least among those who used their cars elsewhere before coming to Vermont. Having registered a car in Vermont, they are similarly situated for all relevant purposes. Each is a Vermont resident, using a car in Vermont, with an equal obligation to pay for the maintenance and improvement of Vermont's roads.

The purposes of the statute would be identically served, and with an identical burden, by taxing each. The distinction between them bears no relation to the statutory purpose. As the Court said in *Wheeling,* appellants have not been "accorded equal treatment, and the inequality is not because of the slightest difference in [Vermont's] relation to the decisive transaction, but solely because of the[ir] different residence."

In some ways, this is not a typical sales and use tax scheme. The proceeds go to a transportation fund rather than to general revenue. Perhaps, as a result, the sales tax is narrower than most, in that it applies not to all sales within the jurisdiction, but only to residents. Conversely, the use tax is broader than most, in that it applies to items purchased by nonresidents and taxed by other States. The general sales and use tax provisions of Vermont, for example, have neither of these features.

Applied to those such as appellants, the use tax exceeds the usual justifications for such a tax. A *use tax* is generally perceived as a necessary complement to the sales tax, designed to "protect a state's revenues by taking away the advantages to residents of traveling out of state to make untaxed purchases, and to protect local merchants from out-of-state competition which, because of its lower or nonexistent tax burdens, can offer lower prices" [*Leverson,* 144 Vt., at 527, 481 A. 2d, at 1032, quoting *Rowe-Genereux, Inc. v. Department of Taxes,* 138 Vt. 130, 133-134, 411 A. 2d 1345, 1347 (1980)].

This customary rationale for the use tax has no application to purchases made out-of-state by those who were not residents of the taxing State at the time of purchase. These home-state transactions cannot be seen as lost Vermont sales, and are certainly not ones lost as a result of Vermont's sales tax. Imposing a use tax on them in no way protects local business. In short, in its structure, this sales and use tax combination is exactly the *opposite* of the customary provision—there is no disincentive to the Vermont resident's purchasing outside the State, and there is a penalty on those who bought out-of-state but could not have been expected to do otherwise. The first provision limits local commerce, the second does not help it.

Despite *Leverson*'s passing reference to the standard rationale for use taxes, the only plausible justification for imposing the tax on those in appellants' position in the first place—apart from the simple desire to raise funds—is the principle that those using the roads should pay for them. In *Leverson,* the Vermont Supreme Court supported the tax by reference to "Vermont's basic policy" of making those who use the highways contribute to their maintenance and improvement.

Yet this does not explain the exemption for a resident who bought a car elsewhere and paid a tax to another State, which, as the dissent points out, is "directly contrary" to the user-pays principle. This "basic policy" arguably supports imposition of the use tax on appellants, and the denial of a credit to them, but it provides no rational reason to spare Vermont residents an equal burden.

The same response applies to the Vermont court's statement that to allow an exemption for people in appellants' position, or for Vermonters who purchase in nonreciprocal States, "would run counter to the state's present policies of requiring user contributions and encouraging purchases within the state, and would result in the loss of tax revenues to the state." This is no less true with regard to the Vermonter who purchases a car in a reciprocal State. Granting the resident a credit for sales tax paid to the other State is similarly "counter to the state's policies of requiring user contributions and encouraging purchases within the state."

The *Leverson* court's primary explanation of the exemption was that it:

> ... appears to be based upon a policy of encouraging out-of-staters from reciprocal states to purchase their vehicles in Vermont and pay a sales tax to Vermont, secure in the knowledge that they will not be subject to a duplicate tax in their home states, and upon a legislative assumption that few, if any, tax dollars will be lost through this exercise in comity.

However, the exemption cannot be justified as an indirect means of encouraging out-of-staters to purchase in Vermont and pay Vermont sales tax, for the straightforward reason that Vermont does not impose its sales tax on nonresidents.

Appellees take a different tack, suggesting that the exemption is designed to encourage interstate commerce by enabling Vermont residents, faced with limited automobile offerings at home, to shop outside the State without penalty. This justification may sound plausible, but it fails to support the classification at issue. Those in the appellants' position pay exactly the penalty for purchasing out-of-state that Vermont spares its own residents.

The credit may rationally further Vermont's legitimate interest in facilitating Vermonters' out-of-state purchases, but this interest does not extend to the facilitation of Vermonters' out-of-state use. Vermont may choose not to penalize old residents who used their cars in other States, but it cannot extend that benefit to old residents and deny it to new ones. The fact that it may be rational or beneficent to spare some the burden of double taxation does not mean that the beneficence can be distributed arbitrarily.

Finally, the Vermont court pointed out that Leverson was "treated in exactly the same manner as all non-exempt persons, including the resident who purchases his vehicle in a nonreciprocal state." Yet the fact that all those not benefited by the challenged exemption are treated equally has no bearing on the legitimacy of that classification in the first place.

A State cannot deflect an equal protection challenge by observing that in light of the statutory classification all those within the burdened class are similarly situated. The classification must reflect pre-existing differences; it cannot create new ones that are supported by only their own bootstraps. "The Equal Protection Clause requires more of a state law than nondiscriminatory application within the class it establishes" [*Rinaldi v. Yeager,* 384 US 305, 308 (1966)].

In sum, we can see no relevant difference between motor vehicle registrants who purchased their cars out-of-state while they were Vermont residents and those who only came to Vermont after buying a car elsewhere. To free one group and not the other from the otherwise applicable tax burden *violates* the Equal Protection Clause.

The Court's holding. Our holding is quite narrow, and we conclude by emphasizing what we do not decide. We need not consider appellants' various arguments based on the right to travel, the Privileges and Immunities Clause, and the Commerce Clause. We again put to one side the question whether a State must in all circumstances credit sales or use taxes paid to another State against its own use tax.

It is conceivable that, were a full record developed, it would turn out that in practice the statute does not operate in a discriminatory fashion. Finally, in light of the fact that the action was dismissed on the pleadings, and given the possible relevance of state law, we express no opinion as to the appropriate remedy.

We hold only that, when the statute is viewed on its face, appellants have stated a claim of unconstitutional discrimination. The decision below is accordingly reversed, and the case is remanded for further proceedings not inconsistent with this opinion.

It is so ordered.

> **Note**
>
> There was both a concurring opinion and a dissenting opinion.
>
> The dissenting opinion is summarized and redacted below.

STUDY QUESTIONS

10. The U.S. Supreme Court in **Williams et al. v. Vermont et al** did which of the following?

   a. Decided that a state must *always* credit sales or use taxes paid to another state against its own use tax

   b. Determined the appropriate remedy in the case

   c. Determined that the statute in question was *unconstitutional* when viewed on its face

---

11. The ***Williams et al. v. Vermont et al*** decision was based on an Equal Protection Clause challenge and did *not* consider arguments by the appellant related to the Commerce Clause. ***True or False?***

12. The Vermont statute in question, as construed by the Vermont Supreme Court in ***Leverson,*** did *not* provide an exemption for which of the following taxpayers?

  a. A taxpayer who purchased and registered a car outside of Vermont, but who immediately afterward became a Vermont resident.
  b. A Vermont resident who purchased and registered a car in another state before registering the car in Vermont.
  c. A Vermont resident who purchased a car in another state but first registered it in Vermont.

13. Which of the following statements is *true* in regards to the ***Williams et al. v. Vermont et al*** majority decision?

  a. The U.S. Supreme Court determined that there was a legitimate purpose for the exemption in question.
  b. The holding by the U.S. Supreme Court was broad.
  c. The Court noted that states have a lot of leeway in making classifications and drawing lines when structuring internal taxation schemes.

Dissenting Opinion

Justice Blackmun, with whom Justice Rehnquist and Justice O'Connor join, dissenting.

The Court in this case draws into question the constitutionality of a statute that was not intended to discriminate against anyone, does not discriminate against appellants, and, for all that appears, never has been applied in a discriminatory fashion against anyone else. Nevertheless, the Court has imagined a fanciful hypothetical discrimination, and then has threatened that the statute will violate equal protection unless the Vermont Supreme Court or the Vermont Legislature rejects the Court's conjecture.

As the Court recognizes, Vermont's use tax is designed to help defray the State's cost for building and maintaining its roads. Generally speaking, if one purchases an automobile in Vermont, one pays a sales tax on the purchase. If one purchases a car elsewhere but registers it in Vermont, the use tax is assessed. The end result is that likely users of the State's roads are assessed a tax for their use.

The overlapping series of credits and exemptions built into this vehicle tax system are designed to resolve a number of less-common cases that fall outside the typical pattern of a Vermonter's purchase of a car either in Vermont or elsewhere. However complex and redundant, the exceptions and credits accomplish two related legitimate purposes:

1. They facilitate the flow of interstate commerce by ensuring that residents and nonresidents alike are not penalized for purchasing cars in a foreign State.
2. They protect against the possibility that someone using the roads primarily in only one State will be forced to pay taxes in two States.

Thus Vermont, along with apparently every other State, will *not* charge a sales tax to an out-of-state purchaser of an automobile [See Vt. Stat. Ann., Tit. 23, §463, and Tit. 32, §8903(a) (Supp. 1984); *J. C. Penney Co. v. Hardesty,* W. Va., 264 S. E. 2d 604, 613 (1980)].

This exemption ensures that out-of-state purchasers who do not use Vermont roads except to leave the State will *not* be made to pay for their use.

The credit at issue in this litigation accomplishes much the same purpose. If a Vermont resident, for whatever reason, *does* pay an out-of-state sales tax, then, when he returns to Vermont with his car, he will be excused from payment of Vermont's use tax to the extent of the amount paid by way of the sales tax, if the other State provides a reciprocal credit. Again, the credit facilitates the interstate purchase of automobiles, and helps ensure that a car buyer is not paying for the use of two States' roads when using only one.

Vermont's tax credit system worked exactly as it was intended to work in the cases of Mr. Williams and Ms. Levine.

Vermont's asserted purposes being concededly legitimate, and the means used to achieve those purposes rational in the abstract and effective in these particular instances, the tax exemption should easily pass the minimal scrutiny this Court routinely applies to tax statutes. The Court, however, has subjected Vermont's motor vehicle tax laws to a kind of microscopic scrutiny that few enactments could survive, and has managed, it feels, to find a way in which the statute can be understood to discriminate against appellants.

The phantom beneficiary of Vermont's discrimination is a Vermont resident who leaves the State to purchase an automobile, pays the sales tax and registers the car in the foreign State of purchase, lives there for a while, and then returns to Vermont and registers the car there. This resident is said to be entitled to the exception of Vt. Stat. Ann., Tit. 32, §8911(9) (1981), while the similarly situated nonresident such as Mr. Williams is not. The phantom's car is said to be entitled to the credit because it is "acquired outside the state by a resident of Vermont" under the terms of the statute.

Hypothetical interpretation. The majority correctly understands that if its hypothetical Vermonter is not entitled to the exception, the discrimination disappears. That being the case, the problem the Court identifies seems to me to be largely of its own making. For the discrimination it finds was neither pleaded in the complaint nor discussed in any opinion of the Vermont courts.

The Court *rejects* the State's submission that the exception would not be applied to this hypothetical Vermonter, has never been applied in that situation, and was not intended to be so applied. It rejects this understanding of the statute because the statute is ambiguously worded, and because the Supreme Court of Vermont in *Leverson* apparently failed to consider explicitly and accept the State's view of the statute.

Thus a statute is placed under a constitutional cloud because a state court failed to go out of its way to reject a hypothetical interpretation of one of the statute's terms. If appellants were in fact concerned about this type of discrimination, they should have made that concern clear in their pleadings, so the Vermont courts could address the issue.

While it is idle to speculate as to how the Vermont Supreme Court will interpret §8911(9) on remand, it is not inappropriate to observe that there is force in the State's position that in context an equally plausible interpretation of the phrase "acquired outside the state" in §8911(9) is that the car is purchased outside the State but registered immediately in Vermont. This reading of the statute best comports with the legislative purpose in enacting exceptions to the automobile use tax. Section 8911(9) was designed to prevent people who buy their cars out-of-state but live in Vermont from being doubly taxed.

Nothing in the exception/credit scheme suggests that Vermont ever wished to protect a resident who took up temporary residency elsewhere and, therefore, ultimately used the highways in two States, rather than in just one. Allowing such residents this credit would be directly contrary to the purpose of the tax, which is to have the users of the State's roads pay for the maintenance and improvement of those roads. There is also support for this construction of the statute in the language of §8911 itself. Nor is there any evidence in the legislative history or the administrative practice that supports the Court's contrary reading of the statutory language.

Legitimate purpose. Even if the Court is correct in its understanding of §8911(9), however, the identified discrimination still is created by a classification rationally related to a legitimate governmental purpose sufficient to satisfy the minimal scrutiny the Court routinely applies in similar equal protection challenges to tax provisions.

The reason nonresidents who purchase cars out-of-state are taxed if they subsequently relocate in Vermont, while resident out-of-state purchasers are not, is that it was presumed that people will use their cars primarily in the States in which they reside. Most people who do not reside in Vermont and do not purchase their cars in that State, will not use their cars primarily in Vermont.

If at some time in the future they move to Vermont and register their automobiles there, the assumption is that they will have used their cars in two different States. On the other hand, most people who reside in Vermont and purchase their cars out-of-state will return to Vermont immediately with their cars. Thus, the out-of-state purchaser is taxed, while the Vermont purchaser is exempted to the extent that he already has paid a sales tax.

This distinction is hardly irrational, and the fact that there may be a Vermont resident who both purchases and uses his car out-of-state, and is therefore situated similarly to Mr. Williams, surely does not render the scheme irrational. A tax classification does not violate the demands of equal protection simply because it may not perfectly identify the class of people it wishes to single out. A State "is not required to resort to close distinctions or to maintain a precise, scientific uniformity with reference to composition, use or value" [*Allied Stores of Ohio, Inc. v. Bowers,* 358 US 522, 527 (1959)].

The Court disagrees, and finds that "residence at the time of purchase is a wholly arbitrary basis on which to distinguish among present Vermont registrants—at least among those who used their cars elsewhere before coming to Vermont." The Court, however, ignores the purpose of the tax and of the classification. Vermont does not wish to "distinguish among present Vermont registrants," but to distinguish those who will likely use Vermont's roads immediately after they have purchased cars out-of-state from those who will not. Residency is a rational way to enact such a classification.

Concocted Applications. Having interpreted the statute so as to generate some discrimination, and then having declared the discrimination "wholly arbitrary," the Court felicitously retreats to a holding sufficiently narrow as to strip its decision of any constitutional significance. The problem is not that the statute actually discriminates, we are told, but that the Vermont Superior Court dismissed the equal protection challenge before there was record evidence of "the actuality of [the statute's] operation."

The implication is that equal protection challenges to tax statutes may never be dismissed on the pleadings when the plaintiff can concoct a discriminatory application of the statute, no matter how far-fetched. This follows because the State need take only one of a number of actions to save its statute. It may produce an administrative regulation clarifying the scope of the exception [see Vt. Stat. Ann., Tit. 32, §8901 (1981)].

It may introduce evidence at trial concerning the statute's application. Or it may introduce evidence to show that a classification based upon residency is a rational way to assess for road use—a proposition that until today I thought was self-evident. And if the state courts on remand find that the statute does not discriminate as applied, or that the discrimination is rationally related to a legitimate governmental purpose, that, too, should end this litigation.

I would affirm the judgment of the Supreme Court of Vermont.

CONCLUSION

The U.S. Constitution provides a set of safeguards that taxpayers can rely upon to know that a particular tax has been constitutionally imposed.

Taxpayers need to be familiar with these provisions so they can identify potentially unconstitutional taxes before they are forced to comply with their provisions. By being aware of the potential problems that may be encountered, taxpayers will be better prepared to respond appropriately when they suspect there is a problem.

STUDY QUESTIONS

14. The dissenting opinion in *Williams et al. v. Vermont et al* stated all of the following *except:*

   a. The U.S. Supreme Court subjected Vermont's motor vehicle tax laws to a microscopic scrutiny that few enactments would survive.

   b. Section 8911(9) was designed to allow people who buy cars out-of-state but live in Vermont to be doubly taxed.

   c. A tax classification does not violate the demands of equal protection simply because it does *not* perfectly identify the class of people it attempts to single out.

15. If a taxpayer believes that a tax is *unconstitutional,* and the effect on the taxpayer is material, the taxpayer should consider challenging the related taxing statute. *True or False?*

CPE NOTE: When you have completed your study and review of chapters 5–7, which comprise Module 2, you may wish to take the Quizzer for this Module.

For your convenience, you can also take this Quizzer online at: **www.cchtestingcenter.com.**

MULTISTATE CORPORATE TAX COURSE (2011 EDITION)
Answers to Study Questions

MODULE 1 — CHAPTER 1

1. a. Incorrect. Most states, including Alabama, impose a corporate income tax.
b. Incorrect. The California corporate franchise tax is computed essentially in the same manner as an income tax.
c. Incorrect. Although Florida does not levy a personal income tax, it *does* impose a corporate income tax.
d. Correct. South Dakota is one of only a handful of states that does not levy a corporate income tax.

2. a. Incorrect. This is a limitation of P.L. 86-272. For example, Public Law 86-272 provides no protection against the imposition of a sales tax collection obligation.
b. Correct. This is not a limitation of P.L. 86-272. Public Law 86-272 protects only sales of *tangible* personal property. It does *not* protect activities such as leasing tangible personal property, selling services, selling or leasing real estate, or selling or licensing intangibles.
c. Incorrect. This is a limitation of P.L. 86-272. If a salesperson exercises authority to approve orders within a state, or performs non-solicitation activities (such as repairs, customer training or technical assistance), the company does *not* qualify for protection under P.L. 86-272.

3. a. Correct. This is an advantage of state conformity to federal tax provisions, as it simplifies tax compliance for multistate corporations. The use of the federal tax base as the starting point for computing state taxable income is referred to as piggybacking.
b. Incorrect. This is a disadvantage of state conformity to federal tax provisions. States must be aware that changes to the federal tax law could significantly affect state tax revenues.
c. Incorrect. This is a disadvantage of state conformity to federal tax provisions. Complete conformity would allow the federal government to determine state tax policy.

4. a. Incorrect. This is a true statement. UDITPA principles have been adopted, at least in part, by most states.
b. Incorrect. This is a true statement. Under UDITPA, business income is defined as 'income arising from transactions and activity in the regular course of the taxpayer's trade or business and includes income from tangible

and intangible property if the acquisition, management, and disposition of the property constitute integral parts of the taxpayer's regular trade or business operations.' Nonbusiness income is all income that is not business income.

c. Correct. This is not a true statement. Under the UDITPA approach, a taxpayer apportions a percentage of its business income to each state in which it has nexus, but it specifically allocates the entire amount of any nonbusiness income to a single state.

5. a. Incorrect. Assigning more weight to the sales factor than to the property or payroll factor tends to increase the percentage of an out-of-state corporation's income that is subject to tax, because the out-of-state corporation's principal activity in the state is likely its sales, and it may have little or no property or payroll in the state.

b. Correct. Assigning more weight to the sales factor tends to reduce the tax on in-state corporations that have significant amounts of property and payroll in the state, but that have sales throughout the country.

6. a. Incorrect. This only applies to sales to the U.S. government and so-called throwback sales, both of which are assigned to the state from which the goods are shipped.

b. Correct. This is known as the *destination test.*

c. Incorrect. Certain types of nonbusiness income, such as nonbusiness interest and dividend income, are assigned to the state of commercial domicile.

7. a. Correct. Arizona generally requires a taxpayer member of a unitary business group to compute its taxable income on a combined unitary basis.

b. Incorrect. Delaware is one of a handful of states that requires separate-company returns under all circumstances.

c. Correct. Maryland requires separate-company reporting. In contrast, most states require or permit some type of consolidated or combined reporting.

8. a. Incorrect. Inclusion in a combined unitary report generally requires more than 50 percent ownership; however, inclusion in a state elective consolidated return generally requires 80 percent or more ownership.

b. Correct. Inclusion in a state consolidated return generally requires 80 percent or more ownership, which piggybacks on the ownership threshold for inclusion in a federal consolidated return.

9. a. *Correct.* Non-solicitation activities are *not* protected by P. L. 86-272, and generally create income tax nexus.

b. *Incorrect.* Solicitation activities are protected by P. L. 86-272, and generally do *not* create income tax nexus.

c. *Incorrect.* Providing a sales representative with a company car that is used only in solicitation activities is protected by P. L. 86-272, and generally does not create income tax nexus.

10. True. *Incorrect.* Although filing a consolidated return can be beneficial, such as when one affiliate has losses that can be offset against the income generated by other affiliates, there can also be disadvantages which should be considered before making that election.

False. *Correct.* There are advantages to filing a consolidated return, but there are also disadvantages that should be considered before determining whether or not to make that election. One disadvantage is that filing consolidated can limit a taxpayer's ability to use intercompany transactions to shift income from affiliates based in high-tax states to affiliates based in low-tax states.

11. a. *Incorrect.* In *Geoffrey,* the South Carolina Supreme Court held that a trademark holding company that licensed its intangibles for use in South Carolina had nexus for income tax purposes, despite the lack of any physical presence in South Carolina.

b. *Incorrect.* In *Lanco,* the New Jersey Supreme Court ruled that the Delaware trademark holding company of Lane Bryant had income tax nexus in New Jersey, even though it had no physical presence there.

c. *Incorrect.* In *MBNA,* the West Virginia Supreme Court of Appeals found that the physical presence test does not apply to state corporate income taxes, and that MBNA had "a significant economic presence sufficient to meet the substantial nexus" test under the Commerce Clause.

d. *Correct.* In *Quill,* the U.S. Supreme Court ruled that a corporation satisfies the Commerce Clause's "substantial nexus" requirement only if the taxpayer has a physical presence in the state. However, *Quill* was a sales and use tax case, and the U.S. Supreme Court has yet to rule on whether that finding applies to taxes based on net income.

12. a. *Incorrect.* The Ohio Supreme Court determined in *SFA Folio* that common ownership alone does not create nexus for an out-of-state affiliate. Other state courts have generally agreed.

b. *Correct.* State courts in Illinois, Michigan and New York have adopted the "more than a slightest presence" test, under which a company's in-state physical presence need not be substantial to satisfy the *Quill* "substantial nexus" requirement. Instead, it must be "demonstrably more than a slightest presence."

c. Incorrect. State supreme courts in Massachusetts and Virginia have determined that deliveries in company-owned trucks is a protected activity under Public Law 86-272.

13. a. Incorrect. This method assumes that the sale is apportioned based on the percentage of actual performance, which is not how the UDITPA cost-of-performance rule works.

b. Incorrect. This method assumes that the sale is evenly distributed to all states that incurred costs, which is not how the UDITPA cost-of-performance rule works.

c. Correct. The UDITPA cost-of-performance rule attributes the entire sale to the state in which the greatest proportion of the costs of performance is incurred.

14. True. Correct. Under the market-based approach, receipts from services are attributed to the state based on where the service recipient is located. This approach provides a more accurate measure of the taxpayer's customer base, and has the political appeal of reducing the tax burden on service providers that have in-state facilities but provide services primarily to out-of-state customers.

False. Incorrect. Under the market-based approach, receipts from services are attributed to the state based on where the service recipient is located. Examples of states that have adopted this approach for sales of services include Georgia, Illinois, Iowa, Maine, Maryland, Michigan, Minnesota, Utah, and Wisconsin.

15. a. Correct. Separate-company reporting can provide taxpayers with opportunities to shift income through intercompany royalty and interest payments. For this reason, combined reporting, as opposed to separate-company reporting, is used as a mechanism by the states to limit tax base erosion.

b. Incorrect. This mechanism is used by states because combined reporting eliminates the tax benefits of intercompany transactions, such as royalty and interest payments.

c. Incorrect. The highest courts in several states have ruled that an economic presence, such as the licensing of trademarks for use within the state by affiliated companies, is sufficient to create constitutional nexus for income tax purposes. This mechanism limits the ability of taxpayers to shift income to out-of-state intangible property holding companies.

MODULE 1 — CHAPTER 2

1. a. *Incorrect.* Although the business is commercially domiciled in State A, the income is *not* allocated there. The income would most likely be allocated to State A if it were from the sale of intangible property that is not an integral part of the taxpayer's regular business.

b. *Correct.* The income should be specifically allocated to State B because:

- **The income is nonbusiness income since the sale is not in the taxpayer's regular course of business.**
- **The real property is located in State B.**

c. *Incorrect.* The income should be specifically allocated to a *single* state, rather than apportioned among the states because it is nonbusiness, rather than business, income.

2. a. *Incorrect.* Since each state can choose the type and number of factors and the computations it will use to determine the amount of business activity conducted within its borders, a corporation's apportionment percentages may not add up to 100 percent. In other words, there can be *double taxation* (i.e., the apportionment percentages sum to more than 100 percent) or *nowhere income* (i.e., the apportionment percentages sum to less than 100 percent).

b. *Incorrect.* *Allocation* refers to the specific assignment of nonbusiness income to a particular state. *Business* income is apportioned among all of the states in which the taxpayer has nexus.

c. *Correct.* A taxpayer apportions its income by computing the percentage of its business income that is taxable in each state in which it has nexus by using those states' apportionment formulas.

3. a. *Correct.* When a corporation as a whole is profitable, but incurs a loss in one state as determined by a separate geographic accounting, the use of an apportionment formula results in the corporation's incurring an income tax liability in the state in which the loss occurs.

b. *Incorrect.* Not all corporations are allowed to apportion their income. The requirements for being allowed to apportion income vary by state, but generally involve doing on business in another state or being taxable in another state. Some states allow apportionment *only* if the corporation actually files returns and pays tax in another state.

c. *Incorrect.* UDITPA §18 allows taxpayers to petition for an alternative to the allocation and apportionment provisions of UDITPA if those provisions do not fairly represent the extent of the taxpayer's business activity in a state. However, UDITPA §18 also allows tax administrators to require an alternative method in these circumstances.

4. a. *Incorrect.* Most California taxpayers must use a three-factor apportionment formula. Effective for tax years beginning on or after January 1, 2011, certain taxpayers may make an annual election to use a single-factor sales-only formula, but it is not required. Vermont currently requires an apportionment formula that that places a 50 percent weight on the sales factor, and a 25 percent weight on both the property factor and the payroll factor.

b. *Correct.* Georgia and Wisconsin both completed phasing in a sales-only formula beginning in 2008.

c. *Incorrect.* North Carolina uses a double-weighted sales formula. Beginning in 2010, a *capital investment corporation* may apportion its business income using a sales-only formula, but a sales-only formula is not required. Beginning in 2010, Pennsylvania taxpayers will use an apportionment formula that weights the sales factor at 90 percent, and the property factor and payroll factor each at five percent.

5. True. *Correct.* These industries are specifically excluded under UDITPA §2. Many states provide special rules for computing apportionment percentages for financial organizations and public utilities because their in-state activity may not be fairly represented by the standard apportionment formula.

False. *Incorrect.* Financial organizations and public utilities are specifically excluded under UDITPA §2 because the standard formula may not fairly apportion the income of these taxpayers.

6. a. *Incorrect.* MTC Reg. IV.18(e) provides that aircraft ready for flight are includible in a state's numerator, based on the ratio of in-state departures to the total departures everywhere (both weighted by the cost and value of aircraft). Therefore the total cost of aircraft ready for flight is *not* included.

b. *Incorrect.* This calculation is correct, except it should be based on in-state *departures* rather than in-state arrivals.

c. *Correct.* MTC Reg. IV.18(e) provides that an airline's sales factor numerator is the taxpayer's total in-state revenue, which includes:

- **The total transportation revenue multiplied by the ratio of in-state departures to the total departures everywhere, (both weighted by the cost and value of aircraft), PLUS**
- **Any nonflight revenues directly attributable to the state**

7. a. *Correct.* MTC Reg. IV.18(h) covers apportionment of a multistate television or radio broadcaster's business income, including broadcasting over the public airwaves by cable, *as well as* by satellite transmission or any other method of communication.

b. *Incorrect.* This statement is true. Some states have adopted the MTC formula for trucking companies, while other states have adopted their own special formulas, such as formulas based solely on revenue miles.

c. *Incorrect.* This statement is true. Under MTC Reg. IV.18(g), a *trucking company* is a motor common carrier, a motor contract carrier, or an express carrier that primarily transports others' tangible personal property by motor vehicle for payment.

8. a. *Correct.* **Outer-jurisdictional property should be pro-rated to a state based on the ratio of uplink and downlink transmissions in the state to the total number of uplink and downlink transmissions everywhere.** *Only* **if that information is not available should outer-jurisdictional property be pro-rated based on the ratio of time the property was used to make transmissions.**

b. *Incorrect.* This statement is true. The payroll factor is based on the normal UDITPA rules for sourcing payroll. The numerator of the payroll factor is the total compensation paid in the state, and the denominator of the payroll factor includes all compensation paid everywhere by the taxpayer.

c. *Incorrect.* This statement is true. Under MTC Reg. IV.18(j), a throwback rule applies if the purchaser is the U.S. government or the taxpayer is *not* taxable in a state where the printed materials are delivered.

9. True. *Incorrect.* Although the MTC has not promulgated a special apportionment formula for insurance companies, states that impose a corporate income tax on insurance companies usually require them to apportion their income using a *single-factor premiums* formula.

False. *Correct.* **States that impose a corporate income tax on insurance companies usually require them to apportion their income using a** *single-factor premiums* **formula, not a single-factor property apportionment formula.**

10. a. *Incorrect.* This denominator is used in Illinois to apportion income from providing transportation services *other than* airline services. Income from providing airline transportation services is apportioned to Illinois based on a ratio of revenue miles.

b. *Incorrect.* Receipts from telecommunications services or mobile telecommunications services are generally attributed to Illinois if the customer's service address is in Illinois. They are *not* attributed based on where a call is completed.

c. Correct. This was a change made by Illinois effective for tax years ending December 31, 2008 or later. Also, receipts from investment or trading assets and activities are attributed to Illinois if they are properly assigned to a fixed place of business within Illinois. If the fixed place of business that has a preponderance of substantive contacts cannot be established, the asset or activity is assigned to the taxpayer's state of commercial domicile.

MODULE 1 — CHAPTER 3

1. a. Correct. If the acquisition is structured as a stock purchase, once the acquirer attains a controlling interest in the target's stock, the acquirer may either retain the target as a separate subsidiary or liquidate the target to acquire direct control of the target's assets.
b. Incorrect. This occurs if the acquisition is structured as an asset purchase rather than a stock purchase.
c. Incorrect. If the acquisition is structured as a stock purchase, the target's NOL carryforwards and other tax attributes remain with the target, which is then controlled by the acquirer.

2. a. Correct. This is a requirement for an acquirer to be eligible for a Section 338(g) election. Stock acquired through a related party or a tax-free exchange is not included in the 80 percent requirement.
b. Incorrect. In order for an acquirer to be eligible for a Section 338(g) election, the acquirer must make the election no later than the 15th day of the *ninth* month beginning after the month in which the acquisition occurs.
c. Incorrect. In order for an acquirer to be eligible for a Section 338(g) election, the acquirer must make the election on Form 8023. Form 8883 is required for allocating basis to the acquired assets.

3. a. Incorrect. In a Section 338(h)(10) election, the gain or loss on the actual sale of the target's stock is ignored. Therefore, a single level of taxation is created by a Section 338(h)(10) election.
b. Incorrect. A Section 338(h)(10) election results in a single level of taxation. A Section 338(g) election results in two levels of taxation. Because of this, Section 338(h)(10) elections are more popular than Section 338(g) elections.
c. Correct. A Section 338(h)(10) election causes a deemed sale of the target's assets that results in both gain or loss recognition and a step-up or step-down in the basis of the target's assets.

4. a. Correct. In *McKesson Water Products Company*, the New Jersey Tax Court ruled that a gain from a Section 338(h)(10) election was *non-operational income* allocable to California.

b. Incorrect. In *General Mills,* the Massachusetts Supreme Judicial Court ruled that gains from a deemed asset sale were properly included in Massachusetts apportionable income, consistent with the federal tax treatment of the transaction.

c. Incorrect. In *Newell Window Furnishing,* the Tennessee Court of Appeals ruled that where a corporation sold the stock of its subsidiary and the sale was treated as a sale of assets under Section 338(h)(10), the gain from the deemed asset sale must be included in the subsidiary's Tennessee income tax base as apportionable business income.

5. True. Incorrect. Pursuant to law changes made in 2004 (H.B. 4744), when an acquiring corporation makes a Section 338 election, the target corporation will be treated as having sold its assets for purposes of computing the sales factor.

False. Correct. Effective for tax years beginning on or after January 1, 2005, for apportionment purposes, if an acquiring corporation makes a Section 338 election (treating certain stock purchases as asset acquisitions), the target corporation will be treated as having sold its assets.

MODULE 1 — CHAPTER 4

1. a. Incorrect. This statement is a direct quote from the Supreme Court's opinion in *Allied-Signal.*

b. Correct. This statement is *not* true. In *Allied-Signal,* the Supreme Court stated that although the payee and the payer need not be engaged in the same unitary business as a prerequisite to apportionment in all cases. What is required is that the "capital transaction serve an operational rather than an investment function."

c. Incorrect. This statement is true. In *Mobil Oil Corp.,* the Supreme Court stated that "the linchpin of apportionability in the field of state income taxation is the unitary business principle."

2. a. Correct. The gain on the sale of land that has nothing to do with the business activities of the taxpayer in the taxing state is the most likely candidate for treatment as nonbusiness income. The land does not appear to be part of the unitary business that the taxpayer is conducting in the taxing state.

b. Incorrect. In *Mobil Oil,* the U.S. Supreme Court ruled that a state could tax an apportioned percentage of dividends received by the taxpayer from its unitary subsidiaries. Thus, the dividends are probably *business* income.

c. Incorrect. The interest is probably *business* income. In *Allied-Signal,* the Supreme Court stated that apportionable income includes "interest earned on short-term deposits in a bank . . . if that income forms part of the working capital of the corporation's unitary business."

3. a. *Incorrect.* This is true of *business* income under UDITPA, not nonbusiness income.

b. *Correct.* **Under UDITPA, *business income* is apportioned among the states in which the taxpayer has nexus, but *nonbusiness income* is exclusively allocated to a single state.**

c. *Incorrect.* Each state can adopt its own definition of nonbusiness income, subject to U.S. Constitutional limitations. This can result in inconsistent treatment and can cause double taxation of income.

4. a. *Incorrect.* This describes the *transactional* test.

b. *Correct.* **This is a description of the *functional* test.**

c. *Incorrect.* This is a question asked in applying the transactional test.

5. True. *Correct.* **Also, in 2003 the MTC amended its Reg. IV.1(a) to state that *business income* includes income that meets *either* the transactional test or the functional test.**

False. *Incorrect.* The majority view is that UDITPA's definition of *business income* includes *both* a transactional test and a functional test, and that income is correctly considered to be business in nature if *either* test is met.

6. a. *Incorrect.* In 2001, the Alabama Legislature added a functional test to the statutory definition of business income.

b. *Incorrect.* In response to the ***Phillips Petroleum*** decision, the Iowa Legislature amended the Iowa statute to include a functional test.

c. *Incorrect.* The Tennessee Legislature added a functional test to the business income statute after the ***Associated Partnership I*** case.

d. *Correct.* **All of the above states have added a functional test to their statutory definitions of business income.**

7. a. *Incorrect.* In ***Kemppel***, the Ohio Supreme Court ruled that gains realized by an S corporation from the liquidating sale of its assets were nonbusiness income because the gains were from a liquidation of assets followed by a dissolution of the corporation, and were not from a sale in the regular course of a trade or business.

b. *Incorrect.* In ***Phillips Petroleum Co.***, the Iowa Supreme Court determined that a taxpayer's gain from a disposition of assets was nonbusiness income because it was a once-in-a-corporate-lifetime occurrence and failed the transactional test.

c. *Incorrect.* In ***Uniroyal Tire Co.*** the Alabama Supreme Court held that the Alabama statute contained only a transactional test.

d. *Correct.* **In *Jim Beam Brands*, the California Court of Appeal determined that the functional test did *not* include a partial liquidation exception or a requirement that the disposition of property be an integral part of the taxpayer's trade or business operations.**

8. a. *Incorrect.* Nonbusiness royalty income from real property is generally allocable to the state where the real property is located.

b. *Incorrect.* Nonbusiness rental income from realty is usually allocable to the state where the rental property is located.

c. *Correct.* Nonbusiness capital gains from the sale of intangible assets are generally allocable to the state of commercial domicile, as is nonbusiness interest and dividend income.

d. *Incorrect.* Nonbusiness capital gain income from real property is generally allocable to the state where the property in question is located.

9. True. *Incorrect.* Generally, expenses attributable to nonbusiness income may be offset *only* against the related nonbusiness income.

False. *Correct.* If an item is treated as nonbusiness income, any expenses attributable to that item generally cannot be deducted against apportionable business income.

10. True. *Correct.* Many states have broadened their definition of *business income* to include all income that may be treated as apportionable business income under the U.S. Constitution.

False. *Incorrect.* States such as Georgia, Illinois, and Pennsylvania have expanded their definition of business income to include all income that can be apportionable business income under the U.S. Constitution. Other states have refined their definition of nonbusiness income to make clear that it includes both a transactional and a functional test.

MODULE 2 — CHAPTER 5

1. a. *Incorrect.* This is not the amount of time that most states allow the taxpayer to report errors. When reviewing for errors, taxpayers may also want to consider the appeal of any penalty included in the assessment.

b. *Correct.* Most states allow 30 or 60 days to report errors that should be corrected before the final assessment is issued. Taxpayers should also verify that any interest or penalty calculations in the preliminary assessment are correct.

c. *Incorrect.* States *do* impose a time limitation for the reporting of errors, although it varies. However, regardless of the time limitation, taxpayers should promptly contact the auditor when errors are found.

2. a. *Correct.* The ordinary negligence penalty is the penalty that is most commonly imposed as the result of a sales and use tax audit. Many states extend this penalty to errors that are similar to those found in previous audits.

b. Incorrect. The gross negligence penalty is *not* the most common penalty imposed as the result of a sales and use tax audit. For those taxpayers who are assessed this penalty, the rate ranges from 20 to 30 percent.

c. Incorrect. The fraud penalty is *not* the most common penalty as it is imposed when a taxpayer deliberately misleads the auditor or hides the truth. If the fraud is on a large enough scale, it can be a criminal offense.

d. Incorrect. The substantial understatement penalty is *not* the most common penalty imposed as the result of a sales and use tax audit. This type of penalty is more commonly imposed in income tax audits.

3. a. Incorrect. When a taxpayer does not exercise the degree of care that would be expected of a reasonable person in similar circumstances, that is considered to be ordinary negligence. This would not be as serious as a reckless disregard for the law.

b. Correct. When a taxpayer exhibits a careless or reckless disregard for the law, that is considered gross negligence. This would include a taxpayer's failure to have sufficient procedures in place to meet its tax responsibilities.

c. Incorrect. A fraud penalty is the *most* serious penalty. It is imposed when a taxpayer intentionally misleads the auditor or conceals the truth about transactions to avoid paying tax. Most states impose either a 50 or 100-percent penalty for fraud.

d. Incorrect. The substantial understatement penalty is imposed when the amount of tax voluntarily reported throughout the audit period is substantially less than the amount of tax that was subsequently found to be due as a result of the audit.

4. a. Incorrect. If an auditor has behaved inappropriately, such as displaying prejudice in a minority-owned firm, this would be a reason to request his or her removal.

b. Incorrect. If an auditor has been extremely unreasonable, such as making demands that are extreme and unnecessary, and is unwilling to be flexible, a taxpayer may want to request his or her removal.

c. Correct. Being late to meetings is an issue that should be handled by talking directly with the auditor and not involving the supervisor. Requesting a supervisor to remove an auditor can damage the working relationship with the state, so it should only be done for the reasons listed in a, b, and d.

d. Incorrect. If an auditor has shown obvious bias against the taxpayer in the audit, this would be a reason to request his or her removal.

5. True. Incorrect. The interest assessment should still be tested, including the state's allocation assumptions that are used in the computation.

False. *Correct.* Although the use of computers has reduced the importance of the interest assessment review, taxpayers should still test the calculation for accuracy.

6. a. *Incorrect.* If the taxpayer has a good audit history, this should be pointed out as an argument for leniency in the current period. However, this does *not* mean the taxpayer made a food-faith effort to comply with the tax law in the current period.

b. *Incorrect.* Staffing issues should be brought up as a defense when the taxpayer was unable to comply with the tax law because of high staff turnover or other staffing problems.

c. *Incorrect.* Just because the taxpayer cooperated with the auditor does not mean it made a good-faith effort to comply with the tax law. This defense is normally used in conjunction with other defenses.

d. *Correct.* **The taxpayer can establish that it was making a good-faith effort to comply with the tax law by demonstrating self-compliance through its self-assessment procedures.**

7. a. *Correct.* **There would be a favorable cost benefit of $29,000 ($20,000 versus $49,000 (70 percent x $70,000)).**

b. *Incorrect.* This answer is incorrect because it does not consider the cost of mounting an appeal.

c. *Incorrect.* This answer is incorrect because it does not consider the probability of success.

8. True. *Correct.* **Taxpayers should not be subject to penalties for errors that occurred before a final audit determination. For this reason, taxpayers should carefully note the completion dates of their audits.**

False. *Incorrect.* Since the audit determination was not made until the midst of the third year of the next audit period, the taxpayer should not be subject to penalties for the same errors that occurred during the first three years of that period.

9. a. *Incorrect.* This statement is true. The amount of potential liability for issues that may be appealed, including related interest and penalty, should be recorded on the books. If it is expected that the issue will extend into future years, estimated audit reserves should also be established for those years.

b. *Correct.* **Being considered a responsible person *can* have personal financial consequences. State responsible person statutes impose personal liability on a responsible person if that person improperly withholds the payment of tax. Some states also impose negligence or fraud penalties on the responsible person.**

c. Incorrect. This statement is true. If the final audit determination does not occur until a later audit period, the taxpayer should not be subject to penalties for similar errors that have already occurred in that later audit period.

10. a. Incorrect. Participating states are required to use *statistical* sampling, not nonstatistical sampling.

b. Incorrect. When joint audits are conducted and errors identified, the states involved must issue assessments or refunds within *90* days of completion of the audit.

c. Correct. Each participating state must provide a matrix of all definitions of tangible personal property and services. Sellers will be held harmless due to errors made by the state in its matrix.

MODULE 2 — CHAPTER 6

1. a. Incorrect. This was an argument *in favor* of requiring National Bellas Hess to collect the tax. In his dissenting opinion, Justice Fortas noted that the *large-scale, systematic, continuous solicitation and exploitation* of the Illinois consumer market is a sufficient *nexus* to require Bellas Hess to collect from Illinois customers and to remit the use tax—especially when coupled with the use of the credit resources of residents of Illinois, dependent as that mechanism is upon the State's banking and credit institutions.

b. Incorrect. This was an argument *in favor* of requiring National Bellas Hess to collect the tax. In his dissenting opinion, Justice Fortas noted that Bellas Hess enjoyed the benefits of, and profits from the facilities nurtured by the State of Illinois the same as if it were a retail store or maintained salespeople there.

c. Correct. National Bellas Hess had no physical presence in Illinois, so this was *not* an argument in favor of requiring the company to collect sales tax. If the company had a physical presence, it would have been required to collect sales tax.

2. a. Incorrect. The *majority* opinion was based on *Miller Bros.*

b. Correct. In his dissenting opinion, Justice Fortas stated that *Scripto* was not "meaningfully distinguishable" from *National Bellas Hess.*

c. Incorrect. The *Quill* case was decided *after National Bellas Hess.*

3. a. Incorrect. This would have been a reason *not* to reverse the Illinois decision. However, National Bellas Hess argued, and The U.S. Supreme Court agreed, that the liabilities that Illinois imposed upon it *did* violate the Due Process Clause of the Fourteenth Amendment and created an unconstitutional burden upon interstate commerce.

b. *Correct.* The U.S. Supreme Court noted that it had never held that a State may impose the duty of use tax collection and payment on a seller when its *only* connection with customers in the State was by common carrier or the U.S. mail—as was the case in *National Bellas Hess.*
c. *Incorrect.* If the Court had considered the facts of the case to be similar to those in *Scripto,* it probably would not have reversed the Illinois Supreme Court decision.

4. True. *Correct.* The Court found that a use tax requirement would create an unfair administrative burden on a remote seller with no physical presence.
False. *Incorrect.* After the finding in *National Bellas Hess,* which *required* a physical presence, some states passed statutes known as "anti-*Bellas Hess*" statutes that would allow those states to impose a use tax requirement on taxpayers with *no* physical presence.

5. a. *Correct.* The Commerce Clause requires substantial nexus unlike the Due Process Clause which only requires a minimum connection.
b. *Incorrect.* The Commerce Clause, not the Due Process Clause, concerns the effects of state regulation on the national economy.
c. *Incorrect.* The Due Process Clause, not the Commerce Clause, concerns the fairness of governmental activity.

6. a. *Incorrect.* Since the State A residents come to State B to buy the products, this would not cause the company to have nexus with State B since it has no physical presence there.
b. *Correct.* Since the company has employees selling and delivering products in State A, it has a physical presence there and would have nexus with State A.
c. *Incorrect.* The company has no physical presence in State B since it is selling goods over the Internet and is located in another state.

7. a. *Incorrect.* The Court noted that *Bellas Hess* is *not* inconsistent with *Complete Auto Transit* and other cases decided since *Bellas Hess* such as *National Geographic Society.*
b. *Incorrect.* The Court pointed out that although cases subsequent to *Bellas Hess* regarding other types of taxes may not have followed the *Bellas Hess* rule, it still remains good law.
c. *Correct.* The Court stated that the continuing value of a bright-line rule and the doctrine and principles of *stare decisis* show that the *Bellas Hess* rule remains good law.

8. True. *Correct.* A taxpayer may have a minimum connection with a state as required by the Due Process Clause, but not the substantial nexus that is required by the Commerce Clause.

False. *Incorrect.* The Due Process Clause only requires a minimum connection. A taxpayer may have a minimum connection but not the substantial nexus that is required by the Commerce Clause in order for the state to impose a collection requirement for a sales tax.

9. a. *Incorrect.* Although an independent sales representative is not an employee of the taxpayer, his or her activities in a state on behalf of a taxpayer can have the same nexus implications as if the taxpayer performed the activities.

b. *Incorrect.* An employee is an extension of the company, and his or her activities in a state related to that company would have the same nexus implications.

c. *Correct.* The *Scripto* Court reasoned that the level of representation in the state was essentially the same whether the representation was by an employee or independent contractor at least to the extent it related to the carrying out of a sale.

10. a. *Incorrect.* Just because an agent works for more than one principal does not necessarily mean that the agent cannot create nexus for any of those principals. The *Scripto* Court noted that there was no Constitutional basis why an agent that works for several principals could not create nexus.

b. *Incorrect.* It does not matter what label is put on an agent when determining whether nexus is created. What matters is the functions the agent performs for the principal.

c. *Correct.* As stated in *Miller Bros.*, there must be "some definite link, some minimum connection, between a state and the person, property, or transaction it seeks to tax."

11. True. *Correct.* The *Scripto* Court noted that Miller Bros. had no solicitors in Maryland; there was no "exploitation of the consumer market"; and no regular, systematic displaying of its products.

False. *Incorrect.* Scripto argued that based on the decision in *Miller Bros.*, the Court must find that it had no nexus. However, the Court disagreed. It distinguished *Miller Bros.* and noted that the goods on which Maryland tried to force Miller Bros. to collect its tax were sold to residents of Maryland when they were present at Miller's store in Delaware.

12. a. *Incorrect.* The needs of business generally determine the activities undertaken by a business and usually take precedence over tax filing requirements. In any case, taxpayers must be careful when making nexus determinations to avoid unnecessarily exposing the remote selling entity to liability for uncollected taxes.

b. *Incorrect.* The *Borders Online* case provides guidelines for what *not* to do when trying to avoid a tax collection responsibility.

c. *Correct.* This is a lesson to be learned from the *Borders Online* case. If entities are trying to avoid a tax collection responsibility, they should operate as independently as possible and stay clear of the types of connections that existed in that case.

13. a. *Incorrect.* Borders did not consent to act as Online's principal so this was not a reason why Borders was considered Online's agent. However, the consent to act as a principal's agent would mean an agency relationship exists.

b. *Correct.* Online's return policy, which allowed customers to return their products to Borders stores, was viewed by the court as an activity that created substantial nexus.

c. *Incorrect.* The court did not determine that Online controlled Borders so this was not a reason why Borders was considered Online's agent. However, had Online had the ability to control Borders, this would be a factor to determine that an agency relationship existed.

14. a. *Incorrect.* Simply belonging to the same parent would not cause one company to be the agent of another.

b. *Correct.* If a company refers customers to its affiliate, it is a representative of the affiliate for the purpose of selling its goods and thereby is an *agent* of the affiliate.

c. *Incorrect.* Accepting a return on occasion from an out-of-state affiliated mail-order business, such as what occurred in *Bloomingdale's,* would not be enough to cause an agency relationship. However, if the stated return policy of the mail-order business advised customers that they could make returns to the in-state store, an agency relationship could be created.

15. True. *Incorrect.* There are four factors that courts consider when determining agency issues, but these factors are not all-inclusive.

False. *Correct.* Although there are four factors that courts consider when determining agency issues, there is no *bright-line* four-factor test to determine agency. Those factors are:

- **Whether the agent has power to alter legal relationships of the principal**
- **Whether the agent acts as the fiduciary of the principal**
- **Whether the principal can control the agent**
- **Whether the agent consents to act as the principal's agent**

MODULE 2 — CHAPTER 7

1. a. *Incorrect.* The Commerce Clause bars states from interfering with interstate commerce because only the U.S. Congress is allowed to make laws in that area.

b. *Correct.* The Equal Protection Clause prohibits jurisdictions from making laws that single out specific taxpayers and impose tax on their activities in a discriminatory manner. In order for a tax to be considered constitutional, a state must be able to demonstrate that there is a rational basis for imposing the tax on a specific group of taxpayers.

c. *Incorrect.* The Due Process Clause restricts jurisdictions to only tax activities that have a substantial nexus or level of activity in that jurisdiction.

2. a. *Incorrect.* The Supreme Court noted that not only had the philosophy underlying the *Spector* rule been rejected, but the rule itself has been stripped of any practical significance since it was based on the use of particular words in a statute. Therefore, it overruled the *Spector* decision.

b. *Incorrect.* The decision in *Complete Auto Transit* presented four specific elements that are necessary for a tax to be considered unconstitutional.

c. *Correct.* The U.S. Supreme Court held that the Mississippi tax that was challenged in *Complete Auto Transit* was *not* unconstitutional since the appellant's only claim was that it was unconstitutional *per se* because it was a tax on the privilege of doing business.

3. a. *Correct.* One of the prongs of the four-prong test for constitutionality presented in *Complete Auto Transit* is that the tax must be fairly related to services enjoyed by the taxpayer in the state, such as police protection.

b. *Incorrect.* One of the four requirements delineated by the U.S. Supreme Court in *Complete Auto Transit* is that the tax must be applied to an activity that has a *substantial* nexus with the taxing state.

c. *Incorrect.* One of the four requirements delineated by the U.S. Supreme Court in *Complete Auto Transit* is that the tax must be *fairly apportioned,* which does not necessarily mean that it will be apportioned primarily to the state in question.

4. True. *Incorrect.* The Court found the order *unconstitutional.* The fact that the milk dealers that paid the order premiums were not competitors of Massachusetts farmers was an argument made by the State, but the Court rejected the argument.

False. *Correct.* The Court found the order *unconstitutional* and repudiated this argument stating that previous cases have determined that imposing a "differential burden on any part of the stream of commerce ... is invalid, because a burden placed at any point will result in a disadvantage to the out-of-state producer."

5. a. *Incorrect.* Pure subsidies funded out of general revenue usually do *not* impose a burden on interstate commerce. However, the milk order was not a pure subsidy.

b. *Correct.* A pure subsidy funded out of general revenue usually simply assists local business and does not impose a burden on interstate commerce. However, the milk order was funded principally from taxes on the sale of milk produced in other states. Therefore, it not only helped local farmers, but burdened interstate commerce. Because of this, the Supreme Court determined that the milk pricing order violated the fundamental principle that a State may not "benefit in-state economic interests by burdening out-of-state competitors."

c. *Incorrect.* The State argued that the milk order was the combination of two independently *lawful* regulations. However, the Supreme Court stated that even if each part of the pricing order would be constitutional standing alone, the pricing order with the combination of the two regulations was unconstitutional.

6. a. *Correct.* The Court rejected this argument. It noted that if it did accept it, this would undermine almost every discriminatory tax case. It also pointed out that state taxes are ordinarily paid by in-state businesses and consumers, yet if they discriminate against out-of-state products, they are unconstitutional.

b. *Incorrect.* The concept that a discriminatory tax does not hinder interstate commerce "merely because the burden of the tax was borne by consumers" in the taxing State was completely rejected in ***Bacchus Imports.***

c. *Incorrect.* This idea was not based on previous Supreme Court decisions. One decision in particular totally dismissed this concept.

7. a. *Incorrect.* This was another part of the State's argument, which was rejected by the Court.

b. *Incorrect.* The Court noted that it is irrelevant for purposes of Commerce Clause analysis whether a state is trying to augment "thriving and substantial business enterprises" or "subsidize … financially troubled" ones.

c. *Correct.* The Court rejected this argument, noting that accepting it would encourage the bad practice that the rule against discrimination condemns. It stated that "Preservation of local industry by protecting it from the rigors of interstate competition is the hallmark of the economic protectionism that the Commerce Clause prohibits."

8. True. *Incorrect.* Chief Judge Rehnquist *agreed* with the Supreme Court's majority opinion when it stated that ***Bacchus*** can be distinguished in this way. However, he disagreed as to the effect that should have on the ***West Lynn Creamery*** decision.

False. *Correct.* Chief Judge Rehnquist *agreed* with the Supreme Court's majority opinion when it stated that *Bacchus* can be distinguished in this way. However, he pointed out that this was not only a distinction, but was an important difference. He noted that, "No decided case supports the Court's conclusion that the negative Commerce Clause prohibits the State from using money that it has lawfully obtained through a neutral tax on milk dealers and distributing it as a subsidy to dairy farmers."

9. a. *Correct.* Justice Scalia believed that this methodology was so far removed from what the Court had previously held to be unconstitutional, that prohibiting it would be an extension of the Court's negative-Commerce-Clause jurisprudence and, therefore, was unacceptable. He believed that previous negative-Commerce-Clause cases had, in effect, already approved the use of this type of subsidy.
b. *Incorrect.* This methodology has previously been determined to be invalid. For example, see *Maryland v. Louisiana*, 451 US 725, 756 (1981).
c. *Incorrect.* It has been settled through previous cases that this methodology is unconstitutional under the negative Commerce Clause. For example, this methodology was found to be unconstitutional in *Guy v. Baltimore*, 100 US 434, 443 (1880).

10. a. *Incorrect.* The Court's decision specifically stated that it was *not* determining the issue of whether a state must always credit sales or use taxes paid to another state against its own use tax.
b. *Incorrect.* The U.S. Supreme Court reversed the Vermont Supreme Court's decision, but it did *not* express an opinion as to the proper remedy.
c. *Correct.* The Court could not see a significant difference between motor vehicle registrants who purchased their cars out-of-state while they were Vermont residents and those who came to Vermont after buying a car in another state. To free one group from the tax and not the other violated the Equal Protection Clause.

11. True. *Correct.* The Court did *not* consider the appellants' arguments based on the Privileges and Immunities Clause or the Commerce Clause.
False. *Incorrect.* The Court did not consider arguments based on the right to travel, the Privileges and Immunities Clause, or the Commerce Clause. It *also* did not determine whether a state must always credit sales or use taxes paid to another state against its own use tax.

12. a. *Correct.* **The appellants in the case bought and registered cars outside of Vermont before becoming Vermont residents and had to pay the full use tax in order to register their cars in Vermont.**

b. *Incorrect.* The State of Vermont asserted in *Williams et al. v. Vermont et al* that the tax credit applied *only* to Vermont residents who *first* registered their cars in Vermont. However, the U.S. Supreme Court noted that the Vermont Supreme Court, in ruling on the equal protection claim in *Leverson,* indicated that the statute did not require Vermont residents who purchased their cars out of state to pay the use tax, *even if the cars were first registered in that other state.* Therefore, a Vermont resident who purchased and registered a car in another state before registering the car in Vermont would be entitled to the exemption.

c. *Incorrect.* The statute clearly did not require Vermont residents who purchased their cars out of state and first registered them in Vermont to pay the use tax.

13. a. *Incorrect.* The Court concluded that there was *no* legitimate purpose for the "discriminatory" exemption in question. It stated that "residence at the time of purchase is a wholly arbitrary basis on which to distinguish among present Vermont registrants—at least among those who used their cars elsewhere before coming to Vermont."

b. *Incorrect.* The holding was very narrow, and did not consider a number of the appellant's arguments. This meant that it would *not* have a great deal of constitutional significance.

c. *Correct.* **The Court noted that it had often pointed out that in structuring internal taxation schemes the states have a lot of leeway in making classifications and drawing lines which in their judgment produce reasonable taxation systems.**

14. a. *Incorrect.* Justice Blackmun, in his dissenting opinion, noted that the Court subjected Vermont's motor vehicle tax laws to a kind of microscopic scrutiny that few tax laws could survive, and managed to find a way to interpret the related statute so as to discriminate against the appellants in *Williams et al. v. Vermont et al.*

b. *Correct.* **In his dissenting opinion, Justice Blackmun pointed out that §8911(9) was designed to *prevent* people who buy their cars out of state but live in Vermont from being doubly taxed.**

c. *Incorrect.* In his dissenting opinion, Justice Blackmun stated that a tax classification does *not* violate the demands of equal protection simply because it may not perfectly identify the class of people it intends to single out. He went on to note that a state does not have to resort to close distinctions or sustain a "precise, scientific uniformity with reference to composition, use or value."

15. True. *Correct.* However, all factors, such as legal fees compared to the tax liability and the likely outcome should be weighed before determining whether to challenge such a statute.

False. *Incorrect.* The most likely way to change a state tax statute is to challenge it in court. However, all factors such as cost/benefit and likelihood of success should be considered.

MULTISTATE CORPORATE TAX COURSE (2011 EDITION)

Index

MULTISTATE CORPORATE TAX COURSE (2011 EDITION)

CPE Quizzer Instructions

The CPE Quizzer is divided into two Modules. There is a processing fee for each Quizzer Module submitted for grading. Successful completion of Module 1 is recommended for **7 CPE Credits.*** Successful completion of Module 2 is recommended for **8 CPE Credits.*** You can complete and submit one Module at a time or all Modules at once for a total of **15 CPE Credits.***

To obtain CPE credit, return your completed Answer Sheet for each Quizzer Module to **CCH Continuing Education Department, 4025 W. Peterson Ave., Chicago, IL 60646**, or fax it to (773) 866-3084. Each Quizzer Answer Sheet will be graded and a CPE Certificate of Completion awarded for achieving a grade of 70 percent or greater. The Quizzer Answer Sheets are located after the Quizzer questions for this Course.

Express Grading: Processing time for your Answer Sheet is generally 8-12 business days. If you are trying to meet a reporting deadline, our Express Grading Service is available for an additional $19 per Module. To use this service, please check the "Express Grading" box on your Answer Sheet and provide your CCH account or credit card number **and your fax number.** CCH will fax your results and a Certificate of Completion (upon achieving a passing grade) to you by 5:00 p.m. the business day following our receipt of your Answer Sheet. **If you mail your Answer Sheet for Express Grading, please write "ATTN: CPE OVERNIGHT" on the envelope.** NOTE: CCH will not Federal Express Quizzer results under any circumstances.

NEW ONLINE GRADING gives you immediate 24/7 grading with instant results and no Express Grading Fee.

The **CCH Testing Center** website gives you and others in your firm easy, free access to CCH print Courses and allows you to complete your CPE Quizzers online for immediate results. Plus, the **My Courses** feature provides convenient storage for your CPE Course Certificates and completed Quizzers.

Go to **www.cchtestingcenter.com** to complete your Quizzer online.

---

* Recommended CPE credit is based on a 50-minute hour. Participants earning credits for states that require self-study to be based on a 100-minute hour will receive ½ the CPE credits for successful completion of this course. Because CPE requirements vary from state to state and among different licensing agencies, please contact your CPE governing body for information on your CPE requirements and the applicability of a particular course for your requirements.

Date of Completion: The date of completion on your Certificate will be the date that you put on your Answer Sheet. However, you must submit your Answer Sheet to CCH for grading within two weeks of completing it.

Expiration Date: December 31, 2011

Evaluation: To help us provide you with the best possible products, please take a moment to fill out the Course Evaluation located at the back of this Course and return it with your Quizzer Answer Sheets.

CCH is registered with the National Association of State Boards of Accountancy (NASBA) as a sponsor of continuing professional education on the National Registry of CPE Sponsors. State boards of accountancy have final authority on the acceptance of individual courses for CPE credit. Complaints regarding registered sponsors may be addressed to the National Registry of CPE Sponsors, 150 Fourth Avenue North, Suite 700, Nashville, TN 37219-2417. Web site: www.nasba.org.

CCH is registered with the National Association of State Boards of Accountancy (NASBA) as a Quality Assurance Service (QAS) sponsor of continuing professional education. State boards of accountancy have final authority on the acceptance of individual courses for CPE credit. Complaints regarding registered sponsors may be addressed to NASBA, 150 Fourth Avenue North, Suite 700, Nashville, TN 37219-2417. Web site: www.nasba.org.

CCH has been approved by the California Tax Education Council to offer courses that provide federal and state credit towards the annual "continuing education" requirement imposed by the State of California. A listing of additional requirements to register as a tax preparer may be obtained by contacting CTEC at P.O. Box 2890, Sacramento, CA, 95812-2890, toll-free by phone at (877) 850-2832, or on the Internet at www.ctec.org.

Processing Fee:
$84.00 for Module 1
$96.00 for Module 2
$180.00 for all Modules

Recommended CPE:
7 hours for Module 1
8 hours for Module 2
15 hours for all Modules

CTEC Course Number:
1075-CE-9707 for Module 1
1075-CE-9708 for Module 2

CTEC Federal Hours:
N/A hours for Module 1
N/A hours for Module 2
N/A hours for all Modules

CTEC California Hours:
3 hours for Module 1
4 hours for Module 2
7 hours for all Modules

One **complimentary copy** of this Course is provided with copies of selected CCH Tax titles. Additional copies of this Course may be ordered for $37.00 each by calling 1-800-248-3248 (ask for product **0-0968-200**).

MULTISTATE CORPORATE TAX COURSE (2011 EDITION)
Quizzer Questions: Module 1

1. The most recent U.S. Supreme Court case on constitutional nexus is:

    a. *National Bellas Hess, Inc. v. Department of Revenue*
    b. *Quill Corp. v. North Dakota*
    c. *Scripto, Inc. v. Carson*
    d. None of the above

2. Which of the following is a limitation of P.L. 86-272?

    a. It does not apply to taxes based on gross receipts.
    b. It does not apply to taxes on net income.
    c. It does not apply to sales of tangible personal property.
    d. It does not apply to solicitation of orders.

3. Income arising from transactions and activity in the regular course of the taxpayer's trade or business comprises the ___ test in determining whether an item of income is business or nonbusiness.

    a. Classification
    b. Functional
    c. Transactional
    d. None of the above

4. Most states use which of the following apportionment formulas?

    a. A single-factor sales formula
    b. A single-factor property formula
    c. An evenly weighted three-factor formula
    d. A three-factor formula that super-weights the sales factor

5. Which of the following is *not* an advantage of filing a consolidated return?

    a. Ability to offset the losses of one affiliate against the profits of other affiliates
    b. Allows a taxpayer to create legal structures to shift income from affiliates in high-tax states to affiliates in low-tax states
    c. Deferral of gains on intercompany transactions
    d. Use of credits that would otherwise be denied because of a lack of income

6. Which judicial test for determining the existence of a unitary business specifically looks to functional integration, centralization of management, and economies of scale?

   a. Three-unities test
   b. Contribution or dependency test
   c. Flow-of-value test
   d. Factors-of-profitability test

7. To acquire the right to apportion its income, the corporation generally must have nexus in at least one state other than its state of commercial domicile. In such cases, whether a corporation's activities or contacts in another state are considered adequate to justify apportionment is generally determined by:

   a. Reference to the tax laws of the domicile state
   b. Reference to the tax laws of states other than the domicile state
   c. Reference to the tax laws of all states
   d. None of the above

8. Creating nexus in a state would *not* be beneficial in which of the following situations?

   a. The corporation wants to include loss affiliates in the consolidated return of another state.
   b. The corporation currently does *not* have the right to apportion its income.
   c. The corporation makes significant sales into a state which has a high tax rate.
   d. The corporation wants to avoid the application of a sales throwback rule.

9. Although there is diversity among the states' apportionment formulas, a corporation can never have more than 100 percent of its income subject to state taxation. *True or False?*

10. Most states that impose corporate income taxes tie the computation of taxable income directly to a corporation's federal tax return. *True or False?*

11. Nexus created by the licensing of trademarks for use within the state by out-of-state affiliated companies which have no property or payroll in the state is referred to as:

a. Agency nexus
b. Affiliate nexus
c. Economic nexus
d. Physical presence nexus

12. Which of the following states imposes a gross receipts tax in lieu of a corporate income tax?

a. Alabama
b. California
c. Ohio
d. South Dakota

13. A corporation sells a service. Ten-percent of the income-producing activity is performed in State A, 15 percent in State B, and 75 percent in State C. Under the cost-of-performance rule in UDITPA §17(b), how is the sale allocated?

a. 100 percent to State C
b. 83 percent to State A and 17 percent to State B
c. 10 percent to State A, 15 percent to State B, and 75 percent to State C
d. 100 percent to the state where the service recipient is located

14. A corporation sells a service. Ten-percent of the income-producing activity is performed in State A, 15 percent in State B, and 75 percent in State C. Under the market-based approach, how is the sale allocated?

a. 100 percent to State C
b. 83 percent to State A and 17 percent to State B
c. 10 percent to State A, 15 percent to State B, and 75 percent to State C
d. 100 percent to the state where the service recipient is located

15. All states conform to the federal tax treatment of a partnership as a pass-through entity that is not subject to any entity-level taxes. *True or False?*

16. How many states currently use the UDITPA equally weighted three-factor apportionment formula?

    a. None
    b. Fewer than 20
    c. More than 20 but not all
    d. All

17. A business is taxable in States A, B, and C. It is commercially domiciled in State A, but most of its facilities are located in State C. The business sells some intangible property at a gain. The sale is not in the regular course of the taxpayer's trade or business, and the intangible property is not an integral part of the taxpayer's regular business operations. Where should the income arising from the sale be allocated?

    a. State A only
    b. State C only
    c. States A and C
    d. States A, B, and C

18. If a business is taxable in several states and the apportionment percentages for those states add up to 110 percent, then:

    a. The apportionment percentages must have been calculated incorrectly.
    b. The taxpayer has nowhere income.
    c. There is double taxation of the taxpayer's income.
    d. None of the above

19. UDITPA §18 provides that, if the allocation and apportionment provisions of UDITPA do not fairly represent the extent of the taxpayer's business activity in a state, then _____ may request or demand an alternative formula.

    a. The taxpayer, but not the tax administrator
    b. The tax administrator, but not the taxpayer
    c. Either the taxpayer or the tax administrator

20. Which of the following states has enacted legislation that will allow certain taxpayers to make an election to use a single-factor sales-only formula effective in 2011?

    a. Colorado
    b. California
    c. Oregon
    d. Vermont

21. The Multistate Tax Commission has promulgated special apportionment regulations covering all of the following industries *except:*

a. Radio broadcasters
b. Publishers
c. Trucking companies
d. Professional sports franchises

22. The MTC's Proposed Model Regulation for Apportionment of Income from the Sale of Telecommunications and Ancillary Services provides that:

a. Outer-jurisdictional property is included in the property factor.
b. The payroll factor is determined under the standard UDITPA rules for sourcing payroll.
c. The sales factor is determined under the standard UDITPA rules for sourcing sales.
d. None of the above

23. Which of the following statements is true?

a. *All* states impose special franchise taxes on financial institutions.
b. *No* state provides a special apportionment formula for financial institutions.
c. The MTC's model statute for financial institutions adopts a sales-only apportionment formula.
d. The MTC's model statute for financial institutions adopts an equally weighted three-factor apportionment formula.

24. In *Moorman Manufacturing Co.*, the Supreme Court ruled that a three-factor formula is constitutionally *required*. **True or False?**

25. In *FedEx Ground Package System, Inc.*, the Pennsylvania Supreme Court upheld the lower court's decision that the company could use its average receipts per mile in Pennsylvania to calculate its revenue miles in Pennsylvania, since this was consistent with the plain language of the statute. **True or False?**

26. For federal tax purposes, if an acquirer makes a Section 338 election:

    a. The purchase of a controlling interest in the target's stock is treated as a stock purchase.

    b. The target recognizes *no* gain or loss on the deemed asset sale.

    c. The acquirer's basis in the target's assets reflects the actual purchase price of the company.

    d. None of the above

27. For federal tax purposes, under a Section 338(g) election:

    a. The basis of the old target's assets is carried over to the new target corporation.

    b. The acquirer must formally liquidate the new target corporation.

    c. Any gain or loss resulting from the deemed asset sale is included in the acquirer's current year tax return.

    d. Gain recognition in respect to the target's appreciated assets is triggered.

28. For federal tax purposes, a Section A 338(h)(10) election:

    a. Results in gains from the deemed asset sale to be taxed to the stock purchaser

    b. Is made *only* by the target corporation, using Form 8023

    c. May *not* be made by S Corporation shareholders

    d. None of the above

29. States generally treat gains and losses from a deemed asset sale under Section 338 as:

    a. Allocable nonbusiness income

    b. Apportionable business income

    c. Nonrecognized gains or losses

    d. None of the above

30. Many states apportion the gains resulting from a target corporation's deemed asset sale under Section 338 by using their standard apportionment rules. ***True or False?***

31. In *MeadWestvaco*, the U.S. Supreme Court stated that the operational function concept as described by the Court in *Allied Signal*:

   a. Was properly applied by the Illinois courts
   b. Modifies the unitary business principle by adding a new ground for apportionment
   c. Recognizes that an asset can be a part of a taxpayer's unitary business, even if there is no unitary relationship between the payor and the payee
   d. None of the above

32. The *unitary business principle* allows a state to tax an apportioned percentage of income generated by a corporation whose interstate activities form a *unitary business*. **True or False?**

33. The majority view of the UDITPA definition of *business income* is that it includes:

   a. A transactional test only
   b. A functional test only
   c. Neither a transactional or functional test
   d. Both a transactional and a functional test

34. Which of the following statements is true of *nonbusiness income*?

   a. It can be defined differently in different states.
   b. It is apportioned among the states in which the taxpayer has nexus.
   c. It includes income from property that is an integral part of the taxpayer's regular trade or business operations.
   d. It includes income that meets *either* the transactional or the functional test.

35. The *functional test*:

   a. Is *not* recognized by the MTC regulations
   b. Has been added to a number of state statutes following state supreme court decisions interpreting the statutory definition of business income to be transactional in nature
   c. Considers the frequency and regularity of the income-producing activity in relation to the taxpayer's regular trade or business operations
   d. None of the above

36. Which of the following states continues to *only* recognize a *transactional test* for determining whether income is business or nonbusiness?

a. Alabama
b. Iowa
c. Tennessee
d. None of the above

37. Which of the following items of *nonbusiness income* is generally allocated to the state where the income-producing asset is physically located?

a. Capital gains from the sale of stock
b. Royalties from real property
c. Interest
d. Dividends

38. Which of the following statements is *not* true?

a. Expenses related to nonbusiness income are generally deductible against business income.
b. The commercial domicile of a corporation may be in a state other than the state of incorporation.
c. Nonbusiness royalty income is allocable to the state in which the intangible asset is used, unless the royalties are not taxable in that state.
d. Nonbusiness income from intangible property is generally allocated to the state of commercial domicile.

39. The trend has been to broaden the statutory definition of nonbusiness income such that more income is considered to be nonbusiness. ***True or False?***

40. In which of the following cases did the U.S. Supreme Court determine that California's interest-offset rule was unconstitutional?

a. *Kroger Co.*
b. *Hunt-Wesson*
c. *American General Realty*
d. *Downey Toy Co.*

MULTISTATE CORPORATE TAX COURSE (2011 EDITION)

Quizzer Questions: Module 2

41. The deadline for appeal of an assessment in most states is usually how long after the notice was mailed or received?

    a. 30 or 60 days
    b. 90 or 120 days
    c. Six months
    d. One year

42. Which of the following is **not** a common reason for imposition of a penalty?

    a. Not filing a return
    b. Late filing
    c. Error in current return
    d. Late payment

43. Which type of penalty would most likely result if a taxpayer does not pay tax to some vendors and does **not** have proper self-assessment procedures in place?

    a. Fraud
    b. Substantial understatement
    c. Gross negligence
    d. Ordinary negligence

44. Discussions related to the trading off of issues should be made at the beginning of negotiations with the auditor. **_True or False?_**

45. Which of the following statements is true?

    a. The rate of interest on deficiencies ranges from six to eight percent in most states.
    b. The use of computers has increased the importance of reviewing the interest assessment.
    c. Most states assess compound interest.
    d. A sample should be allocated across the audit period on a monthly basis to calculate interest.

46. Which of the following defenses should *not* be used when a penalty is imposed on an uncontroversial transaction?

    a. The taxpayer has a good audit history.
    b. The taxpayer has had significant staff turnover.
    c. The administration of the tax law is complex.
    d. The tax deficiency is low compared to the amount of tax voluntarily paid during the period.

47. Which of the following statements is *not* true?

    a. Most states will refuse to discuss issues with an outside advisor if the advisor is not duly authorized to act on the taxpayer's behalf.
    b. If another taxpayer has been unsuccessful in appealing the same issue, the taxpayer should not appeal, even if its facts are different.
    c. Intangibles of litigation, such as public disclosure, should be determined if the cost-benefit analysis yields a *positive* result.
    d. In order to properly estimate the probability of success of an appeal, the litigation environment in the state should be considered.

48. A taxpayer is under a four-year audit, with two years under waiver because of expiration of the statute of limitations. The audit is completed in the second year of the next audit cycle. In which years of the next audit cycle should the taxpayer be required to demonstrate corrective action?

    a. Years two through four
    b. Years three through four
    c. All four years, because the taxpayer has sufficient time to correct them before the next audit.
    d. None of the years, because the audit cycle began before the audit was completed.

49. If the tax law is *not* complied with, in some states a return preparer who has substantial authority for the payment of tax could have a penalty imposed for negligence or fraud. *True or False?*

50. Which of the following is likely to occur in the near future?

    a. Sampling will play a *lesser* role in sales and use tax audits.
    b. The use of penalties will *decrease.*
    c. The use of database programs in the performance of audits will *decrease.*
    d. Taxpayers will have more opportunities to perform all or part of audits themselves.

51. The majority opinion in *National Bellas Hess* was based *primarily* on the previous decision in which of the following cases?

   a. *Miller Bros.*
   b. *Scripto*
   c. *Quill*
   d. *Sears, Roebuck*

52. Which of the following is a primary reason why the U.S. Supreme Court determined that National Bellas Hess did **not** have nexus with Illinois for sales and use tax purposes?

   a. National Bellas Hess did not enjoy any of the benefits of the State of Illinois.
   b. National Bellas Hess had no administrative or recordkeeping requirements with Illinois for sales and use tax purposes.
   c. National Bellas Hess had no *physical presence* in Illinois.
   d. None of the above

53. Like some other states, North Dakota enacted an "anti-*Bellas Hess*" statute which is still in effect today. **True or False?**

54. According to the *Quill* Court, which of the following is *true* concerning the Commerce Clause and/or Due Process Clause?

   a. The nexus requirements of the two clauses are identical.
   b. The Due Process Clause requires substantial nexus.
   c. The Commerce Clause requires *minimum contacts.*
   d. None of the above.

55. The *Quill* Court determined that:

   a. The Commerce Clause did not bar enforcement of use tax against Quill.
   b. The Due Process Clause did not bar enforcement of North Dakota's use tax against Quill.
   c. *Neither* the Commerce Clause nor the Due Process Clause barred enforcement of North Dakota's use tax against Quill.
   d. *Both* the Commerce Clause and the Due Process Clause barred enforcement of North Dakota's use tax against Quill.

56. The Commerce Clause of the U.S. Constitution:

a. Requires some definite link with a state for the imposition of a sales and use tax

b. Requires a *minimum connection* with a state for the imposition of a sales and use tax

c. Requires substantial *nexus* with a state for the imposition of a sales and use tax

d. None of the above

57. Which of the following statements is **not** true?

a. A corporation may have the minimum contacts with a state required by the Due Process Clause to impose a tax, but not the substantial nexus required by the Commerce Clause.

b. The **Quill** Court determined that **Bellas Hess** was not consistent with **Complete Auto Transit.**

c. The **Quill** Court refused to override the **Bellas Hess** decision.

d. The **Quill** Court determined that Quill's economic presence in North Dakota was *not* enough to create nexus.

58. The primary finding in the **Scripto** decision is that:

a. An independent contractor can create nexus for a taxpayer.

b. If an independent contractor works for several principals, the contractor cannot create nexus for any of the principals.

c. The *minimum connections* required by the Due Process Clause cannot be made by an independent contractor working for a taxpayer.

59. The required minimum connections for nexus that were not present in *Miller Bros.* were present in *Scripto.* **True or False?**

60. The **Borders Online** Court noted that the key question when testing a state's taxing authority against the dormant Commerce Clause is:

a. Whether the foreign company has agents *soliciting* sales in the state

b. Whether the activities of the retailer's in-state representatives are significantly associated with its ability to *establish and maintain* a market in the state for sales

c. Whether the retailer's in-state representatives are actually *making* sales

61. In which of the following cases did the U.S. Supreme Court, in regard to sufficient nexus, note that minor "differentiations are without constitutional significance?"

    a. *Nardis Sportswear*
    b. *Miller Bros.*
    c. *General Trading Co.*
    d. *Complete Auto Transit*

62. Which of the following cases presented a four-part test that would sustain a tax **against** a Commerce Clause challenge?

    a. *Nardis Sportswear*
    b. *Miller Bros.*
    c. *General Trading Co.*
    d. *Complete Auto Transit*

63. In which of the following cases did the U.S. Supreme Court find for the taxpayer because the taxpayer's only connection with customers in the state was by common carrier or U.S. mail?

    a. *National Bellas Hess*
    b. *Scholastic*
    c. *Scripto*
    d. *Borders Online*

64. Congress has the ability to determine whether, when, and to what extent the States may burden interstate mail-order and Internet businesses with a duty to collect use taxes. **True or False?**

65. Which of the following statements is *true?*

    a. *Physical presence* in a state is necessary to create sales and use tax nexus in that state.
    b. *Economic nexus* with a state is enough to create sales and use tax nexus in that state.
    c. An employee or property must be present in a state to create a *physical presence* in that state.

66. Which clause of the U.S. Constitution prohibits jurisdictions from interfering with interstate commerce?

a. Commerce Clause
b. Equal Protection Clause
c. Due Process Clause
d. Interstate Clause

67. Which of the following cases identified four essential elements that were necessary for a tax to be considered *unconstitutional?*

a. *Spector*
b. *Complete Auto Transit*
c. *West Lynn Creamery*
d. *Williams v. Vermont*

68. If a state imposes a tax that allows a credit to taxpayers performing an activity in the state, but does not allow a credit performing the same activity outside the state, which clause of the U.S. Constitution is the state most likely *violating?*

a. Commerce Clause
b. Equal Protection Clause
c. Due Process Clause
d. Privileges and Immunities Clause

69. Which of the following is one of the four essential elements necessary for a tax to be considered *unconstitutional* under the Commerce Clause?

a. There must be at *least* a minimal nexus with the taxing state.
b. The tax must be fairly apportioned.
c. The tax must *not* discriminate against intrastate commerce.
d. The tax must be fairly related to the services provided to the state by the taxpayer.

70. Which clause of the U.S. Constitution prohibits taxing jurisdictions from making laws that single out specific taxpayers and impose tax on their activities in a discriminatory manner?

a. Commerce Clause
b. Equal Protection Clause
c. Due Process Clause
d. Privileges and Immunities Clause

71. A state taxing statute will not be deemed to be unconstitutional unless it is challenged and found to be unconstitutional in the courts. ***True or False?***

72. The case in ***West Lynn Creamery*** was challenging which of the following clauses of the U.S. Constitution?

    a. The Commerce Clause
    b. The Equal Protection Clause
    c. The Due Process Clause
    d. The Privileges and Immunities Clause

73. Which of the following arguments by the State of Massachusetts in ***West Lynn Creamery*** was accepted by the U.S. Supreme Court?

    a. The milk pricing order did *not* cause protectionism because only in-state consumers felt the effect of any price increase.
    b. Because the milk order achieved its goals through lawful means, the order as a whole was *constitutional.*
    c. The order's incidental burden on commerce was *justified* by the local benefit of saving the dairy industry from collapse.
    d. None of the above

74. Which of the following is a situation described by Judge Scalia where a self-executing "negative" Commerce Clause comes into play?

    a. When there is a state law that is distinguishable from a type of law previously held unconstitutional by the U.S. Supreme Court
    b. When there is a state law that is indistinguishable from a type of law previously held constitutional by the U.S. Supreme Court
    c. When there is a state law that facially discriminates against interstate commerce
    d. When there is a state law that facially discriminates against intrastate commerce

75. The tax in question in the ***West Lynn Creamery*** case was found to be *unconstitutional* by the U.S. Supreme Court, although there was a dissenting opinion. ***True or False?***

76. The U.S. Supreme Court in *Williams et al. v. Vermont et al* did which of the following?

    a. Determined that the statute in question was *constitutional* when viewed on its face

    b. Determined the appropriate remedy in the case

    c. Decided that a state must always credit sales or use taxes paid to another state against its own use tax

    d. None of the above

77. The dissenting opinion in *Williams et al. v. Vermont et al.* made its argument using all of the following comments *except:*

    a. The U.S. Supreme Court's decision was so narrow that it had *no* constitutional significance.

    b. The discrimination the U.S. Supreme Court found was neither pleaded in the complaint nor discussed in any Vermont court opinions.

    c. The U.S. Supreme Court subjected Vermont's motor vehicle tax laws to a kind of microscopic scrutiny that few enactments could survive.

    d. The U.S. Supreme Court's remedy was not constitutional.

78. The *Williams et al. v. Vermont et al* case was a challenge based on which of the following Constitutional Clauses?

    a. Commerce Clause

    b. Equal Protection Clause

    c. Due Process Clause

    d. Privileges and Immunities Clause

79. The U.S. Supreme Court in *Williams et al. v. Vermont et al* agreed with the Vermont Supreme Court that the statute in question was *constitutional.* **True or False?**

80. If a taxpayer believes a tax is *unconstitutional,* the taxpayer should:

    a. Pay the tax because it can only be changed by the state legislature

    b. Simply *not* pay the tax if confident that it is unconstitutional

    c. Consider challenging the tax in court

    d. None of the above

MULTISTATE CORPORATE TAX COURSE (2011 EDITION)   (0775-3)

Module 1: Answer Sheet

NAME _____

COMPANY NAME _____

STREET _____

CITY, STATE, & ZIP CODE _____

BUSINESS PHONE NUMBER _____

E-MAIL ADDRESS _____

DATE OF COMPLETION _____

CFP REGISTRANT ID (for Certified Financial Planners) _____

CRTP ID (for CTEC Credit only) _____ (CTEC Course # 1075-CE-9707)

On the next page, please answer the Multiple Choice questions by indicating the appropriate letter next to the corresponding number. Please answer the True/False questions by
marking "T" or "F" next to the corresponding number.

A $84.00 processing fee will be charged for each user submitting Module 1 for grading.

Please remove both pages of the Answer Sheet from this book and return them with your
completed Evaluation Form to CCH at the address below. You may also fax your Answer
Sheet to CCH at 773-866-3084.

You may also go to **www.cchtestingcenter.com** to complete your Quizzer online.

METHOD OF PAYMENT:

☐ Check Enclosed   ☐ Visa   ☐ Master Card   ☐ AmEx

☐ Discover   ☐ CCH Account* _____

Card No. _____ Exp. Date _____

Signature _____

* Must provide CCH account number for this payment option

EXPRESS GRADING: Please fax my Course results to me by 5:00 p.m. the business
day following your receipt of this Answer Sheet. By checking this box I authorize
CCH to charge $19.00 for this service.

☐ Express Grading $19.00   Fax No. _____

Mail or fax to:
CCH Continuing Education Department
4025 W. Peterson Ave.
Chicago, IL 60646-6085
1-800-248-3248
Fax: 773-866-3084

MULTISTATE CORPORATE TAX COURSE (2011 EDITION)   (0775-3)

Module 1: Answer Sheet

Please answer the Multiple Choice questions by indicating the appropriate letter next to the corresponding number. Please answer the True/False questions by marking "T" or "F" next to the corresponding number.

1. ___	11. ___	21. ___	31. ___
2. ___	12. ___	22. ___	32. ___
3. ___	13. ___	23. ___	33. ___
4. ___	14. ___	24. ___	34. ___
5. ___	15. ___	25. ___	35. ___
6. ___	16. ___	26. ___	36. ___
7. ___	17. ___	27. ___	37. ___
8. ___	18. ___	28. ___	38. ___
9. ___	19. ___	29. ___	39. ___
10. ___	20. ___	30. ___	40. ___

Please complete the Evaluation Form (located after the Module 2 Answer Sheet) and return it with this Quizzer Answer Sheet to CCH at the address on the previous page. Thank you.

MULTISTATE CORPORATE TAX COURSE (2011 EDITION)   (0776-3)

Module 2: Answer Sheet

NAME _____

COMPANY NAME _____

STREET _____

CITY, STATE, & ZIP CODE _____

BUSINESS PHONE NUMBER _____

E-MAIL ADDRESS _____

DATE OF COMPLETION _____

CFP REGISTRANT ID (for Certified Financial Planners) _____

CRTP ID (for CTEC Credit only) _____ (CTEC Course # 1075-CE-9708)

On the next page, please answer the Multiple Choice questions by indicating the appropriate letter next to the corresponding number. Please answer the True/False questions by marking "T" or "F" next to the corresponding number.

A $96.00 processing fee will be charged for each user submitting Module 2 for grading.

Please remove both pages of the Answer Sheet from this book and return them with your completed Evaluation Form to CCH at the address below. You may also fax your Answer Sheet to CCH at 773-866-3084.

You may also go to **www.cchtestingcenter.com** to complete your exam online.

METHOD OF PAYMENT:

☐ Check Enclosed   ☐ Visa   ☐ Master Card   ☐ AmEx

☐ Discover   ☐ CCH Account* _____

Card No. _____ Exp. Date _____

Signature _____

* Must provide CCH account number for this payment option

EXPRESS GRADING: Please fax my Course results to me by 5:00 p.m. the business day following your receipt of this Answer Sheet. By checking this box I authorize CCH to charge $19.00 for this service.

☐ Express Grading $19.00   Fax No. _____

Mail or fax to:

CCH Continuing Education Department
4025 W. Peterson Ave.
Chicago, IL 60646-6085
1-800-248-3248
Fax: 773-866-3084

MULTISTATE CORPORATE TAX COURSE (2011 EDITION)   (0776-3)

Module 2: Answer Sheet

Please answer the Multiple Choice questions by indicating the appropriate letter next to the corresponding number. Please answer the True/False questions by marking "T" or "F" next to the corresponding number.

41. ___	51. ___	61. ___	71. ___
42. ___	52. ___	62. ___	72. ___
43. ___	53. ___	63. ___	73. ___
44. ___	54. ___	64. ___	74. ___
45. ___	55. ___	65. ___	75. ___
46. ___	56. ___	66. ___	76. ___
47. ___	57. ___	67. ___	77. ___
48. ___	58. ___	68. ___	78. ___
49. ___	59. ___	69. ___	79. ___
50. ___	60. ___	70. ___	80. ___

Please complete the Evaluation Form (located after the Module 2 Answer Sheet) and return it with this Quizzer Answer Sheet to CCH at the address on the previous page. Thank you.

MULTISTATE CORPORATE TAX COURSE (2011 EDITION)   (0968-2)
Evaluation Form

Please take a few moments to fill out and mail or fax this evaluation to CCH so that we can better provide you with the type of self-study programs you want and need. Thank you.

About This Program

1. Please circle the number that best reflects the extent of your agreement with the following statements:

		Strongly Agree				Strongly Disagree
a.	The Course objectives were met.	5	4	3	2	1
b.	This Course was comprehensive and organized.	5	4	3	2	1
c.	The content was current and technically accurate.	5	4	3	2	1
d.	This Course was timely and relevant.	5	4	3	2	1
e.	The prerequisite requirements were appropriate.	5	4	3	2	1
f.	This Course was a valuable learning experience.	5	4	3	2	1
g.	The Course completion time was appropriate.	5	4	3	2	1

2. This Course was most valuable to me because of:

    _____ Continuing Education credit   _____ Convenience of format
    _____ Relevance to my practice/   _____ Timeliness of subject matter
    employment   _____ Reputation of author
    _____ Price
    _____ Other (please specify) _____

3. How long did it take to complete this Course? (Please include the total time spent reading or studying reference materials and completing CPE Quizzer).

    Module 1 _____   Module 2 _____

4. What do you consider to be the strong points of this Course?

5. What improvements can we make to this Course?

MULTISTATE CORPORATE TAX COURSE (2011 EDITION)   (0968-2)

Evaluation Form *cont'd*

General Interests

1. Preferred method of self-study instruction:
    ____ Text ____ Audio ____ Computer-based/Multimedia ____Video

2. What specific topics would you like CCH to develop as self-study CPE programs? ___

    _____

    _____

    _____

3. Please list other topics of interest to you _____

    _____

    _____

About You

1. Your profession:

____ CPA	____ Enrolled Agent
____ Attorney	____ Tax Preparer
____ Financial Planner	____ Other (please specify)
	_____

2. Your employment:

____ Self-employed	____ Public Accounting Firm
____ Service Industry	____ Non-Service Industry
____ Banking/Finance	____ Government
____ Education	____ Other _____

3. Size of firm/corporation:

    ____ 1 ____ 2-5 ____ 6-10 ____ 11-20 ____ 21-50 ____ 51+

4. Your Name_____

    Firm/Company Name _____

    Address _____

    City, State, Zip Code _____

    E-mail Address _____

THANK YOU FOR TAKING THE TIME TO COMPLETE THIS SURVEY!

NOTES

NOTES

NOTES

NOTES

NOTES

NOTES